The
EVERYTHING®
Investing Book

D0509094

Dear Reader:

Woody Allen once said that wealth is better than poverty, if only for financial reasons. Like most good one-liners, this quote hits home because there
is so much truth to it. Of course, there's the age-old debate over whether
money can truly make people happy. My opinion is that it definitely helps.
Studies show that wealthy people are happier, healthier, and more motivated to achieve their goals. The question is how do you find this perfect
place where money and happiness meet? It's an intricate process. But the
best steps toward creating wealth are knowing the lay of the financial land,
preparing a plan, being patient and disciplined, and executing your plan
to the best of your abilities.

That's what this book is all about. Inside, we explain what you need to
know to set you on the path to profit and prosperity. From understanding
the inner machinations of the world's greatest financial markets to figuring
out how to make a fortune trading collectibles on eBay, we'll be your tour
guides on the road to wealth and financial freedom. Here's hoping you
enjoy the ride.

Best of Luck,

Michele Cagan

Brian O'Connell

The EVERYTHING® Series

Editorial

Publishing Director	Gary M. Krebs
Managing Editor	Kate McBride
Copy Chief	Laura M. Daly
Acquisitions Editor	Gina Chaimanis
Development Editor	Katie McDonough
Technical Reviewer	Joe Duarte
Production Editors	Bridget Brace

Production

Director of Manufacturing	Susan Beale
Associate Director of Production	Michelle Roy Kelly
Series Designers	Daria Perreault
	Colleen Cunningham
	John Paulhus
Cover Design	Paul Beatrice
	Matt LeBlanc
Layout and Graphics	Colleen Cunningham
	Holly Curtis
	Erin Dawson
	Sorae Lee
Series Cover Artist	Barry Littmann

Visit the entire Everything® Series at *www.everything.com*

THE
EVERYTHING®
INVESTING BOOK

2nd EDITION

Make money, plan ahead, and
secure your financial future!

Michele Cagan, C.P.A., and Brian O'Connell

Adams Media
Avon, Massachusetts

To JCT: I could never have done this without you.

Copyright ©1999, 2005, F+W Publications, Inc. All rights reserved.
This book, or parts thereof, may not be reproduced
in any form without permission from the publisher; exceptions
are made for brief excerpts used in published reviews.

An Everything® Series Book.
Everything® and everything.com® are registered trademarks of F+W Publications, Inc.

Published by Adams Media, an F+W Publications Company
57 Littlefield Street, Avon, MA 02322 U.S.A.
www.adamsmedia.com

ISBN: 1-59337-358-9
Printed in the United States of America.

J I H G F E D C B A

Library of Congress Cataloging-in-Publication Data
The everything investing book / Michele Cagan and Brian O'Connell. -- 2nd ed.
p.   cm.
ISBN 1-59337-358-9
1. Investments--United States. 2. Stocks—United States.
3. Mutual funds—United States. 4. Bonds—United States. 5. Finance, Personal
—United States.   I. O'Connell, Brian. II. Title. III. Series: Everything series.
HG4910.C34 2005
332.67'8'0973—dc22
2005011017

This publication is designed to provide accurate and authoritative information with regard to the subject matter covered. It is sold with the understanding that the publisher is not engaged in rendering legal, accounting, or other professional advice. If legal advice or other expert assistance is required, the services of a competent professional person should be sought.
          —From a *Declaration of Principles* jointly adopted by a Committee of the American Bar Association and a Committee of Publishers and Associations

Many of the designations used by manufacturers and sellers to distinguish their products are claimed as trademarks. Where those designations appear in this book and Adams Media was aware of a trademark claim, the designations have been printed with initial capital letters.

This book is available at quantity discounts for bulk purchases.
For information, please call 1-800-872-5627.

Contents

Doing Your Homework / 57

Taking the Leap / 73

The Basics of Mutual Funds / 89

Stock Mutual Funds / 105

Choosing the Right Fund Combination / 117

Acknowledgments

Special thanks to my good friend Micki Gorman, whose keen eye and skill with a pen lifted this book to a level higher than I could have dreamed. Thanks, also, to our editor, Gina Chaimanis, whose good humor and endless patience helped make this book a joy to write.

Top Ten Things to Do
Before You Invest $1

1. **Pay off all your credit card debt.** You can earn more than 22-percent returns just by paying your credit cards to zero instead of making meager monthly interest-bearing payments.

2. **Amass an emergency fund.** Start a separate bank account just for emergencies, and keep it filled with enough cash to cover at least three (preferably six) months' worth of living expenses.

3. **Establish a household budget.** Know where your money comes from and where it's going.

4. **Set your financial goals.** Whether you want to save for a vacation next year or a college education in ten years, you need to know your reasons for investing.

5. **Figure out your time frame.** The length of time you intend to be investing plays a big part in choosing the best investments.

6. **Know your risk tolerance.** Investing can involve about as many downs as ups, and you have to know just how much uncertainty you can comfortably stand.

7. **Determine your optimal asset allocation mix.** Figure out before you start what proportion of your investment pile will go toward each asset class (stocks, bonds, and cash, for example).

8. **Gain an understanding of the markets.** This includes the global political and economic forces that drive the markets and affect asset prices.

9. **Set up a brokerage account.** Whether you choose to start out with a financial advisor or to take a more do-it-yourself approach, you'll need a brokerage account in place before you can make your first trade.

10. **Research investments before you buy them.** Buy only those investments that you understand and about which you are at least basically informed; never invest in the unknown.

Introduction

▶ Wall Street is a place full of mazes and shadows—figuratively and literally. Take a walk through the concrete canyons of lower Manhattan, and you'll see for yourself. The tall buildings, most of which are huge financial centers filled with people in suits, largely block out the sun and cast great dark shadows over all. The landscape is mysterious and mind-boggling. An outsider might wander through the area and wonder what on earth goes on there.

In fact, that's how the financial power brokers who reside on Wall Street want things. As far as they're concerned, the secrets to wealth creation and financial freedom should remain just that—secret. Despite what their rosy marketing brochures and bright, happy television commercials promise, the financial powerhouses know it's in their best interest to keep you from really understanding what it takes to make money, create wealth, and achieve financial freedom. After all, billions upon billions of dollars in fat financial fees would be at risk if investors ever cracked Wall Street's devilish code.

Actually, the first secret to understanding Wall Street is figuring out that there is no secret to wealth creation. In fact, it's pretty simple to do, if you're willing to work hard and think logically. Investing legend Warren Buffett agrees. Buffett once famously said that he became one of the wealthiest men in the world by following two simple rules. The first is not to lose money. The second is to never forget the first.

Of course, it helps to be smart. The best step toward successful investing is using those smarts. You might have heard the story of the little girl who went to buy a watermelon. She pointed to a huge watermelon and asked the farmer how much it cost. "That one is three dollars," he replied. The little girl said, "But I've only got thirty cents." The farmer shrugged his shoulders and pointed to a smaller melon nearby. "How about that one?" he asked. The little girl said: "Okay, I'll take it. But leave it on the vine and I'll be back in thirty days to pick it up." Your investments should work the same way. If given time to grow, they can truly make a difference in your financial life.

Inside this book, you'll find a great deal of information on how to keep wealth creation simple and how to use your smarts to secure your financial freedom. All you need to know is right here. There's no smoke, no fun-house mirrors, and none of the tricks Wall Street likes to use to keep you off-balance. This is just straight information, presented in a way you can understand and geared to setting you on the path to financial security. Use it to the best of your ability, and take control of your financial life.

Chapter 1

Getting Organized

In the sixth century B.C., when the Greeks built a temple to the holy oracle of Delphi, they inscribed over the doorway the famous saying, "Know thyself." Though the average Greek citizen making the perilous journey to this site probably didn't realize it, this tiny phrase also makes for great investment advice. Investment professionals talk constantly about the importance of studying the market, knowing the playing field, and learning from the masters. While these guidelines certainly play an important role in a successful investment plan, investment gurus like Michael Price, William F. Sharpe, and Foster Friess would tell you that the key to managing your money effectively is to first know yourself.

Laying the Foundation

Taking control of your personal financial situation is the first step toward building wealth. To set foot on the ladder of financial freedom, you have to know where you stand and how much further you'll need to climb to reach your destination. A daily glance at your investment portfolio isn't enough, though it certainly plays a part. Investment tracking is fun, but there's a lot more involved in taking a true snapshot of your current financial situation.

FACT

According to a recent Federal Reserve survey of consumer finances, the average net worth of Americans aged forty-five to fifty-four is $90,500. The same survey showed that households with incomes in excess of $100,000 could boast a net worth of $485,900.

To eventually succeed in the world of investing, you'll have to start with the basics. This includes things like creating and sticking to a budget, balancing your checkbook, and determining your net worth. No, these options aren't as appealing as getting in on the ground floor at the next Microsoft, but you can't get ahead financially without them. Taking charge of your everyday household finances and understanding your real financial picture are the actions that make up the solid base from which you grow your nest egg. These simple starting points also give you the insights you'll need to make well-informed choices when you're ready to enter the more complex world of investing. You wouldn't enter a black-belt competition knowing nothing about karate, and jumping into the intricate world of high finance is no different. You need to master the fundamentals before you can develop a winning game plan.

Taking Financial Inventory

Taking your personal financial inventory is the first step toward creating a unique guide on which you'll base all of your financial decisions. Although this initial guide will be frozen in time, you'll revisit and reconstruct it regularly to chart the changes. At first, you'll probably need to revise it every three to six months; later, an annual revision will usually suffice (unless you undergo a major life change during the year). Even more important than looking at your personal balance sheet, it is vital that you understand what goes into it. This knowledge will carry you toward setting (and meeting) achievable financial goals.

Your net worth equals the difference between what you have (assets) and what you owe (liabilities). Your assets include things like bank accounts, investment portfolios, retirement accounts, the value of whole life insurance policies, the market value of real estate and vehicles, and any other property (like jewelry). Liabilities encompass everything you owe, typically separated into short-term debt and long-term obligations. Short-term debt covers your regular monthly bills, credit card balances, income taxes, and anything else you might have to pay within the next twelve months. Long-term debts include mortgages and any other installment loans (like for your car). In taking stock of your assets, use current market value for things like real estate and vehicles.

Good news! In addition to things like savings and other accounts, you can also count money that is owed to you by other people as an asset. As long as this money is coming your way in the foreseeable future, it can be regarded as part of your financial inventory.

While getting a formal appraisal may give you the most accurate assessment, it's not necessarily the most efficient way to proceed. To get approximate market values for your house, you can check out your state's property tax assessment Web site. For your car, try the *Kelley Blue Book* (online at ✑*www.kbb.com*). As for smaller items, you can determine which may have significant resale value. Again, you can get a professional appraiser, or you can try looking up similar items on a Web site like eBay to get approximate market values. Once you've ascertained reasonable values for your belongings, add them to your cash and investment accounts for a total asset figure.

Once you've figured out your assets, it's time to take an honest look at your liabilities. For now, we'll just add in your true debt, and leave out your regular monthly bills. (We'll take a look at those later when we talk about your budget.) In this section of your worksheet, include the outstanding balance of your mortgage and other installment loans, everything you owe on credit cards, and any unpaid personal loans. Total these up, and you have an accurate picture of your current debt load.

To calculate your net worth, subtract your total liabilities from your total assets. The result shows what you'd have left if you sold or cashed in all your assets and paid off all your liabilities. Here are some steps you can follow to calculate your net worth:

1. List all of your liquid (cash-like) assets: bank accounts, CDs, stocks, bonds, mutual funds, etc.

2. List your retirement accounts: every IRA, 401(k) plan, ESOP, etc.

3. List all of your physical assets at current market value, starting with your home, other real estate you own, vehicles, and any valuable smaller items (like jewelry) that you choose.

4. Add the value of all these items to get your total assets.

5. List all of your outstanding debts, and add those to get your total liabilities.

6. Subtract your total liabilities (step 5) from your total assets (step 4) to get your personal net worth.

7. Revisit your worksheet every three to six months at first, then at least once a year going forward, to adjust for any changes.

If the number you came up with as your net worth is greater than zero, you have a positive net worth, meaning you'd still have assets left if you settled all outstanding debts. If your bottom line is less than zero, you have a negative net worth, meaning you would still owe money even if you liquidated all your assets and put that cash toward your debts. Regardless of your personal bottom line, you now have a solid base to work from and will be able to make your financial plan accordingly.

Building a Budget

Once you've calculated your personal net worth, your next step will be looking at cash flow. When you're ready to start building your nest egg, you're going to need some cash to do it. However, there are things standing in the way of this cash stream, from your monthly bills to that nagging weekly urge to treat yourself to a dinner out. Frequent expenses like groceries and gasoline won't come as a big surprise to you. But newer cash drains like cell phones and Internet access are quickly working their way into the must-have spending category, knocking even the smartest spender's budget off-balance. New technologies and new products crop up with amazing frequency, making it harder and harder to curb excess spending. The solution is to outline your total expenses, knock off the unnecessary ones, create a budget, and stick to it.

ALERT!

It's remarkably easy to lose track of where your money is going. Many people indulge in small luxuries like buying coffee in the morning, ordering pizza for dinner, and renting a DVD at night (and forgetting to return it on time) more often than they realize. All these little extras add up to some big daily spending. Keep track of these expenditures for a week and see for yourself!

Don't get sucked in to the temptation of using your credit card for all your purchases as a simple way of tracking them. That strategy is great for the credit card companies, but it's not so good for your net worth. Instead, invest a little time in keeping an expense notebook; a mere two-week listing will do. You'll be glad that you don't have a whopping credit card bill at the end of the month, and you won't be making a year's worth of interest payments on a cup of coffee.

Budget Components

Before you get started building your budget, you should take a brief look at what makes up a budget. You may already know that budgets have both income and expense sections, but you may not recognize all the things that qualify for those categories. And since your budget will be used to help you create a nest egg, you should also add a section for savings.

Most budgets start with income. For these purposes, income includes all the cash you have flowing into your household. So, in addition to your regular take-home pay, you'll include items like interest and dividends you receive, any pension payments, and tax refunds. The second section, for expenses, will probably be a lot longer. This category includes things like mortgage or rent payments, utility and phone bills, groceries, cable, child-care costs, and entertainment. Don't forget to add in periodic expenditures, like auto insurance premiums or vet bills. The savings section includes all the cash you put away at the end of the day. For planning purposes, a good savings number to shoot for is 4 to 10 percent of your expenses, at least until you have enough to cover about three months of regular expenses.

To make your budget the best it can be—and not so annoying to work on that you just throw up your hands and walk away—here are a few simple guidelines to follow:

- **Be realistic when forming goals.** If your target budget is too hard to live with, you won't follow it.
- **Use real numbers, not estimates.** Estimates may help you fill in the blanks, but they won't help further your goals. You can find true figures by backtracking through your checkbook.
- **Use your computer to help track your budget.** Create a spreadsheet in Microsoft Excel, or pick up some prepackaged budget software, like Quicken or Microsoft Money.
- **Make your budget easier to read by categorizing some of your expenses.** For example, electricity, gas, water, and heating oil could all go under the heading "Utilities."
- **Include absolutely everything you spend money on.** Don't leave out even occasional expenses, like theater tickets, haircuts, and donations.
- **Initially, track your budget at least once a month.** Even better, update the numbers every time you get a paycheck.
- **Take an in-depth look at your budget each quarter to make sure it's accurate and to see how well you're managing your cash.**

Completing Your Budget

Once you've listed all of your income and expenditures, add the components of each section to come up with totals. Then subtract your total expenses and savings from your total income. The result is your net cash flow. If that number is greater than zero, you have positive cash flow. If it's less than zero, you have negative cash flow. If your bottom line comes out to exactly zero, your cash flow is considered neutral. When your result is positive cash flow, you have options. You can spend the money, hide it away for extra savings, or consider investing the surplus, perhaps in stocks or mutual funds. With a negative cash flow result, you'll first have to concentrate on either increasing your income or cutting back your expenses wherever possible. You might have to sacrifice some favorites, but it'll be worth it if you can save some cash every month.

Throughout this entire process, you may find that sticking to your budget is very difficult to do. You're not alone. Many people struggle to stay inside the boundaries of their personal budgets. You're also not alone if you already have debt to deal with. Try not to let debt discourage you—it's never too late to improve your situation. Luckily, there are ways to get debt under control and find a fresh start.

FACT

The average credit card debt for American households that carry a balance exceeds $10,000. Furthermore, Americans owe more in credit card debt than they do for education. That's scary! Do everything you can to get out and stay out of debt. It's far easier to get in than it is to get out.

The first step to dealing with debt is to stop using your credit cards so frequently. The second is to reduce the balance you're carrying. If you have equity in your home, you may want to consider a home equity loan while interest rates remain low. In addition to reducing your interest burden, you may be able to deduct some of the expense on your tax return (check with your accountant). Another approach is a debt consolidation loan. While the rates typically aren't as low as home equity loans, they are usually considerably lower than the interest credit card companies charge.

Leave Some Money for Investments

After creating your budget, you may find that everything that comes in immediately goes back out to cover expenses. In that case, you might not be able to start your investment plans just yet. However, you can still contribute as much as possible to your employer's retirement program to get yourself going. Generally, it's easier to decrease the amount of money needed for monthly expenses than it is to increase your income. So it's worth taking the time to identify which expenses you can eliminate or reduce. Maybe some of your expenses are luxuries that you could give up. Perhaps a debt refinancing or consolidation plan could reduce your monthly payments.

If you find that you have plenty of income to cover not only your regular monthly expenses but also entertainment (restaurants, movies, etc.) and incidental expenses (postage stamps, an occasional magazine), the time may be right for you to enter the world of investing.

Even when you think you're ready to start investing, you still need to consider a few things. First of all, you should not use money that is needed to cover other obligations in order to jumpstart your investment portfolio. If you are supplementing your income by adding to your credit card debt, any money you have at the end of the month isn't truly left over. Therefore, it would be wise to pay off your credit card debt before embarking on an investment plan. Likewise, if you have loans with high interest rates, you would be better off using any funds left over at the end of the month to pay down that debt.

Creating an Investment Cushion

Keep in mind that once you place your money into an investment portfolio, your funds will not be as readily accessible as they would be in a savings account. In fact, depending on the choices you make for your investments, you might find that your funds will not be liquid (easily accessible) for a considerable time.

Before you start investing, it's a good idea to set aside some money—roughly the equivalent of three to six months worth of living expenses—in a liquid account that you can easily tap into. A liquid account might be a regular savings account at a bank or credit union, one that provides some return on your deposit and from which your funds can be withdrawn at any time without penalty. By creating this cushion, you can feel confident that you will have enough funds to get through a tough situation (such as illness or unemployment) without disrupting your investment plan.

Knowing how much you can safely and reasonably invest is the first step to investing wisely. Since your income, monthly expenses, and lifestyle situations are likely to change over time, you should also re-evaluate your finances regularly to be sure your expense and investment plan is still meeting your needs.

Preliminary Planning

After you've decided you can afford to invest, it's time to take the next step. Sit down and very honestly determine your investment goals and objectives. Without an understanding of what you want your investment portfolio to do for you, it's nearly impossible to assess whether the return on your investment is high enough to meet your goals and whether the investment is safe enough to be reliable when you need it. Knowing and understanding the desired outcome of your investment will help keep you motivated and focused. Knowing and understanding your personal investment goals will help you determine what kind of growth/yield, income, and safety to seek from your investments.

Where to Cut Spending

In order to cut down on your spending, you have to ask yourself a few questions. Does your priority list match your spending habits? Are you spending money only on the important things in your life? Money may be dribbling out of your pockets without your even realizing it.

Consider your daily lunch expenses, assuming you dine out. If the average amount you spend each day is $6, you're spending $30 a week, $120 a month, and $1,440 per year on lunch. Making your own lunch could save you money and allow you to cover other expenses. Consider how you could use that $6 per day to reduce or eliminate your debt, or how you could put it to work as the start of a great investment future. Tracking your spending and comparing it to your priorities will help you identify what spending habits you need to change.

It's not an easy thing to do, but most people can find some areas of their budget where they can make some cuts. Some sacrifices such as cutting your cable service, eating out less, or forgoing the purchase of an SUV might be mildly painful, but keep in mind that they could make a real difference. While these are not fun choices, they may save you from financial troubles.

Do-It-Yourself Filing System

One major key to a good budget is organization. A basic filing system is an easy way to keep all your documents and records handy and in order. Of course, there are a few things you need to do to make this system work. First, you'll have to free up some space for this endeavor. It doesn't have to be very big or very fancy—a simple filing cabinet will do. You'll need to designate enough room to hold your monthly bills and other financial paperwork. Starting with a well-organized space can keep your budgeting tasks flowing more smoothly, saving you lots of time and aggravation.

ESSENTIAL

Once you have a filing system set up, the next tool you need is some financial software, like Quicken or Microsoft Money. These programs come with bill-pay reminders. They also deal with all the calculations, instantly track all of your account balances, and even flow into your tax-return software at the end of the year. You can even hook up to the program's online services so you can track your finances from anywhere.

As soon as you have the proper tools to work with, go through all your financial records. Get rid of everything you no longer need, like old phone bills, gas receipts, even pay stubs. (Read on to learn what you should and should not hold onto during this dumping session.) Toss out the instruction manuals for appliances you don't have anymore; trash the payment books from old loans that you've paid off. If you don't need it anymore—and it has nothing to do with your taxes—throw it out. Remember to shred anything with personal information on it to protect yourself from identity theft. Consider this list of documents you'll need to hold on to for a while; they should be easy to find in case you need them:

- **Tax returns:** Keep these for six years. Include the full return, plus all related receipts for itemized deductions, in your file. Although the IRS usually only has three years from the date you file to audit your return, they occasionally get more time. For example, if they claim you've understated your income by at least 25 percent, they can hold your file open for up to six years.
- **Investment information:** Any time you buy or sell an investment, hold on to the written record of that transaction. In addition, keep the annual summary your broker or fund company sends you at the end of the year. When tax time comes around, you'll need all that information to properly report your income. Also, save all the paperwork for any nondeductible IRAs you contribute to. That way, if the IRS tries to tax you twice, you'll have the proof to show the taxes were already paid.
- **Credit card and bank statements:** Credit card statements are crucial for recreating expenses, and bank statements can remind you of income outside your regular paycheck. When you come across tax-related items, highlight them, and make a note in your tax file. Keep credit card statements for one year and bank statements, including cancelled checks, for three years.
- **Medical bills:** Hold on to receipts for all your co-pays anytime you visit a medical professional or fill a prescription. It's also a good idea to keep benefit statements received from your insurance company, in case there's any dispute with the service provider. If you pay for your own insurance out of pocket (rather than through paycheck deductions), hold on to those statements as well.
- **Real estate records:** For every property you own, you should file the following documentation: the deed, property tax bills and

assessments, receipts for major repairs and improvements, and any home warranties.

- **Personal documents:** In this folder you'll place the records of your life, starting with your birth certificate. Also include your current passport, marriage license, divorce papers, paperwork pertaining to your children, military service records, and any other important personal information.

QUESTION?

Is the value of your donated items deductible?

Yes. Any items that you donate, whether to organizations like the Salvation Army or to a local church, are deductible. Just remember to get a written receipt. With charitable, noncash contributions, the rule is simple: No receipt means no deduction if you get audited.

When you're done going through all that paper and have figured out what you'll be keeping, start setting up your files. Create a folder for each category. Clearly label your folders so you can easily find any documents you're looking for. Put all the folders in your file cabinet—and be glad the most cumbersome part of this process is finished. To make sure no bills fall through the cracks, set up a payment schedule. Add each bill to the schedule the day it arrives, noting the due date. The simplest place to jot the due dates is on a calendar you use regularly. If you don't pay your bills as soon as they come in, set aside time every week to write checks for those bills coming due. Remember to balance your checkbook each time, and reconcile it to your bank statement every month. (Banks usually allows sixty days for you to bring errors to their attention.) And while you're at it, double-check your credit card statements when they come in, just to make sure there aren't any erroneous charges listed.

The Next Step

Once you've compiled a current financial snapshot and gained a good understanding of how you handle your money, it's time to take your first big step forward. Now that you know where you stand, you can decide where you want to go and how best to get there. Take a good look at your goals for the future before you continue.

One thing to do is make your goals specific and measurable. Instead of a vague plan to "save more," define your goal clearly. For instance, decide to save an additional $1,000 by December 31. Also, whenever you get your hands on extra cash—like a pay raise, a bonus, or a loan finally paid off—use it to pay down debt or add to savings. Extra cash is money you weren't counting on. You won't miss it, so use it to move you closer to your goals.

ALERT!

When you begin planning your investment portfolio, take inflation into account. Historically, inflation has averaged about 3 percent annually (although at times it's been much higher or virtually nonexistent). Based on that average 3-percent rate, you can expect prices to double every twenty-four years. For example, today's $25,000 car will cost about $50,000 in twenty-four years, about $37,500 in twelve years, and about $31,250 in six years.

You might also consider investing in the stock market. Over the long run, stock investing appears to be the best way to beat inflation. Sure, the market comes with inherent risk, but you can temper that through diversification. If you have a low risk tolerance and aren't comfortable with the ups and downs of stock investing, devote a smaller portion of your holdings to that asset class. Alternatively, you can shrug off some level of risk by investing (at least initially) in mutual funds, which provide instant stock diversification.

In addition, determine your retirement needs. You can base your initial estimate on your current earnings and lifestyle. If you plan to live it up in retirement, count on needing 100 percent of your current income. If your lifestyle will tone down some, or if you expect to continue earning some amount of income, figure you'll need about 60 to 70 percent of your current income. For more intricate calculations—like the potential effects of inflation and investment returns—check in with a financial planner, or try some financial planning software.

Another thing to do is assess your savings stage and adjust your holdings accordingly. The further you are from retirement, the more risks you can afford to take. In this early phase, you'll focus on building up your nest egg and investing more aggressively. The next phase comes when you're getting closer to retirement, but you still have some time left for your portfolio to grow. During this stage, you'll begin shifting out of the most aggressive investments toward a more conservative portfolio makeup. When you hit the home stretch, about three years before retirement, you'll switch your goal to capital preservation. In this final phase, you'll refocus your portfolio completely toward holding on to your capital rather than growing it. The exact timing of these phases depends almost entirely on you—the current size of your nest egg, your risk tolerance, and your age—with, of course, a nod to the current market conditions.

Finally, save money now. To carry yourself through twenty (or more) years of retirement, you'll need an awful lot of savings—that's why most people work for thirty or forty years before they finally can retire. The sooner you start, the more time your money has to grow. Every dollar you put away today gets you closer to a more comfortable, perhaps even luxurious, retirement. Another wise move is to buy life insurance. The amount you need depends largely on your stage of life. If you have children, you'll need more coverage: think orthodontia, college tuition, weddings, etc. If your kids are grown, you'll need less insurance, but you still want enough to keep your spouse living comfortably. While cash flow is still an issue, term insurance is the way to go. You can usually get a few hundred thousand dollars worth of coverage for a very reasonable monthly payment.

Chapter 2

The Lay of the Land

You may or may not have any preconceptions of Wall Street. Perhaps you imagine a frenetic landscape pulsing with traders in brightly colored jackets, all jumping up and down, voices straining to be heard over each other as deals are made, and bells ringing to signal the start and finish of each trading day. These notions, while still very much a reality, are becoming less representative of today's investment world. Nowadays, more investment is being done in cyberspace, and specialists are becoming obsolete. Nonetheless, it's important that any investor understand the various entities that comprise the investment market.

How Wall Street Works

In 1792, under a buttonwood tree near the then-quiet Wall Street, a handful of businessmen opened what is now known as the New York Stock Exchange. That exchange and "The Street" became known as hard-nosed places where great fortunes could be made—but at great risk. Most investments were kept for a very short term, and traders on the exchange tended to look out for themselves first, with attention going to their clients only if any spoils were left over.

For years, Wall Street insiders had the markets virtually to themselves. A lopsided playing field gave brokers, market makers, traders, and specialists a big advantage over small-account investors. Typically, insiders were in at the start of a stock's run-up, and they bowed out long before the stock tanked. Individual investors were left holding the bag. Information was peddled to the highest bidder, and tipsters—information merchants who delighted in spreading inside information—often provided investment advice. After many decades as a functioning exchange, the fastest form of information became the ticker tape, which reported only prices.

In 1792, twenty-four Wall Street merchants, each of whom paid $400 for a "trading seat" in mutual negotiations, signed the Buttonwood Agreement. This agreement outlined the regulations under which shares of public stock could be bought and sold. These regulations formed the basis for trading rules that still exist today and led to the formation in 1817 of the New York Stock Exchange.

Without adequate information, the investor was at the mercy of the market. After the crash of 1929, financial reformers made substantial gains in cleaning up the markets, and investors eventually benefited. Much improved methods for analyzing risk were developed, along with efforts to introduce what is now called market transparency.

For years, the term "investor" meant "institutional investor." Pension funds, insurance funds, and mutual funds dominated the markets, acting on behalf of individuals but exercising their own special brand of institutional influence. Institutional investors remained in the driver's seat until the NYSE introduced negotiated commissions in 1975. This scheme opened the door for individual investors by allowing discount brokers to begin offering bare-bones brokerage services to them.

Another twenty years and unforeseen new advances in technology—particularly the advent of the Internet—were needed before the full implications of this power shift from institutional to individual investor would be felt. By the beginning of the 1990s, it was clear that individual investors were serious players in the world of Wall Street. It's true that there are no guarantees when it comes to investing. But with the advent of online investing, and an aggressive play for smaller investors by the two leading stock markets—the New York Stock Exchange and the NASDAQ—buying and selling investments that interest you has only gotten easier and less expensive.

FACT

Several markets make up what is known in general as the stock market. Many stocks are traded on the New York Stock Exchange (NYSE), the National Association of Securities Dealers Automated Quotations (NASDAQ), and the American Stock Exchange (Amex). In addition, such cities as Boston, Chicago, Philadelphia, Denver, San Francisco, and Los Angeles have exchanges, as do major international cities like London and Tokyo.

Competition, both domestic and global, continues to make stock transactions more transparent and more accessible to all investors. By understanding how the different stock markets work and compete for your business, you'll be better equipped to succeed in the investing world.

The NYSE

Also known as "the Big Board," the New York Stock Exchange (NYSE) is home to prominent industry players like IBM, AOL, and Disney. The Big Board is not for little-league players. Among other requirements for inclusion on the NYSE, a company must have at least 1.1 million public shares of stock outstanding. It must show pre-tax income of at least $6.5 million over the three most recent fiscal years (with each year equal to or greater than the previous), and the company's market value of public shares must be at least $40 million. In addition, the company's most recent year's pre-tax income must be at least $2.5 million, and its net tangible assets must be a minimum of $40 million.

The NYSE is a 36,000-square-foot facility located in the heart of New York City's financial district, which is wedged eastward between lower Broadway and the South Street Seaport and which extends all the way down to the southern tip of Manhattan. The oldest stock exchange in the United States, the NYSE uses an agency auction market system designed to allow the public to experience the actual trading as much as possible. NYSE members relay open bids and offers on behalf of institutions and individual investors. Buy and sell orders for each listed security meet directly on the trading floor in assigned locations. Every listed security is traded in a unique location, at one of the floor's seventeen trading posts.

The Specialist

Specialists (or specs) are members of the NYSE or American Stock Exchange (Amex) who perform a unique function by acting as the focal point for trading the stocks assigned to them. Specialists play a significant but perhaps diminishing role in the NYSE. Whether they specialize in the shares of blue chips or of small growth companies, the job of the specialist is to help maintain fair and orderly markets in those stocks.

Each stock on the NYSE is allocated to a specialist who trades only in specific stocks at a trading post. All buying and selling of stock occurs at that location. Buyers and sellers—represented on the floor by brokers—meet openly at the trading post to find the best price for a security. The people who gather around the specialist's post are referred to as the trading crowd. Bids to buy and offers to sell are made by open outcry, hence the perceived chaos on the floor. When the highest bid meets the lowest offer, a trade is executed.

ESSENTIAL

The NYSE is home to approximately 450 specialists who work for thirty-eight specialist firms. Their work is published in the Market Lab section of *Barron's* magazine, with a two-week time lag. Why would you want to read two-week-old information? The reason is that these market specialists have an uncanny knack for predicting market movement. If they're betting against the market by selling or short-selling stock, it's a fairly good bet that the market will be going down.

While the majority of volume on the NYSE (approximately 88 percent) occurs with no intervention from the dealer, the specialist is responsible to a large degree for maintaining the market's fairness, competitiveness, and efficiency. Although specialists cannot control the price of a stock, they are responsible for ensuring that changes in price are gradual and that all customers have had a chance to participate at a given price.

Behind the frenzied spectacle that many outsiders picture when they think of the NYSE trading floor is a methodical and organized system of trading, in which the price of any stock is set purely by rule of supply and demand in an auction setting. Specialists help match buyers and sellers, but shares are always sold to the highest bidder.

The End of the Specialist?

In an historic move that could signal the end of its open-outcry auction system, in August of 2004, the New York Stock Exchange announced a plan that would end many limits on electronic trading and expand computer-driven orders. The proposal would create a hybrid market, which would still include the traditional system of floor traders who manually handle orders but would increase the use of the exchange's electronic trading platform, called NYSE Direct. Under the plan, the exchange would eliminate many of the limits on the size, timing, and types of orders that could be placed through NYSE Direct. This proposal still needs to be approved by the U.S. Securities and Exchange Commission, but it has been months in the making. Institutional investors have been demanding greater transaction speed, in addition to the NYSE traditional strengths of pricing and deep liquidity.

Trading practices at the 212-year-old Big Board have been under scrutiny since 2003 in the wake of a trading scandal involving the specialists on the floor of the exchange. More recently, proposed reforms to the structure of the U.S. stock markets have placed a spotlight on the way the Big Board handles trades. The proposal would allow specialists to work electronically, but if instituted, it would change the tenor of the trading floor at the NYSE forever.

The NASDAQ and the Amex

The National Association of Security Dealers Automated Quotations (NASDAQ) and the American Stock Exchange (Amex) united in October 1998, creating the NASDAQ/Amex Market Group. The Amex is now a subsidiary of the National Association of Securities Dealers, Inc. (NASD). With this joining of two of the world's top securities markets comes an alliance that creates an even more globally competitive market. However, the NASDAQ and the Amex are currently still operating as separate entities.

FACT

The NASDAQ is an over-the-counter (OTC) market, which means its securities are traded through telephone and computer networks as opposed to an auction exchange (such as that used on the American Stock Exchange). NASDAQ is also the world's largest stock market in terms of dollar volume.

The NASDAQ began operating in February of 1971, with 250 companies, as the world's first electronic stock market. It has since evolved into a full-fledged stock market with over 5,000 companies listed. Trading volume broke the 500 million shares-per-day barrier in 1996. More initial public offerings (IPOs) are listed on NASDAQ than on any other U.S. stock market.

The NASDAQ market is an inter-dealer market represented by over 600 securities dealers trading more than 15,000 different securities. These securities dealers are called market makers (MMs). Unlike the NYSE, the NASDAQ does not operate as an auction market. Instead, market makers are expected to compete against each other to post the best quotes (that is, the best bid/ask prices).

The NASDAQ has no single specialist through whom transactions pass. NASDAQ's market structure allows multiple market participants to trade stock through a sophisticated computer network linking buyers and sellers from around the world. Together, these participants help ensure transparency and liquidity for a company's stock while maintaining an orderly market that functions under tight regulatory controls.

Two separate markets comprise the NASDAQ Stock Market: the NASDAQ National Market, which includes the NASDAQ's largest and most actively traded securities, and the NASDAQ SmallCap Market for emerging growth companies.

The Amex lists over 700 companies and is the world's second largest auction marketplace. Like the NYSE, the Amex uses an agency auction market system designed to allow the public as much access to public shares as possible.

What's in a Trade?

From the perspective of an investor, the process of buying and selling stocks seems pretty simple. If you use a full-service broker, you can just call her up on the phone and place an order for 100 shares of Coca-Cola. Within a few minutes, you receive a confirmation that your order has been completed, and just like that, you're the proud new owner of stock in Coca-Cola. Behind the scenes, however, there's a lot of action that takes place between your order and the confirmation.

After you place the order with your broker to buy 100 shares of the Coca-Cola Company, the broker sends the order to the firm's order department. The order department sends the order to the firm's clerk, who works on the floor of the exchange where shares of Coca-Cola are traded (the NYSE). The clerk gives the order to the firm's floor trader, who also works on the exchange floor. The floor trader then goes to the specialist's post for Coca-Cola and finds another floor trader who is willing to sell shares of Coca-Cola. The traders agree on a price, and the order is executed. Finally, the floor trader reports the trade to the clerk and the order department. The order department confirms the order with the broker, and the broker confirms the trade with you.

This is how a traditional stock exchange works, but much of the action that takes place when you buy or sell a stock is now being handled with the assistance of computers. Even if you bought a stock that trades on a stock exchange, your order may be executed with little or no human intervention. You can log on to a brokerage firm's Web site, enter an order, have the trade executed, and receive a confirmation—all within sixty seconds or less. And once you become an Internet-proficient investor, you'll find that you don't need a personal broker to execute your trades.

The Stock Indexes

The Dow Jones Industrial Average (DJIA, also called the Dow) is the most prominent stock index in the world. It was named after Charles H. Dow, first editor of the *Wall Street Journal,* and his one-time partner Edward Jones (although Jones was not instrumental in creating the index). Dow's creation revolutionized investing, as it was the first publicly published gauge of the market. The thirty stocks on the Dow, which are all part of the New York Stock Exchange, are all those of established blue-chip companies like McDonald's, Coca-Cola, DuPont, and Eastman Kodak. The Dow was created to mimic the U.S. stock market as a whole, and its companies represent a variety of market segments such as entertainment, automotive, health-care products, and financial services.

General Electric is the only company that was included in the original Dow Jones Industrial Average, created in 1896, that is still part of its makeup today. However, General Electric was dropped in 1898, restored in 1899, taken out again in 1901, and then put back on the list in 1907.

The thirty stocks of the Dow Jones Industrial Average companies are weighted by stock price, rather than market capitalization (which is much more common). Basically, the Dow number is calculated by adding up the prices of all the stocks, then dividing by the number of stocks included in the index, adjusted for stock splits (which makes that divisor higher). The important point to remember is that each company carries equal weight.

Some indexes are capitalization weighted, giving greater weight to stocks with greater market value, while other indexes treat each stock equally. For example, consider Standard & Poor's (S&P) Composite Index of 500 Stocks. The Standard & Poor's 500 Index, commonly known as the S&P 500, is a benchmark that is widely used by professional stock investors. The S&P 500 represents 500 stocks—400 industrial stocks, twenty transportation stocks, forty utility stocks, and forty financial stocks. This index consists primarily of stocks listed on the NYSE, although it also features stocks that are a part of the Amex as well as some over-the-counter (OTC) stocks.

Russell 2000 and Value Line Index (also known as the Value Line Investment Survey) are two other indexes. The Russell 2000 was created to be a comprehensive representation of the U.S. small-cap equities market, which includes companies with market capitalization between $300 million and $2 billion. It measures the performance of the 2,000 smallest companies in the Russell 3000 Index. The Value Line Index tracks 1,700 equally weighted stocks from the NYSE, NASDAQ, Amex, and OTC markets. It acts as a market barometer, widely held to be the best measure of the overall market and a crucial monitoring tool for any investor.

The U.S. Securities and Exchange Commission (SEC)

After the Great Depression, the U.S. Securities and Exchange Commission (SEC) was created to regulate the securities industry as a whole. It was during this time that Congress also passed the Securities Exchange Act of 1934. The SEC oversees the industry to ensure that no illegal activity is being conducted. In addition, the commission sets many standards for both brokers and investors. Companies trading on stock exchanges nationwide must be registered with the SEC.

Essentially, the SEC administers federal securities laws and issues rules and regulations. Its primary mission is to provide protection for investors and to see that the securities markets are fair and honest. The commission makes sure that there is adequate and effective disclosure of information to the investing public. It also regulates firms engaged in the purchase or sale of securities, people who provide investment advice, and investment companies.

In addition to its other duties, the SEC oversees trading activity to ensure that investors are getting the appropriate prices when both buying and selling securities. The SEC also requires that publicly traded companies publish regular financial reports. The reports provided to the SEC for annual or quarterly reports are called Form 10K or Form 10Q, respectively.

Insider information is one of the issues the SEC oversees. Essentially, insider information (also known as insider trading) deals with the buying and selling of stock based on confidential information obtained from an inside source. Because such information is not available to the rest of the public, those insiders have an unfair advantage when it comes to trading. In fact, insider trading typically comes to light long after the fact, when it's much too late for the average investor to recover. And though it makes for splashy headlines—think Martha Stewart, Enron, and WorldCom—a good story does nothing to help people recoup their losses.

The SEC's Division of Enforcement is charged with enforcing the federal securities laws. The division's responsibilities include investigating possible violations of federal securities laws and recommending appropriate remedies for the commission's consideration.

Invest Like the Pros

In the late 1990s, corporations began responding to the growing numbers of individual investors and their demands for information and services.

Continuing advances in technology were suddenly creating fast, comprehensive, and cheap information conduits between investors and corporations. Hundreds of thousands of individuals were tapping into the Web regularly, easily surfing their way to online resources and corporate Web sites, building stock portfolios, compiling information, and conducting transactions online.

Information flowing to the investment community is now equally available to institutional and individual investors. The professionals retain a big advantage, of course, because of their direct access to corporate executives at meetings and through phone conversations. Most individual investors can't pick up the phone and get the CEO of a major corporation on the line. But the tables have turned in favor of individual investors, thanks primarily to the Internet.

The World Wide Web offers advantages and benefits that were previously available only to professional investors. The Internet gives you, the individual investor, the same access to analysts' research on individual companies that a broker at Goldman Sachs might have. You can look at up-to-the-minute stock and index charts and see if things are moving in the direction you expected. (Looking at charts and trends can actually give you a glimpse of what's going on before a big story hits the news.) Anyone can now download vast amounts of stock market data and information at any time, and if you get worried about something you discover in the middle of the night, you don't have to wait until the start of the next business day to retrieve information from your stockbroker. You can follow global markets around the clock, see the impact of international and after-hours trading, even participate in after-hours trading with your online broker. You can access information in real time via the Web, allowing you to make better-informed decisions quickly. And, you don't have to wait to get your broker on the phone to send a trade order to the trading floor—you can do it at the speed of light using online brokerage services.

With a little effort and some practice, you can have a veritable plethora of Internet analysis tools at your fingertips. You can even choose online portfolio tracking tools that automatically place a buy or sell order when an increase or decrease in stock price or a similar event is triggered. All these tools can help you by providing better information you can use in making your investment decisions.

E ALERT!

For all its benefits, cyberspace hasn't completely eroded the institutional investor's biggest advantages—personal connections, portfolio size, and investing skill. Professional traders and analysts can still get the chief financial officer of any company in America on the phone when they need to, but a retail investor with 500 or 1,000 shares can't.

The good news is that publicly traded companies are now allowing high-end individual traders into their initial public offering (IPO) information sessions via the Internet. Known as "road shows," these sessions have been a mainstay on Wall Street for years. The CEO and management team visit a brokerage house or fund firm, lay out a blueprint for the company's future, and (they hope) walk away with a commitment from the money managers to buy hefty chunks of stock when the stock goes public—at favorable prices, of course. The most important aspect of road shows—attendance at the live event itself, rather than an Internet presentation—is still closed to individual investors. If you participate in one of these sessions, you'll probably miss the backslapping and wink-and-nod information sharing that transpires when the cameras are off.

The information now accessible through the Internet—for example, SEC filings, product information, and news reports—is a bit of a double-edged sword. While such information can help you be a savvier player in the market, it can also put individual investors at a disadvantage. Institutions are in a better position to sift through the information and decide what's really important. But don't let yourself get discouraged in the face of all the information you'll encounter as you set out on your journey to build an investment portfolio. The trading turf today is significantly more user-friendly for individual investors that at any other time in Wall Street's history.

Chapter 3

Ladies and Gentlemen, Start Your Portfolios

Whether you're working with a financial advisor or a brokerage firm, you're at the wheel of your own investment vehicle. You decide the pace at which you head into the investment world, and you determine how much risk you're willing to take in order to win. However, you're responsible for more than just making investment decisions. You'll also have to do independent research. That includes due diligence on companies where you're considering parking some of your investment dollars, as well as portfolio tracking and performance monitoring to keep your investment portfolio chugging along in the right direction.

Investment Cornerstones

Having all the ingredients for success is a good start, but you won't get too far without the recipe. If you take all the ingredients for a delicious pastry and throw them together in equal parts, you'll end up with an inedible brick. Developing the art of measuring and mixing your ingredients so that they work together to create investment perfection requires patience and diligence on your part. You need to figure out the delicate balance that will provide the most effective and productive investment portfolio for your needs.

FACT

Most investment portfolios are comprised of five or so components. Usually, they include some combination of the following: liquid assets (cash and equivalents), fixed income (bonds and annuities), equities (stocks), real estate, precious metals, and other investments.

Figuring out which stocks and bonds will comprise your portfolio isn't a difficult process, as long as you apply the tried-and-true investment tenets: knowing your risk levels, having a fixed time horizon, using some form of investment diversification, and having fixed investment goals (such as retirement, college tuition, or starting your own business). Two of the more important factors in your portfolio decision-making process are risk and diversification. Read on to learn more about these factors.

Why Good Poker Players Make Good Investors

"Every serious choice that a man or a woman makes is a leap, more or less frightening, into contingency. Not to make those choices, not to open oneself to misfortune and the fear of misfortune, is a tempting choice, but one gives into it at the risk of never living a fully human life," says Nelson Aldrich, multimillionaire investor and author of the best-selling book *Old Money*. Aldrich is simply stating what is already obvious to legions of risk-loving Americans. Risk is at the core of many favorite pastimes, like betting on poker, and it's what makes those pastimes so appealing to participants.

PartyPoker.com, the world's largest online poker Web site, hosts more than 35,000 simultaneous players during its peak traffic time every day. That is no insignificant achievement, especially considering the site only launched in August of 2001. With the incredible upsurge in poker popularity around the world, greatly driven by televised poker tournaments, poker has undergone a renaissance of sorts, with bricks-and-mortar poker rooms experiencing a 40-percent increase from 2003 to 2004. Online gaming has jumped a whopping 500–600 percent during the same time period.

But even those numbers pale in comparison to the amounts of money pouring into Wall Street these days. According to the Investment Company Institute, mutual fund investors alone account for $7 trillion worth of assets through mid-2004. The New York Stock Exchange's "Shareownership 2000" survey estimated that there were 84 million direct and indirect U.S. shareholders in 2000, representing 43.6 percent of the country's adult population. That figure was up 21 percent from 1995's 69.3 million and up 61 percent from 1989's 52.3 million.

Risk is the reason that those who excel at poker are usually those who excel on Wall Street. Each industry rewards those participants who take matters very seriously and understand risk, just as they understand preparation, discipline, and opportunity. Good poker players, like good investors, also understand human emotion, and they leverage that information to separate other people from their money.

Consider the legendary financier Jay Gould, who made a fortune in the railroad industry and was a dominating force on Wall Street during the latter half of the nineteenth century. Gould was so good at separating people from their money that he earned the moniker "The Devil of Wall Street." Once, when Gould was attending his local church service on Monday, the minister pulled Gould aside and asked him how to invest a $30,000 windfall that had fallen into the congregation's lap. Gould advised the minister to invest the entire sum in shares of Missouri Pacific Railroad. The minister did so and watched happily for a short spell as the stock rose. But after awhile the stock slid precipitously, finally falling below fifty cents per share. The minister, distraught over losing virtually all of the $30,000, poured his woes out to Gould, who snapped open his checkbook and covered the entire loss with one sweep of his pen. Then the minister confessed that despite Gould's request to the contrary, he had passed the stock tip along to other members of the congregation. "Oh, I guessed that," Gould replied merrily. "As a matter of fact, they were the ones I was after."

Gould knew, like good poker players know, that there is little in the investment world that is more delicate and more personal than the trade-off between risk and reward. The more uncertain the investment, the greater the investment risk. The greater the investment risk, the greater the opportunity for hefty investment returns. If you're uncomfortable with too much risk and seek to minimize it, you'll be penalized with lower investment returns. You can't completely eliminate risk. If you don't take any risk, you surely won't make any money.

Investment risk is tied to market volatility—the fluctuations in the financial markets that happen constantly over time. The sources of this volatility are many. Interest-rate changes, inflation, political consequences, and economic trends can all create combustible market conditions with the power to change a portfolio's performance results in a hurry. Ironically, this volatility, by its very nature, creates the opportunities for economic benefit in our own portfolios.

What's Your Tolerance for Risk?

Your comfort level as an investor depends on many factors, including your age, financial needs, number of dependents, and level of debt. If you're twenty-five years old, single, childless, and debt-free, you obviously have far more tolerance for risk than a fifty-five-year-old nearing retirement with two kids in college.

Trying to pin down your tolerance for risk is an uncertain process that's forever susceptible to second-guessing. You can never be quite sure what your tolerance for risk will be from year to year. But the following test, developed by Lincoln Benefit Life, a subsidiary of Allstate Life Group, can help clear things up. Simply choose an answer from the choices given for each question and assess your results at the end.

1. **If someone made me an offer to invest 15 percent of my net worth in a deal he said had an 80-percent chance of being profitable, I'd say:**

   A. No level of profit would be worth that kind of risk.
   B. The level of profit would have to be seven times the amount I invested.
   C. The level of profit would have to be three times the amount I invested.
   D. The level of profit would have to be at least as much as my original investment.

2. **How comfortable would I be assuming a $10,000 debt in the hope of achieving a $20,000 gain over the next few months?**

   A. Totally uncomfortable. I'd never do it.
   B. Somewhat uncomfortable. I'd probably never do it.
   C. Somewhat uncomfortable. But I might do it.
   D. Very comfortable. I'd definitely do it.

3. **I am holding a lottery ticket that's gotten me to the finals, where I have a 1-in-4 chance of winning the $100,000 jackpot. I'd be willing to sell my ticket before the drawing, but for nothing less than:**

   A. $15,000
   B. $20,000
   C. $35,000
   D. $60,000

4. **How often do I bet more than $150 on one or more of these activities: professional sports gambling, casino gambling, or lottery tickets?**

   A. Never.
   B. Only a few times in my life.
   C. Just in one of these activities in the past year.
   D. In two or more of these activities in the past year.

5. **If a stock I bought doubled in the year after I bought it, I'd:**

   A. Sell all my shares.
   B. Sell half my shares.
   C. Not sell any shares.
   D. Buy more shares.

6. **I have a high-yielding certificate of deposit that is about to mature, and interest rates have dropped so much that I feel compelled to invest in something with a higher yield. The most likely place I'd invest the money is:**

   A. U.S. savings bonds.
   B. A short-term bond fund.
   C. A long-term bond fund.
   D. A stock fund.

7. **Whenever I have to decide where to invest a large amount of money, I:**

   A. Delay the decision.
   B. Get someone else, like my broker, to decide for me.
   C. Share the decision with my advisors.
   D. Decide on my own.

8. Which of the following describes how I make my investment decisions?

    A. Never on my own.
    B. Sometimes on my own.
    C. Often on my own.
    D. Totally on my own.

9. My luck in investing is:

    A. Terrible.
    B. Average.
    C. Better than average.
    D. Fantastic.

10. My investments are successful mainly because:

    A. Fate is always on my side.
    B. I was in the right place at the right time.
    C. When opportunities arose, I took advantage of them.
    D. I carefully planned them to work out that way.

Give yourself one point for each answer **A**, two points for each answer **B**, three points for each answer **C**, and four points for each answer **D**.

If you scored nineteen points or fewer, you're a conservative investor who feels uncomfortable taking risks. You probably realize that you will have to take some calculated risks to attain your financial goals, but this doesn't mean you will be comfortable doing so.

If you scored twenty to twenty-nine points, you're a moderate investor who feels comfortable taking moderate risks. You are probably willing to take reasonable risks without a great deal of discomfort.

If you scored thirty or more points, you're an aggressive investor who is willing to take high risks in search of high returns. You are not greatly stressed by taking significant risks.

Typical behavior indicates that most investors either don't understand risk or choose to ignore it. Here's how we know. When the market is rising, money floods into stocks and mutual funds, even as each upward move in price increases risk and reduces potential returns. In a bear market, many investors engage in near-panic selling, even though each drop in price decreases risk and increases potential returns. For most investors, the two most effective ways to manage risk are to limit your aggressive exposure to a small part of the whole portfolio and to stick with your program once you have embarked on it.

Different Types of Risk

There are many different types of risk, and some are more complicated than others. The risk classifications you'll learn about here are the primary forms of risk, which aren't as complex as some. You'll likely run into some of the following five risking categories when investing in your separate account plan.

There are a lot of details that go along with determining risk. But one of the biggest mistakes an investor can make is to sell the impact of investment risk short—whether the investment is in a separate account or not. Spend some time thinking about your tolerance for risk, and then invest accordingly. If you're working with a personal financial advisor, make sure you discuss risk before deciding on the securities that will comprise your separate account portfolio. And never underestimate the power of an exit plan. When you're prepared to react to a drastic change in the markets, your portfolio will have a fighting chance at self preservation.

Stock Specific Risk

Any single stock carries a specific amount of risk for the investor. You can minimize this risk by making sure your portfolio is diversified. An investor dabbling in one or two stocks can see his investment wiped out; although it is still possible, the chances of that happening in a well-diversified portfolio are much more slender. (One example would be the event of an overall bear market, as was seen in the early 1990s.) By adding a component of trend analysis to your decision-making process, and by keeping an eye on the big picture (global economics and politics, for example), you are better equipped to prevent the kinds of devastating losses that come with an unexpected sharp turn in the markets.

Risk of Passivity and Inflation Rate Risk

People who don't trust the financial markets and who feel more comfortable sticking their money in a bank savings account could end up with less than they expect. Because the interest rates on savings accounts cannot keep up with the rate of inflation, they decrease the purchasing power of your investment at the same time—even as they preserve your core investing principle of avoiding risk. For this somewhat paradoxical reason, savings accounts may not always be your safest choice. You may want to consider investments with at least slightly higher returns (like inflation-indexed U.S. Treasury bonds) to help you combat inflation without giving up your sense of security.

A close relative of passivity risk, inflation risk is based upon the expectation of lower purchasing power of each dollar down the road. Typically, stocks are the best investment when you're interested in outpacing inflation, and money-market funds are the least effective in combating inflation.

Market Risk

Market risk is pretty much what it sounds like. Every time you invest money in the financial markets, even via a conservative money-market mutual fund, you're subjecting your money to the risk that the markets will decline or even crash. With market risk, uncertainty due to changes in the overall stock market is caused by global, political, social, or economic events and even by the mood of the investing public. Perhaps the biggest investment risk of all, though, is not subjecting your money to market risk. If you don't put your money to work in the stock market, you won't be able to benefit from the stock market's growth over the years.

Credit Risk

Usually associated with bond investments, credit risk is the possibility that a company, agency, or municipality might not be able to make interest or principal payments on its notes or bonds. The greatest risk of default usually lies with corporate debt: Companies go out of business all the time. On the flip side, there's virtually no credit risk associated with U.S. Treasury-related securities, because they're backed by the full faith and credit of the U.S. government. To measure the financial health of bonds, credit rating agencies like Moody's and Standard & Poor's assign them investment grades. Bonds with an A rating are considered solid, while C-rated bonds are considered unstable.

Currency Risk

Although most commonly considered in international or emerging-market investing, currency risk can occur in any market at any time. This risk comes about due to currency fluctuations that may affect the value of foreign investments or profits, or the holdings of U.S. companies with interests overseas. Currency risk necessarily increases in times of geopolitical instability, like those caused by the global threat of terrorism or war.

Interest Rate Risk

When bond interest rates rise, the price of the bonds falls (and vice versa). Fluctuating interest rates have a significant impact on stocks and bonds. Typically, the longer the maturity of the bond, the larger the impact of interest rate risk. But long-term bonds normally pay out higher yields to compensate for the greater risk.

Economic Risk

When the economy slows, corporate profits—and thus stocks—could be hurt. For example, political instability in the Middle East makes investing there a dicey deal at best. This is true even though much of the region is flush with oil, arguably the commodity in greatest demand all over the planet.

Diversification

Diversification simply means dividing your investments among a variety of types. It's one of the best ways, if not the absolute best, to protect your portfolio from the pendulum swings of the economy and the financial markets. Since a separate account portfolio may invest in many different securities, a decline in the value of one security may be offset by the rise in value of another.

Diversification can take other forms as well. For example, you could diversify your common stock holdings by purchasing stocks representing many different industries. That would be safer than concentrating in a single sector. Or you could diversify your bond holdings by buying a mixture of high-quality bonds and some lower-rated bonds. The high-quality bonds would tend to reduce the overall risk associated with the bond portfolio.

ALERT!

No matter how diversified your portfolio, you can never completely eliminate risk. You can *reduce* the risk associated with individual stocks, but general market risks affect nearly every stock, so it is important to also diversify among different assets. The key is to find a medium between risk and return; this ensures that you achieve your financial goals while still getting a good night's rest.

Another important form of diversification is obtained when you invest in different types of securities—stocks, bonds, real estate, and money market instruments, to name the major investment types. Diversifying your holdings over several asset classes, particularly among those that tend to perform differently under the same economic circumstances, adds an extra layer of protection to your portfolio.

Understanding Asset Allocation

Investors often find the concept of asset allocation confusing or intimidating when they're initially structuring their portfolios. But it's actually quite simple. Asset allocation is nothing more than determining where your investment capital should be placed. This determination is based on variables like net worth, time frame, risk acceptance, and other assets the investor owns. Generally, properly allocating your investment dollars means assembling a portfolio from the three major asset categories: cash, fixed income, and equities. Cash includes money in the bank, short-term investments such as U.S. Treasury bills, and money market mutual funds. Fixed-income investments include bonds, guaranteed investment certificates, and other interest-generating securities. Equities are stock market investments. Equities can be further subdivided into more specific categories, such as value and growth.

Anywhere on Wall Street, the goal of asset allocation is to achieve the best possible return while reducing the risk. But how do you determine what the best performing sectors are and what your asset allocation mix should be? Here are some good questions to ask yourself to determine your investor profile:

1. Do market fluctuations keep you awake at night?
2. Are you unfamiliar with investing?
3. Do you consider yourself more a saver than an investor?
4. Are you fearful of losing 25 percent of your assets in a few days or weeks?
5. Are you comfortable with the ups and downs of the securities markets?
6. Are you knowledgeable about investing and the securities markets?
7. Are you investing for a long-term goal?
8. Can you withstand considerable short-term losses?

If you answered yes to the first four questions, you are most likely a conservative investor. If you answered yes to the last four questions, you are more likely an aggressive investor. If you fall somewhere in between, you could call yourself a moderate investor.

It is a tricky business to achieve the right mix of stock types (small, mid, and large caps, as well as internationals) and bonds (short, medium, and long-term) for maximum return on your volatility tolerance while also maintaining adequate diversification. Even a lot of brokers and fund managers get it wrong. For that reason, considering whether to consult a qualified financial planner or advisor should be at the top of your investment to-do list.

Many financial advisors say, quite sensibly, that your asset allocation plan depends on where you are in life. If you're just starting out, a long-term strategy that emphasizes stocks is advised. This strategy tends to emphasize growth to build assets by investing in more aggressive stocks. In order to moderate risk, it may also include a commitment to income investments, such as bonds. An example of a portfolio that employs a long-term strategy may include 70 percent equities, 25 percent bonds, and 5 percent short-term instruments or cash.

If you're nearing or are in retirement, advisors often advocate a short-term strategy that relies more heavily on bonds to place more emphasis on capital preservation. This strategy is designed to emphasize current income, capital preservation, and liquidity, while maintaining a smaller portion of the portfolio in stocks for growth potential. An example of a portfolio that employs a short-term strategy may include 50 percent bonds, 20 percent equities, and 30 percent short-term instruments or cash.

ESSENTIAL

When establishing an asset allocation strategy, there are a few things you should do. For one, determine how long you'll be investing. Then decide how much risk you can take. Next, pick a target mix that's right for you, and select investments that will help you achieve that mix. Finally, adjust your investments gradually. Start with your future deferrals to match your asset mix, and gradually redirect existing balances to fit into your overall plan.

There are two primary ways of allocating assets. The first method is to use a stable policy over time. Based on your income needs and risk tolerance, you might pursue a balanced strategy. This might require putting 25 percent of your dollars in each class of assets, such as stocks, bonds, cash, and real estate. Then, each quarter or year, you rebalance those dollars back to your original allocation of 25 percent in each class. This forces you to sell off some of the best-performing assets while buying more of the weakest performers. This allocation system eliminates the need to make decisions on the expected return for each class and instead allows for more stable returns over long periods of time.

The second means of allocating assets is through an active strategy. With this method, you first determine your tolerance for risk and your long-term goals. Then you allocate the range of your total portfolio you will invest in each class. Thus, if you need a good mix of growth and income, you might allow your investment in stocks to range from 35 percent to 65 percent of your portfolio, based on the market. You would develop these ranges for each asset class.

An active strategy involves making a prediction of where you expect each class of asset to go. If you believe we are in a fast-growing equities market, for example, you would put the maximum amount of dollars into common stocks or common stock mutual funds. Therefore, you would be lowering the amount of dollars invested in other asset classes. Likewise, if you believe that we are in a period of great risk for the markets, you would put more dollars into cash as a means of protecting your portfolio.

Obviously, an active strategy requires a lot of homework and a good knowledge of the financial markets and what impacts them. You'll have to track your investments at least weekly and adjust your holdings based on your revised expectations—as well as on their actual performance. You'll also have to take into account greater market forces and trends, changes in the global political and economic scene, even seasonal differences in sector performance as you examine your holdings, deciding which to hold on to and which to cut loose. It is a higher-risk strategy. If you make the wrong choices, you put your portfolio at a greater risk than if you had pursued a stable strategy. But if you consistently make the right calls (an outcome that becomes more frequent as you gain experience and insight), you can make substantially higher returns.

Organizing your asset allocation campaign is a fairly straightforward process, once you get the hang of it.

Investor Profile

Managing your own expectations is a big part of your investment planning process. You've probably heard about buy-and-hold investing and why it doesn't really matter what the market's doing when you get in, as long as you stay in. There's a great deal of truth in that line of thinking. Studies show that stocks can grow (on average) up to 10 to 12 percent annually, and bonds can grow at a rate of up to 6 to 8 percent per year, for longer term U.S.

Treasury instruments. Combined with the miracle of compound interest (your accumulated investment returns rolled over year after year), a long-term outlook coupled with a solid, disciplined investment strategy can yield big bucks over twenty, thirty, and especially forty-plus years.

The trick is in staying in the markets and not missing its sharp upturns. People who engage in market timing—market timers, those Wall Street daredevils who try to get in and out of the stock market at the most optimal moments—risk missing those market spikes by weaving in and out of the financial markets. And that's money that's hard to make back.

ALERT!

Market timing in funds used to be viewed as a nuisance, an arcane practice by a handful of cunning investors. But timing is now under the microscope of regulators in Massachusetts and New York, who say the practice is unfair to individual investors—and illegal, in some cases.

Market timers also generally experience higher transaction costs compared to a buy-and-hold strategy. Every time an investor sells or buys securities, a transaction fee is incurred. Even if the market timer achieves above-average returns, the transaction costs could negate the superior performance. Plus, trying to time the market can create additional risk. Take the time period from 1962 to 1991. An investor who bought common stocks in 1962 would have realized a return of 10.3 percent with a buy-and-hold strategy. If that same investor tried to time the market and missed just twelve of the best-performing months (out of a total of 348 months), the return would have been only 5.4 percent. There's a flip side to this theory, it must be admitted. If the investor had jumped out of the market during its worst periods (like the 1987 crash and several subsequent bear markets), the returns would have been even higher.

One additional negative aspect of using market-timing techniques is tax reporting complications. Going in and out of the market several times in one tax year (sometimes several times in a month) generates numerous taxable gain and loss transactions, all of which must be accounted for on your income tax return.

Chapter 4

All About Stocks

It's time to become familiar with the different types of stocks available and what they can mean for your portfolio. The stocks of companies that have stood the test of time are always in great demand. Finding these companies poses the real challenge to investors. Traders, on the other hand, take a more active approach to investing, placing as much or more emphasis on stock price movement than on the solidity of the company. Regardless of which strategy or combination of tactics you apply to your holdings, the same underlying rule applies. Know what and why you're buying (or selling) before you make any trade.

Buy What You Know

One of the side benefits of being a consumer is that you are constantly exposed to products and services that you are probably evaluating every day. This exposure breeds a level of familiarity that takes a lot of the anxiety out of picking stocks. It also gives you valuable insight about honing in on a specific company. Did you recently try out a new gadget at an electronics show that you found intriguing? Have you come across a certain brand of car wax that does wonders for your vehicle's finish? These are experiences you can put to work when you're making your investment decisions.

In addition to your own experiences, observations are another way to gain valuable insight. During your recent trip to Japan, did you notice people consuming huge quantities of a new Coca-Cola product? While waiting to pay for dinner at the local restaurant, did many of the patrons pull out American Express cards? Part of doing your homework as an investor is noticing the companies whose products and services are prominently displayed.

ALERT!

Putting serious thought into your investments early on will most likely pay off in the long run. Unfortunately, many people are introduced to the world of investing through a hot stock tip from their barber, buddy, or bellman. There's really no way to make an easy buck, and by jumping into a stock because of a random tip, you'll probably end up losing income. Remember: The idea of an easy buck in the stock market is a mere fantasy.

You need to understand the difference between investing and trading. Investing is a proposition for the long term, where you buy stocks for income and growth. Trading is a much more active practice in which today's price—and what you hope it will hit tomorrow—is the number to follow. Investing can help you reach long-term goals; trading is much more immediate and much more risky. Buying stock as a means to purchase a house or to attend college within a year's time is also not advisable. Holding quality stocks for long periods of time, as in a *minimum* of five years, is the recommended course. This provides you enough time to ride out any bear markets (the term used to describe the market when it is down) or other downturns that might come about. Could your investments be in a down period right at the time you need to sell? Yes. But with a longer time frame, you're less likely to end up with an overall loss. When it comes to investing in stocks, patience is a virtue, and staying in the market for the long term has proven to be the most successful way to invest.

No matter what type of stock fits your strategy, it's important that you have some just-in-case emergency money set aside (preferably enough to cover expenses for six months) in a risk-free investment. Even the most prestigious blue-chip stocks come with inherent risks. After you've set aside an emergency fund and have reached the conclusion that you are not entirely adverse to risk taking, you can devise your own personal investment strategy.

ESSENTIAL

If you had purchased 200 shares of General Electric at the end of June, 1995, for $5,640, your investment would have been worth more than $20,000 by July of 2002. General Electric is a fairly stable stock; other companies, especially smaller, less-established companies, can fluctuate significantly more in the short term.

The earlier in life you start investing, the longer you can keep your money in the market. Although past performance is no guarantee of the future, history shows that time will probably work in your favor when it comes to investing. Most analysts agree on this one universal truth: Market fluctuations, appearing in varying degrees, are inevitable, and are merely part of the entire investing process. As with most things in life, no ride is completely smooth.

Stock Basics

Purchasing shares of stock is a lot like buying a business. That's the way Warren Buffett, one of the world's most successful investors, views it—and his philosophy is certainly worth noting. When you buy stock, you're actually buying a portion of a corporation. If you wouldn't want to own the entire company, you should think twice before you consider buying even a piece of it. If you think of investing in these terms, you'll probably be a lot more cautious when singling out a specific company.

It's important to become acquainted with all of the details of the company you're considering. What products and services does the company offer? Which part of the business accounts for the greatest revenue? Which part of the business accounts for the least revenue? Is the company too diversified? Who are its competitors? Is there a demand for the company's offerings? Is the company an industry leader? Are any mergers and acquisitions in the works? Until you understand exactly what the company does and how well it does it, it would be wise to postpone your investment decision.

Let's say you want to buy a convenience store in your hometown. You've reviewed such factors as inventory, the quality of the company's employees, and customer service programs. In addition to selling staple grocery items, the company also rents videos and operates a gas pump. The grocery side of the business may only account for a small percentage of the overall revenue. It would be in your best interest to value each part of the business separately in order to get a complete and accurate picture of the company's profit potential. Many companies may have traditionally been associated with a specific business, yet that same company may have expanded into totally new venues.

FACT

The Altria Group, formerly known as Philip Morris, is commonly associated with tobacco products though it has many other holdings as well. The company also profits from food and beer subsidiaries, including 84 percent of Kraft (featuring popular brands like Jell-O, Oscar Mayer, and Post) and 36 percent of SABMiller Brewing (home of Miller beers).

Disney, for example, has historically been associated with the Disneyland and Disney World theme parks. The reality is that Disney is also involved in a host of other ventures. Among other things, the multifaceted company also has interests in television and movie production, including Touchstone Pictures and Buena Vista Home Entertainment. Disney's ABC, Inc., division includes the ABC television network, as well as numerous television stations and shares in various cable channels like ESPN.

As with any other career, making money through investing requires work. The more research and thought you put into your strategy, the more likely you are to reap rewards. Although there are no guarantees in the world of investing, the odds will be more in your favor if you make educated and well-informed investment decisions. When you make an investment, you are putting your money into a public company, which allows you—as part of the public—to become an owner or to have equity in the company. That's why stocks are often referred to as equities.

Types of Stocks

Common stocks are securities, sold to the public, that constitute ownership in a corporation. They come in all sizes. You can invest in a mega-company or a micro-cap company that has just begun to soar. While some individuals prefer to invest in well-established companies, other investors prefer investing in smaller, growth-oriented companies.

No matter what type of company fits in with your overall strategy, it's important to research every potential stock you buy. Just because a company has been around for decades doesn't mean it's the best investment vehicle for you. Furthermore, companies are always changing, and it's important to make sure that the information you are reviewing is current. Mergers and acquisitions have practically become commonplace. It's essential to know if a company you are considering buying is undergoing, or is planning to undergo, such a transaction.

QUESTION?

What is an SPDR?
Nicknamed "spiders," Standard & Poor's Depositary Receipts are a relatively new type of investment called exchange-traded funds (a single investment holding several securities, like a mutual fund, that trades in real-time, like a stock). SPDRs are traded on the American Stock Exchange under the ticker symbol SPY. They track the S&P 500, and trade at 1/10 of its value. Dividends are paid to owners of SPDRs every quarter.

It's also a good idea to research a company's market capitalization. The market value of all outstanding shares of a particular stock is synonymous with its market capitalization (or cap). Market capitalization is calculated by multiplying the market price by the number of outstanding shares. The number of outstanding shares refers to the number of shares that have been sold and that now are therefore shares outstanding. Larger companies usually have a lot more outstanding shares than their smaller counterparts. Shares that are issued are outstanding until they are redeemed, reacquired, converted, or canceled.

A public company with 20 million shares outstanding that trade at $40 each would have a market capitalization of $800 million. Although there are no concrete rules to categorize stocks, they can be differentiated as follows:

- **Large cap:** $5 billion and over
- **Mid cap:** Between $1 billion and $5 billion
- **Small cap:** Between $300 million and $1 billion
- **Micro cap:** Below $300 million

There are also different categories of stock to suit almost every personality. The variety includes blue chip, growth, small cap, large cap, cyclical, defensive, value, income, and speculative stocks, and socially responsible investments (SRI).

Blue Chip and Growth Stocks

Blue chip are considered to be the most prestigious, well-established companies that are publicly traded, many of which have practically become household names. Included in this mostly large-cap mix are IBM (which trades on the NYSE under the acronym IBM), Disney (NYSE: DIS), and Coca-Cola (NYSE: KO). A good number of blue-chip companies have been in existence for more than twenty-five years and are still leading the pack in their respective industries. Since most of these organizations have a solid track record, they are good investment vehicles for individuals leaning to the conservative side in their stock picks.

FACT

Morgan Stanley created a new way to invest in blue chips called Blue Chip Baskets. Basically, instead of using your money to buy one or two stocks, you buy one share of a basket that includes tiny portions of stock in several blue chip companies. For example, a $50 basket may include 1/10 of a share of Microsoft, 1/5 of a share of Disney, 1/8 of a share of Coca-Cola, and so on. This allows you to spread out your investments without having to choose the specific companies.

As the name suggests, growth stocks comprise companies that have strong growth potential. Many companies in this category have sales, earnings, and market share that are growing faster than the overall economy. Such stocks usually represent companies that are big on research and development; for example, pioneers in new technology are often growth stock companies. Earnings in these companies are usually put right back into the business.

Growth stocks may be riskier than their blue-chip counterparts, but in many cases you can also reap greater rewards. In recent years, growth stocks have outperformed value stocks (defined later in this section), though that has not been the case at times in the past, and the trend may well turn around in the future. A word of caution: Beware of stocks whose price seems to be growing faster than would make sense. Sometimes momentum traders will help run growth stock prices to sky-scraping levels, then sell them off causing the stock to plummet.

Small-Cap and Large-Cap Stocks

The small-cap stock category comprises many of the small, emerging companies that have survived their initial growing pains and are now enjoying strong earning gains, along with expanding sales and profits. Today's small-cap stock may be tomorrow's leader—it can also be tomorrow's loser. Overall, such stocks tend to be very volatile and risky. A safer way of adding these to your portfolio can be through a professionally managed small-cap fund. That way, you'll have exposure to potentially explosive profits without the added risk of investing in a particular company.

Large-cap stocks are a broad subset of the stock market. Generally considered integral to an investor's diversified portfolio, they tend to have fairly similar characteristics and so are grouped together. As a whole, large-cap stocks are an important part of the economy and therefore essential to assest allocation.

Larger companies tend to have a more established business presence and less uncertainty in sales or profits than smaller companies (that is, the small-cap stocks). Although there are exceptions, larger companies often have slower growth rates, but they are less risky investments than many smaller companies. Large-cap stocks are considered long-term investments, and fifty-plus years of historical market returns yield slightly lower than short-term returns, but with less volatility.

Cyclical, Defensive, and Value Stocks

Companies with earnings that are strongly tied to the business cycle are considered to be cyclical. When the economy picks up momentum, these stocks follow this positive trend. When the economy slows down, these stocks follow, too. Cyclical stocks would include companies like DaimlerChrysler (NYSE: DCX), United Airlines (NYSE: UAL), and Phelps Dodge (NYSE: PD)—the copper mining and smelting company considered the bellwether of the cyclical sector.

Defensive stocks, on the other hand, are relatively stable under most economic conditions, no matter how the market is faring. Stocks with this characteristic include food companies, drug manufacturers, and utility companies. For the most part, you can't live without these companies' products no matter what the economic climate at any given time. The list of defensive stocks includes General Mills (NYSE: GIS) and Johnson & Johnson (NYSE: JNJ).

Value stocks, finally, look inexpensive when compared to earnings, dividends, sales, or other fundamental factors. When there is a big run on growth stocks, value stocks may be ignored. However, many investors believe that value stocks are a good deal given their reasonable price in relation to many growth stocks. Warren Buffett would probably vouch for that.

Income and Speculative Stocks and Socially Responsible Investing (SRI)

Income stocks, which include real estate investment trusts (REITs), may fit the bill if generating income is your primary goal. One example of an income stock is public utility companies; such stocks have traditionally paid higher dividends than other types of stock. In addition, preferred stocks make excellent income vehicles, typically providing steady dividends and high yields. As with any stock, it's wise to look for a solid company with a good track record.

ALERT!

Diamonds aren't just a girl's best friend anymore! When you buy a share of a Diamond (symbol DIA), you are buying a fraction of each of the stocks in the Dow Jones Industrial Average. Like SPDRs, Diamonds are exchange-traded funds bought and sold on the American Stock Exchange.

Bewared of speculative stocks. Any company that's boasting about its brilliant ideas but doesn't have the earnings and revenue to back them up would be classified as a speculative stock. Since these companies have yet to prove their true worth, they make risky investments.

Another investment strategy that is growing in popularity is socially responsible investing (SRI). Here, investors put capital into companies that represent their personal values. Such individuals may avoid tobacco or liquor companies or any company whose products or services damage the environment. Socially responsible investors favor companies that have a positive influence on society.

Preferred Stocks

Preferred stocks have as much in common with bonds as they do with common stock. Essentially, this type of stock comes with a redemption date and a fixed dividend—and the income received has nothing to do with the company's earnings. If the company has financial difficulties, holders of preferred stock have priority when it comes to dividend payments.

ALERT!

Think plastics are going to go sky-high this year? Maybe you're interested in the bio-tech sector? Holding company depositary receipts (or HOLDRs) allows you to invest in entire market sectors, as opposed to individual companies. This form of investment, originally created by Merrill Lynch, serves as a nice tool for those hot on a particular industry who don't want to do all the work of researching specific companies. HOLDRs are traded on the American Stock Exchange.

As the owner of preferred stock, you normally have none of the ownership rights that come with common stock ownership (like voting). However, preferred stock can be a good portfolio addition for income-oriented investors. This book focuses on common stock because, like its name, it's the far more common choice for stock investors.

Penny Stocks

Penny stocks are stocks that sell for $5 or less, and in many cases you're lucky if they're worth even that much. Most penny stocks usually have no substantial income or revenue. You have a high potential for loss with penny stocks. If you have a strong urge to invest in this type of company, take time out to follow the stock to see if it has made any headway. Learn all you can about the company, and don't be tempted to act on a hot tip that may have been passed your way.

ESSENTIAL

Penny stocks trade in either the pink sheets, a forum operated by the National Quotations Bureau, or on the NASDAQ small-cap market. Pink sheets, in brief, are listings and price information literally printed on pink sheets of paper that go to select brokers.

The companies behind these stocks are thinly capitalized and are often not required to file reports with the SEC. They trade over the counter, and there is a limited amount of public information available. This in itself is reason for concern. How many astute investors want to put their money into an investment offering little to no information? Nonetheless, people do invest in these stocks.

One of the most interesting—and alarming—aspects of penny stock dealing is that brokers are not always acting as a third party but instead set prices and act as the principals in the transaction. In other words, the broker selling the stock owns large chunks of it. Penny stocks most often do not have a single price but a number of different prices at which they can be purchased or sold. Like bonds on the market, penny stocks have asking and bidding prices. Unlike bonds, you often cannot find the price listed that is being quoted to you by a penny stock dealer.

Okay, so there's little information about the company, the price, or anything else to investigate. But the guy on the phone—making a cold call—says it will be the next Starbucks! This is where they get you. Thanks to the Internet and the selling of phone lists, penny stocks dealers can reach out far and wide. They use high-pressure sales tactics and armies of callers to tell you anything to make you buy the stocks. Beware!

FACT

The U.S. Securities and Exchange Commission (SEC) offers on its Web site (✍www.sec.gov) the opportunity to investigate any questionable activities. They also offer a host of services, including free literature, complaint tracking, and a toll-free information line at 1-800-SEC-0330.

Typically, unscrupulous brokers hype up and promote companies that have either no assets or minimal assets. Called "pump and dump," these hard-selling wheeler-dealers hype the stocks, making outrageous claims about the company that are substantiated by absolutely nothing. They bring the price up so that they can cash in on an artificial price that is high for a company that is worth nearly nothing, or not in business at all. Fraudulent practices by brokers also include unauthorized trading, churning, bait-and-switch, and other methods of pulling the wool over the eyes of unsuspecting new investors. Their goal is to convince naive investors that these stocks are an incredible bargain, so cheap that nobody should pass them by. And, when they become the next Lucent, you'll be rich!

All of this is not to say that there are no low-priced legitimate stocks on the market. There are. They are usually small grassroots companies that can grow over time—if you pick the right one and wait a while. You should invest cautiously and conservatively at first. Look for a new company with good leadership in an industry where you see growth potential. It's also advantageous to find a company that holds the patent on a new product. If the product takes off, so could your stock. You must seek out all of this information—it will not come to you via a cold caller.

Stock Options

A stock option is a specific type of option, with a stock as the underlying instrument (that is, the stock is the security that the value of the option is based on). An option is a contract giving you the right, but not the obligation, to buy or sell shares of stock, at a predetermined or calculable price. (When you buy options, you exercise what is known as a call contract; to sell is to exercise a put contract; and the predetermined option price is called the strike price.) Options trade over exchanges, just like the underlying stocks.

For example, you could own an option to buy a share in XYZ Corp. for $100 one month from today. If the actual stock price in one month is $105, then you would exercise (use) your option and buy a stock from whoever sold you the option for $100. You could then either keep the stock, or sell it on the open market for $105, netting a profit of $5.

However, if the stock price in a month is only $95, you would not exercise your option. If you really wanted a share in XYZ Corp, you would be much smarter to buy it in the open market for $95 rather than using your option to buy it for $100. If you have an option, you have virtually unlimited profit potential, and your losses are limited to what you paid for the option. A stock option's value is determined by five principal factors: the current price of the stock, the strike price, the cumulative cost required to hold a position in the stock (including interest and dividends), the time to expiration (usually within two years), and an estimate of the future volatility of the stock price. Also available are longer term options called long-term equity anticipation securities (or LEAPs), which typically don't expire for two to three years. Other than that distinction, LEAPS trade like regular options.

You have probably heard of employee stock options. Stock options for a company's own stock are often offered to upper-level employees as part of their compensation package. Non-executive employees are occasionally offered options, especially in the technology sector, in order to give all employees an incentive to help the company become more profitable and to lure quality employees to work. Employee stock options differ from the options that are traded on exchanges as securities primarily in the time frame under which they can be exercised. Employee stock options can typically be exercised over a time frame of up to ten years.

Chapter 5

Doing Your Homework

Most educators will tell you that 75 percent of all learning is gained by doing homework; this is true of investing as well as school. When you are interested in investing, it's important that you do your homework, including research, analysis, and investigation. Look up the stock you own on the Internet and find any company news listings. Read the company newsletter, its annual or semiannual reports, and ask your broker for any updated news about the company. An educated investor is more likely to be a patient and relaxed investor.

Researching Stocks

Would you pay any amount to buy a car or a house? Probably not. Most people want to feel like they've gotten a good deal. They're looking for a price that's proportionate to what they want or need from the purchase and to what they have to spend. The price of a particular stock is an important part of the buying and selling equation. In most instances, you have to take the stock price into account. Taking a business attitude toward investing is important—it is wise to base your investment decisions on a variety of factors. That's the only way to ensure profitability in the long run. You want high quality at a fair (or better than fair) price.

FACT

Since 1926, large company stocks have generated annual returns of 11.3 percent. Over the same time period, the return has been 5.7 percent on long-term corporate bonds and 3.8 percent on U.S. Treasury bills. Compare that with the 3.1 percent annual rate of inflation during the same period.

Fortunately, good-quality companies in this country are plentiful. However, finding these companies is something of a challenge. Some investors are more inclined to look for the current hot stock, while others prefer to hunt out a great deal. The terms "growth investing" and "value investing" describe these differing approaches.

Essentially, growth investors want to own a piece of the fastest-growing companies around, even if it means paying a hefty price for this privilege. Buying on momentum is a common practice among investors of this type. Growth companies are organizations that have experienced rapid growth, such as Microsoft. They may have outstanding management teams, highly rated developments, or plans for aggressive expansion into foreign markets. Such stocks rarely pay significant dividends, and growth investors do not frown upon this shortcoming. Here, growth is the name of the game. Growth companies put a lot of their revenue right back into the business to accelerate even more growth. Among other things, those who engage in growth investing pay close attention to company earnings. If growth investing melds well with your overall investment strategy, look for companies that have demonstrated strong growth over the past several years.

ALERT!

Of the "Nifty 50" growth companies of the 1970s, only seventeen are growth companies today. In fact, many do not even exist anymore. This alone is proof that the market can change dramatically, so don't hang your hat on any company before doing your research.

Value investors are on the prowl for bargains, and they're more inclined than growth investors to analyze companies using such data as sales volume, earnings, and cash flow. The philosophy here is that value companies have already taken some sort of beating, so the risk of their getting hit again is low. In other words, the value investor believes that such companies really have nowhere to go but up. Dividends are more important to value investors. Such investors are often willing to ride out stock price fluctuations because of the extensive research they have done prior to committing to a particular stock.

Both styles of investing can be lucrative. The idea is to hone in on a style of investment that fits your personality and investment strategy. You need to make investments that are comfortable for you. Sometimes you may lean toward growth investing; other times, you may feel that taking a value-investing approach is the way to go. Still other times you may want growth and value all wrapped up in one neat package. In that case, you would be looking for growth at a reasonable price (known as the GARP approach).

The Role of the Internet

The Internet is one of the modern investor's most important tools for research and analysis. It has quite possibly been the most significant factor in making the individual investor so important in today's market. It provides curious investors with the ability to transcend the informational boundaries that existed for years. Now, you can easily find the best investment information in real time. This access to information has given individual investors the confidence and incentive to do their own research and make their own decisions without the help of a broker.

Lower costs and easier access to good information are driving an increasing trend toward stock market research on the Web. More and more, investors both young and old are turning to Web sites to limit their reliance on expensive financial advisors. A professional money manager will typically charge an annual fee of 1 to 1.5 percent of a client's assets. As an investor with a $250,000 portfolio (about the minimum size that most professionals consider worthy of their attention), you're looking at paying out $2,500 to $3,750 every year. By contrast, many free Internet sites are full of information and advice to help you optimize your finances, and others charge just a few dollars per month.

Prospective investors seek industry comparisons and financial data such as valuation ratios, annual reports, balance sheets, and income statements before they make their investment decisions. After you become a shareholder, you will find that your top information needs are timely news releases, income statement and balance sheet data, and profiles of company ownership.

There is no shortage of good market research available to you as an investor. Part of your job is to determine which sources work best for your needs. You may want to look at free Internet sites such as *www.cnbc.com*, *www.fool.com*, *www.forbes.com*, and *www.thestreet.com*, all of which provide a wide range of in-depth information. Other good sites to check out include *www.hoovers.com*, *www.wsj.com* (the electronic version of the *Wall Street Journal*), and *www.investors.com* (the *Investors Business Daily* site), though these sites may charge for premium information.

How the Great Ones Choose Stocks

Investors generally favor one of two stock-picking techniques: fundamental analysis or technical analysis. Technical analysis focuses on price movement, and it relies on charts and graphs to determine patterns. Fundamental analysis, more common among beginning investors, involves studying the company itself, with a focus on financial statements and performance. For optimum results, many savvy investors combine both techniques when making trade decisions. For example, a stock with great fundamentals and sagging price trends could indicate trouble on the horizon.

Technical analysis focuses on charts and graphs showing past stock price patterns. There are a number of patterns technical analysts recognize to be historically recurring. The trick is to identify the pattern before it is completed. Those who use this technique believe that you can forecast future stock prices by studying past price trends. Therefore, they buy and sell stock based on stock price movements. Technical analysts tend to do much more buying and selling than fundamental analysts.

QUESTION?

What's a good first step in selecting stocks?
Learn about all the products and/or services offered by the company you're considering. A company may have one high-profile product and several other products and/or services that are not as visible. Even if a high-profile product is getting rave reviews and profits, the company's lesser-known products may be taking a toll on the total profits. Or it may very well be the other way around. This being the case, you need to closely examine each company to determine its future potential.

Fundamental analysis is a long-used, common way to review stocks. The technique involves an analysis of the company's ability to generate earnings and an examination of the value of the company's total assets. Value investing and growth investing are two subdivisions of fundamental analysis. Proponents of fundamental analysis believe that stock prices will rise as a result of growth. Earnings, dividends, and book values are all examined, and a buy-and-hold approach is usually followed. Fundamental analysis advocates maintain that stock in well-run, high-quality companies will become more valuable over time.

Understanding Great Companies

Once you've narrowed your focus to a handful of companies, you need to fine-tune your research even more. One of the primary reasons to buy a particular stock is because of its future outlook. As explained earlier, it's wise to buy and hold onto a stock for the long term. That's why buying quality is such an important part of your investment strategy. Among other factors, you want to purchase stock in a company that you believe has the following traits:

- **Sound business model:** You want to single out a company that has a solid business plan and a good grasp of where it wants to be in the years ahead and a plan to get there. A company with a clear focus has a better chance of reaching its goals and succeeding than a company that just rolls along without a concrete plan.
- **Superior management:** An experienced, innovative, and progressive management team has the best chance of leading a company into the future. Star managers have had a major impact on their prospective companies, and a company will often witness dramatic changes when a new management team comes on board. When key management leaves an organization, you will often see major changes in the way a company operates.
- **Significant market share:** When a majority of individuals rely upon the products and/or services of a designated company, odds are that the company has good insight into consumer preferences. Industry market leaders usually have a well-thought-out vision. However, the strongest company performance doesn't always indicate the best stock to buy. Be careful and look more closely at markets with a glut of competitors; sometimes the second-best company makes the best stock investment.
- **Competitive advantages:** A company that is ahead of the pack will often be on top of cutting-edge trends and industry changes in

areas like marketing and technology. You want to single out those companies that are—and are likely to stay—one step ahead of the competition.

- **New developments:** If a company places a high priority on research and development, it's likely to roll out successful introductions. Those new introductions could be anything from a drug to treat arthritis to vegetarian chili to a quick-dry nail polish. If the product or service takes off, the stock price may very well follow.

If the future outlook for a particular company appears promising—that is, as long as a company continues to exhibit these traits and act upon them—owning a portion of that company might make good business sense.

Most individuals want to emulate the successful investors. And why not? Warren Buffett, for example, has earned his fame by investing in quality companies instead of relying on technical analysis strategies (although not every choice has been a winner). Buffett believes that if you buy stock in quality companies, you have no reason to sell your investments unless there is a serious underlying problem behind a price dip. Buffett believes that investors should understand a company and its industry before making any investment decisions. He says that this understanding is important in focusing on a specific company.

E ALERT!

When evaluating an analyst's report, make sure you read the fine print. If the author is a representative of the company being profiled, the report is not objective. If it's based on research paid for by the company, avoid that investment.

Although Buffett wants to buy companies at prices below their potential, price is not the sole consideration in his stock-selection process. Buying quality companies for the long haul is key. If one of your star companies suffers a dip in its stock price, Buffett says, it might be a good chance to pick up some additional shares.

Know the Basics

After you've narrowed your focus to a handful of companies, continue your research efforts by reviewing a few factors for each company. Find out about each company's earnings per share, price/earnings ratio, book value, price volatility, dividends, number of shares outstanding, and total return. These factors will give you greater insight into the stocks.

Earnings Per Share and Price/Earnings Ratio

The term "earnings per share" (often abbreviated EPS) describes the company's net income divided by the number of common shares outstanding. Simply, it is the portion of the company's profit (or net income) for each share of stock. A company's growth rate is often determined in terms of earnings per share. Finding a company with a strong earning growth is advisable. You also want to review the company's earnings per share over the past several years to see if the company is growing on a consistent basis.

Reviewing a company's price-to-earnings (P/E) ratio is also an integral part of the stock selection process. P/E ratio is the stock price divided by the earnings per share, so the result tells you how much you'll be paying for one dollar of the company's earnings. Essentially, since stock prices reflect investor demand, this ratio tells you the price investors are currently willing to pay in proportion to the company's earnings. A P/E ratio of 20 means investors are willing to pay twenty times more for a stock than the stock's earnings per share. More important, though, is the relationship of one stock's P/E ratio to others in the same class (a combination of size and industry), which you'll learn more about in a moment. In most instances, you can find a company's P/E ratio, and those of its peers, in the newspaper or online.

When investigating a particular stock, compare its P/E ratio with that of other companies in the same industry. Since every industry has its own unique qualities, you want to find out what the average P/E is for that sector. If a company has an exceptionally low P/E compared to others in its industry, you will want to find out why (for example, the company's growth could be stagnant, or it could be burdened with excessive debt).

Book Value and Price Volatility

A company's book value is determined by subtracting its liabilities from its assets, then dividing by the number of shares outstanding. Essentially, book value represents a company's cash flow reckoned per share. Many experts say that a good way to find value stocks is to look for companies whose stock price is less than their book value.

Price volatility refers to the difference between a stock's high and low prices over a certain period. This factor is important in determining the risk of an investment. You probably wouldn't be as willing to pay a lot for a stock if you knew that its price had jumped up and down dramatically over the past few months. In stocks, the term that describes price volatility is "beta." To figure a stock's volatility (that is, its beta factor), its price must be compared to something stable. Beta measures the changes in a stock's price against the S&P stock index. (Refer to Chapter 2 for more information on the S&P 500.) Changes in the S&P 500 are given a fixed value of 1. Accordingly, a stock with a beta of 2 moves up and down two times as much as the S&P 500. That stock can be expected to rise in price by 40 percent if the S&P 500 rises by 20 percent. Similarly, a stock with a beta of 2 can be expected to drop by 40 percent if the S&P 500 falls by 20 percent.

FACT

To be entitled to dividends, you must actually own the shares on the record date, which is when the board declares a dividend. Find out the current dividend and compare it with the dividend rate for the past five years. When a company's primary goal is growth, dividends may be small or nonexistent. Usually, stock dividends are paid by large-scale companies.

Dividends and Shares Outstanding

Dividends are payments to shareholders that are not based on the stock price but are made simply because the company has reaped healthy profits and chooses to reward shareholders. Depending on the company's profits, the board of directors will decide whether to pay a dividend to shareholders, as well as how often and when dividends will be paid. Dividends are usually most important to investors looking for income, and stocks that pay dividends are thus known as income stocks. Many companies pay dividends on a quarterly basis, and special one-time dividends may also be paid under certain circumstances.

The term "shares outstanding" refers to the number of shares a company has issued to the general public, including its employees. It's a good idea to start your investing career by looking at companies with at least 5 million shares outstanding. This indicates that the stock is heavily traded and, as a result, will not be difficult to sell if you so decide.

Total Return

Most investors in stocks tend to think about their gains and losses in terms of price changes, not dividends, whereas those who own bonds pay attention to interest yields and seldom focus on price changes. Both approaches are problematic. Although dividend yields are obviously more important if you are seeking income, and changes in price play a greater role in growth stocks, the total return on a stock is extremely important. Knowing a stock's total return makes it possible for you to compare your stock investments with similar types of investments, such as corporate or municipal bonds, treasuries, mutual funds, and unit investment trusts.

To calculate total returns, add the stock's price change (or subtract it if the price has gone down) and dividends for the past twelve months and then divide by the price at the beginning of the twelve-month period. For example, suppose you buy a stock at $42 per share and receive $2.50 in dividends for the next twelve-month period. At the end of the period, the stock is selling for $45 per share. Your calculations would look like this:

Dividend: $2.50
Price change: up $3.00 per share
$2.50 + $3.00 per share = $5.50
$5.50 divided by $42.00 = 13 percent

Your total return is a 13-percent increase.

But suppose, instead, that the price had dropped to $40 per share by the end of the period. Then your calculation would look like this:

Dividend: $2.50
Price change: down $2.00 per share
$2.50 - $2.00 per share = $0.50
$0.50 divided by $42.00 = 1 percent

Your total return is only a 1-percent increase.

Avoiding the Herd Mentality

As much as you'd like to make your investment decisions with the cold calculation of a computer chip, your emotions and behaviors often won't let you. This can complicate the process of evaluating investments that don't fit the traditional mold. Past history comes into play as well. As the technology bubble of the late 1990s demonstrated, it's easier and less complicated to follow the herd than to do your homework and get a reliable barometer on a stock's potential direction. But when a bubble bursts, investors learned an unforgettable lesson in financial behavior.

ALERT!

You can't outperform the market if you buy the market. Bernard Baruch, an important government economic advisor, was a firm believer in this principal of market investing, saying repeatedly, "Never follow the crowd." If you buy with the crowd, you will achieve the same results as everyone else, whether good or bad.

Learning from the Past

You may remember what happened with the 1990s technology bubble. In the days when dot-com millionaires walked the earth and shares of certain Internet stocks sold for about the same price as a new microwave oven, few investors wanted to hear about bubbles. Perhaps that's why so many investors were carried away by the herd when the technology bubble finally burst in 2000. They were unable to sell their dot-com stocks and technology funds before it was too late.

The 1990s bubble was a classic case of everyone following the herd—right off a cliff. The enthusiasm for technology stocks and the sustained bull market was based on the shaky premise that since everyone was buying, everyone should buy.

Understanding Behavioral Finance

Following the crowd is a major component of behavioral finance. This is a new, developing mode of analysis that many investment professionals now use as part of their overall strategies. Traditional market analysis is founded on the idea that investors behave rationally and make their decisions only after carefully considering all available information. Behavioral finance adds a more human component by combining basic psychology with investing.

FACT

Corporate Web sites are an invaluable source of information in helping you make your investment decisions. In a recent study of individual investors, 74 percent said they visit a company's Web site before investing in a company and 53.6 percent visit often before making a final decision to invest.

It turns out that many individual investors often act irrationally when it comes to making their buy and sell decisions—for example, they might trade based on the popularity of a stock rather than value or growth potential. This emotional trading leads to losses, more often than not, yet the investors continue to make the same types of investment decisions again and again. In the relatively new field of behavioral finance, these poor decision-making strategies are examined and linked to market irregularities like crashes and bubbles.

Here's how behavioral finance tends to work. People jump to buy a stock because it's hot. That drives up the price, and still they snap up shares. It makes no difference that the company has an unproven track record or is loaded with debt—all that matters in the heat of the trading moment is the excitement of owning this very popular stock. The number of investors who jump on that bandwagon alters the patterns and directions of the stock market—and not necessarily for the better.

The irony is that while many investors have no problem plowing their hard-earned money into portfolios stuffed with complicated creatures like biotech or nanotechnology stocks, these very same investors give pause when given the opportunity to invest in a classic alternative investment like a hedge fund or a real estate trust.

When to Sell

Knowing when to hold and when to sell a particular stock is an art in itself. You may have every intention of sticking with your investments for the long haul, but instead you find yourself rushing to sell at the first sign of turbulence. History has revealed that holding onto solid stocks for a minimum of five to ten years has produced the best results. Therefore, buying good companies and holding them for the long term is a sound strategy for most investors.

QUESTION?

Whose advice should you avoid when it comes to choosing investments?
No one's! Always get as many opinions as you can about which companies to invest in. There is something to be learned even from bad advice. Consult coworkers, friends, family, and any other resources available. Once you can discern between good and bad guidance, you'll be better equipped to make an informed decision and the choice that's best for you.

Determining whether a company is "good" means thoroughly researching its balance sheet, income statement, and subsequent ratio analyses. You need to take all these measures because you're deciding whether as well as when to buy. It's most advantageous to buy stock at the lowest possible price before it begins to rise again.

It's important to examine the price chart for each potential stock investment. Trends can be identified by looking at a company's price chart over time, then used to determine an entry point, or good time to buy. You might use the fifty- or 200-day moving average (the average value of the stock price over the specified amount of time) as a starting point to help determine your entry point. It's also important to identify the lower and upper trending ranges for stocks to help determine entry and selling points.

Other technical analyses will also help to make entry point determinations, and they can provide information crucial to your decision whether and when to purchase a stock. For example, good investors follow the money. To identify a ceiling, or possible selling point, they watch how quickly money is flowing into a stock. Money flow and on-balance volume are indicators that help make their determinations.

Your Place in the Equation

Understanding yourself is an integral component to mapping out an investment plan. What's right for one investor might be disastrous for another. If the market were to drop 20 percent after you purchased stock, would you lose sleep? Would you be able to work the next day? Worse yet, would you "panic sell"? Determining how much risk you can tolerate is even more critical when dealing with stocks than it is with other types of investments such as bonds and mutual funds. Stocks have a tendency to be more volatile than the majority of mutual funds and a lot more volatile than bonds, where you're usually aware up front of how much profit you can expect.

If you find at any point after you've invested that you simply cannot handle the market's mood swings, you may want to re-evaluate your strategy. Your investment plan is not set in stone, but you should be fully aware of your reasons for changing your original strategy. Maintaining realistic expectations will keep beginning investors from growing frustrated, disappointed, and disillusioned. It's unrealistic to expect a 15-percent return on your investment if you aren't willing to take any risks. Understanding how the market works is a necessity that needs to be addressed early on in the learning process.

Until you have enough market exposure to make actual trades with your hard-earned money, a good way to gradually enter the world of investing is through "paper trading." Before you commit actual cash to an investment, test out your skills by buying and selling stocks on paper only. By keeping a record of your paper trades, you can get a feel for what it's actually like to invest and gauge your tolerance for risk and market fluctuations.

Once you have developed a strategy that you are comfortable with, don't analyze it on a daily basis, and don't even try to predict stock prices for either the long or short term. Predicting actual stock prices for any period of time is impossible. No matter what your investing strategy, you have a good shot at success if you invest in high-quality companies that you believe will—among other things—continue a track record of good financial execution and financial management.

Chapter 6

Taking the Leap

Now that you've learned the basics, studied the different types of stocks out there, and done your homework on companies you might want to invest in, it's time to take the next step and put some of your hard-earned dollars out there. You've got the fundamentals down, and you're prepared to enter the world of stock trading. Whether you make your entrance on your own or with the help of a broker, this chapter provides you with the necessary information to elevate you from student to player.

Executing Stock Trades

As an individual investor in the stock market, your first concern is how to go about executing a stock trade. When you're ready to place an order, either online or with a broker, you have several options: a market order, a limit order, a stop/limit order, or a stop/loss order. You can also determine the length of time your order is in effect, so that it is either good for the specific day it is placed or good til canceled (or GTC).

Market Order

When you want to buy or sell a stock at the current market price, you place a market order. This means that you want to buy or sell a stock at whatever price the stock is trading for when your order reaches the floor. In other words, you're buying or selling a given stock at the going rate. Depending on whether you're buying or selling, the market price may differ. The broker's terms for these prices are the bid (buy) or ask (sell), and the difference between these two prices is known as the spread. For example, Coca-Cola's bid price may be $65.25 (usually notated as 65¼), while its asking price is $65.50 (or 65½). In this case, the spread is one quarter.

ALERT!

Set target prices—but not in stone! If you've studied the past history of the stocks you're looking to purchase, you should have a good idea of the 52 week highs and lows. This will help you set target prices for when to sell. As the stock approaches the target price you can start selling off shares, and then gauge to what degree you believe it might pass the target. Don't use the target as an absolute figure but as a barometer.

Unlike Coca-Cola, securities that are thinly (infrequently) traded often have bigger spreads. Dealers in a security generally keep a large part of the spread in exchange for playing the role of middleman. Like all middlemen, dealers are in the business of selling goods at a higher price than what they initially paid. Stock prices, especially in heavily traded stock, can change in just seconds. By the time your order is filled with a market order, you might find a slight difference in the price you were quoted.

Limit Order

Limit orders are placed if you don't want to purchase stock for more or sell a stock for less than a predetermined price. A limit order, like other types of orders, can be placed as a day order or as a good-til-canceled (GTC) order. A day order is only good until the end of the trading day; a GTC order is good until it is canceled. Your limit order may not fill with either one of these two options; however, you have a greater chance of your order being filled with a GTC order since it can remain open for a longer period of time.

Limit Order Buy

If you want to buy a stock for a specified price, you can place a limit order. Let's say Cisco is currently trading at $105. You want to buy 100 shares of Cisco, but only if it dips to $100. In this case, you place a limit order for 100 shares of Cisco at $100 per share. The order may fill for $100 per share if the price dips to that level. If it does not, your order will remain unfilled. Your order to buy stock may also be filled for *less* than $100 per share if the stock hits $100 and continues to fall. In that case, your order would fill at the first available price under $100 (since price movement can move more quickly than trades can be settled). However, your order will not fill for more than $100.

Limit Order Sell

If you own Cisco, you might want to sell the stock if it dips to $95 per share. If so, you would place a limit order to sell. In this case, your order will fill for at least $95 per share. Your order to sell the stock may be filled for more than $95 per share if the stock hits $95 and continues to rise. In this circumstance, your stock would be sold at the first opportunity at $95 or higher; again, stock prices move faster than sell orders. However, your order will not fill for less than $95 per share.

Stop Order

Stop orders are crucial for investors who are concerned about a stock's price falling too low. Using either a fixed dollar amount or percentage, the investor sets a stop point; that is, a price at which the stock is automatically put up for sale. This is a good way to help lock in profits or prevent excessive losses, and it also takes the emotion out of making critical trading decisions. With a stop order, once your stock reaches your stop point, it becomes a market order.

Company size, or market capitalization, is an important consideration when making an investment. Remember: To determine a company's market capitalization, multiply the number of outstanding shares of stock by the price per share. If a company has 2 million outstanding shares of stock trading at $10 per share, then the market capitalization for that company is $20 million. Many blue-chip companies have market capitalization in the billions.

Stop Order Buy

You can also place a stop order to buy. Let's say Disney is currently selling at $35 per share. If the price climbs to $40, you want to buy because you think the price will continue to rise. Therefore, you put in a stop order to buy at $40. Once Disney hits $40 per share, your stop order automatically becomes a market order. Your order might be filled at your stop point of $40. However, since the stop order becomes a market order at your set stop point, you might also end up paying more or less for the stock. The price might rise to $40.50, for instance, before your order is filled. Conversely, the stock might hit $40 and then drop; you might end up buying it for $39.50 or less, depending on the market price at the time your order is filled.

Stop Order Sell

Let's say you bought that Disney stock at $40 per share. You can now place a stop order to sell if the stock price drops to $30. Once the stock hits your set stop point, your stop order to sell becomes a market order. Again, that means your order might end up being filled at a higher or lower price, depending on the market price at the time your order is filled.

Initial Public Offerings (IPOs)

You probably remember hearing a lot about initial public offerings (IPOs) during the tech bubble of the 1990s. IPOs are exciting and frightening propositions, both for those involved in managing a company as it enters an IPO and for those who choose to invest in one. A company makes an IPO when it chooses to go public, which means it will be issuing stocks to the public for the first time. By selling shares of its stock, a growing company can raise capital without incurring debt. Investors, in turn, expect to earn profits by purchasing stock in the growing company. (If a company has already gone public and issued stock, it can hold a primary offering during which additional new stock is issued.)

FACT

Before the company has its initial public offering (IPO) and its stock goes public, the SEC must make sure that everything is in order. This can take some time. In the meanwhile, a red herring is usually issued, which is a prospectus informing the public about the company and the impending stock offering. When the stock is ready to go public, a stock price is issued in accordance with the current market.

An investment bank—Credit Suisse, for example—usually handles the detailed process of issuing stock. The company works with the investment bank to determine how much capital is needed, the price of the stock, how much it will cost to issue such equities, and so forth. The company must file a registration statement with the SEC, which then investigates the company to ensure that it has made full disclosure in compliance with the Securities Act of 1933. The SEC then determines whether the company has met all the criteria to issue common stock and go public.

The best way to find out about an IPO is to have a broker who is in on all breaking financial news. *Investment Dealer's Digest* lists all IPOs that are registered with the SEC. Once the stock is issued, the publication will print an IPO update. Companies awaiting an IPO often call the leading brokerage houses and/or brokers they are familiar with, who will inform their clients about such an offering. As is the case with anything new, these stocks can be very risky due to their potentially volatile nature. It's a good idea to wait until the stock settles before you determine whether it would be a viable investment. The vast majority of stocks that you will be researching have probably already been actively trading.

An IPO Example

In August of 2004, one of the most highly anticipated IPOs in more than a decade took place with a resounding thud. The founders of Google, the Internet search engine company, took their brainchild public, using a Dutch auction system to price the company's stock in an effort to revolutionize the way Wall Street handles IPOs. This goal may have been worthwhile given Wall Street's past methods of handling IPOs (not always popular). However, Google still managed to upset both institutional and individual investors.

Companies may repurchase or do a buyback of their own stock for many reasons. In theory, the buyback should not be a short-term fix to the stock price but a rational use of cash, implying that a company's best investment alternative is to buy back its stock. Normally these purchases are done with free cash flow, but not always. If earnings stay constant, the reduced number of shares will result in higher earnings per share. All else being equal, this should result in a higher stock price.

Individual investors who were supposed to benefit from the offering were turned off by the overly high suggested share price, which Google set at $108 to $135. (The stock ended up trading at $85.) Google's decision to issue two classes of stock also turned individual investors off. The founders got stock that gives them ten times the voting power of the hoi polloi. Google said it wanted to be democratic, but the way it structured its IPO told individual investors that management, not investors, would continue to have the prima-

ry say in how to run the company. And what of the investors who did participate, despite some dissatisfaction with the methods? They saw quick profits,
as the stock hit around $200 a share within just a few weeks.

Dividend Reinvestment Plans (DRIPs)

Dividend reinvestment plans offer shareholders a simple and inexpensive
way to purchase stock directly through a company. This type of investment
plan does not require the services of a broker. Such plans enable investors to
purchase small amounts of common stock directly through the company—
in many cases, as little as $25 worth. Depending on the company, there
may be a small fee for handling your account, and you often need to have
already purchased at least one share of the stock from a broker.

Close to 900 companies, most of them blue-chippers, have dividend
reinvestment plans. If you are involved in ten different dividend reinvestment plans with ten different companies, you will get ten different statements. This may not be ideal for individuals who like one comprehensive
investment statement. Dividend reinvestment plans, however, may be a
good choice for long-term investors who want to continue to buy shares of a
certain stock on an ongoing basis. You can probably find a listing of companies that offer dividend reinvestment plans at your local library, or you can
call a company directly to find out if they offer this service.

Working with a Stockbroker

As an investor, you have multiple options available to you in terms of choosing a stockbroker. Before you make your selection, you need to evaluate your
needs, comfort levels, personal commitment, and available time for research,
as well as your desire to be personally involved in your investment portfolio.
Also be sure you are aware of any fees associated with your choice.

Discount Brokers

If you are ready, willing, and able to investigate potential companies on
your own, then a discount broker may fit the bill. Many individuals find that

taking charge of their investments is an empowering experience. Once they become acquainted with all of the available information, many investors feel like they are in the best position to handle their investments, and they are happy to be in the driver's seat.

Commissions charged by brokerage houses were deregulated in 1975, and this decision was truly the beginning of the ascent of the discount broker. Trades could be conducted for far less money than investors were used to paying at full-service brokerage firms like Merrill Lynch and Morgan Stanley Dean Witter. Discount brokers are now offering more services than ever before. Combine that with today's new and faster technology, and investors have all of the investment information they need right at their disposal.

Another type of broker available to you as an investor is an online broker (Ameritrade, for example). Online brokers are a subset of discount brokers. While they offer discount prices on trades and much more, the online brokerage is only available online. Whereas you can walk into a traditional discount broker's office and talk to someone, face to face, that service is not available with the strictly online version. Online brokers are expanding the range of services they offer over the Internet and are starting to catch up with full-service brokers in areas like float allocation and research distribution.

With the explosive development of the Internet, the opportunity for self-education is virtually limitless. Beginning investors now have access to many of the same resources as full-service brokers. With this access to data, the demand for full-service brokers has been diminishing. A little enthusiasm and determination can pay off with a wealth of online information that will keep you well informed about everything from a company's new introductions to the ten most highly traded stocks on any given day.

Some of the best Internet sites were created by financial institutions, and investors have access to everything with just the click of a mouse—from real-time quotes to analyst reports to stock market basics. You can even communicate with other investors, who may offer you some great investment ideas. The proliferation of online discount brokers has made it possible to trade around the clock for a nominal fee. In some cases, you can make trades for under $10. Trading online is ideal if you have done your homework and know exactly which stock you want to own.

Full-Service Brokers

If you want someone else to do most of the legwork, you might opt for a full-service broker. Of course, full-service brokers charge a premium for their input. There is no guarantee that a full-service broker will steer you in the direction of massive capital gains. It is also true that many such brokers tend to pay more attention to their large accounts (clients investing over $250,000, for example) than the smaller ones.

ALERT!

If you want to work with a full-service broker, it's advisable to get a reference from someone you know and trust. Be on the lookout for brokers who engage in churning, term for trades conducted purely to generate commissions. If a broker is overly eager to buy and sell your stocks on a continual basis for no apparent reason, you may be the victim of churning. Churning is especially beneficial to brokers who work on commission—the more trades they make, the more pay they take home.

With ease of access to the Internet, full-service brokers have been losing market share because it's becoming increasingly more difficult for them to justify their high rates. Some experts believe that if you have investments totaling more than $100,000, you may want to explore the possibility of using a full-service broker. If you choose to go the full-service route, find a broker who both shares your basic investment philosophy and gives you several investment options to choose from. Choose a broker with a minimum of five years of investment experience. You want someone who has traded in both bull and bear markets.

It's perfectly acceptable to interview potential brokers with questions about how long they have been in this business and about their formal education, their investment philosophy, and what sources they use to get the majority of their information. You may want to find out which investment publications they regularly read and which they find most helpful (and why). Find out if they rely only on their brokerage firm's reports when making stock recommendations. You can also ask more pointed questions, like how their clients fared during the bear market of 2000 to 2003, or what strategies they use to protect their clients from downturns. Also make sure the broker provides you with a written list of up-front fees you'll be charged, along with an explanation of when charges will be incurred. If the broker gives you the runaround or refuses to answer your questions, find someone else to work with.

Broker Fees

Becoming acquainted with the broker fee structure is crucial. In many cases, you may be charged for services that you didn't know you were getting—and wouldn't use even if you knew you could. You also want to inquire about the fees associated with opening, maintaining, and closing an account; getting checks; participating in investment profiles; buying and selling securities; and attending various seminars. To circumvent potential discrepancies, it's important that you obtain this information in writing and in advance—and not after the fact.

The National Association of Securities Dealers (NASD) can answer your questions about the practices of a particular broker by looking up his or her past record regarding any disciplinary actions taken or complaints that have been registered against the broker. They can also confirm whether the broker is licensed to conduct business in your state.

The NASD Regulation, Inc., is the independent subsidiary of the NASD. This body is charged with regulating the securities industry and the NASDAQ Stock Market. Through its many departments and offices, NASD Regulation's jurisdiction extends to more than 5,400 firms with more than 58,000 branch offices, and more than 505,000 securities industry professionals.

Financial Planners

Another option is to hire a professional financial planner. These people go beyond handling just your investments—they can aid you in matters relating to insurance, taxes, trusts, and real estate. The cost of doing business with a financial planner can vary considerably. If you opt for a financial planner, it may be better to pay a set fee rather than commissions. If the planner works on commission alone, it may be in his or her best interest to encourage heavy trading. While some planners charge a flat hourly rate, others may charge a fee that is based on your total assets and trading activity. In this type of arrangement, you are responsible for paying the financial planner even if you do not follow any of his or her suggestions. Other planners operate with a combination of fee-based charges and commission. Here, you may pay less per trade, but you are also responsible for paying additional fees.

Buying Bargain Stocks

If you're like the average American consumer, you're on the lookout for a great bargain. You might clip coupons and watch for sales in your pursuit of a great deal on merchandise, clothing, food, cars, and houses. But the stock market works differently than other markets. It's an enormous mistake to buy a stock simply because it's inexpensive in absolute dollar value terms. Instead, look for a stock that is considered undervalued or underpriced (as in the case of growth stocks on the upswing that still have a fair way to climb), regardless of what it actually costs.

FACT

The average per-share price of the best-performing stocks of the last forty-five years was $28 per share before they doubled or tripled (or more!). Though the actual per-share cost seems high, the earnings and growth potential make these top performers worth considering for your portfolio.

The price of a stock is often dependent on its earnings per share. Many other factors can affect the price of a stock: a company's product or service, operating costs, debt, and management, as well as overall market sentiment. It may be better to own a few shares of a high-priced stock with good earnings growth than many shares of a low-priced stock with poor earnings growth. It may seem tempting to go for low-priced stocks; just remember that you get what you pay for.

Stock Tables

A stock table provides you with essential information about the company's stock price (valuation). In order to monitor your stock investments accurately, it is vital that you become adept in understanding stock tables. Stock table information may vary slightly among different publications, but the basic information is generally presented in a similar manner. Stocks are always listed alphabetically, from A to Z.

There are a few things you should know about stock tables. For one, the date on a stock table is the date at which the trading activities occurred, not the date of the newspaper. Additionally, you will need to learn some stock table terminology, including the following:

- **High-low:** Generally the first column in a stock table, the high-low is the highest and lowest price at which the stock was sold in the past year (52 weeks).
- **Company symbol:** The second column is usually the abbreviated name of the firm issuing the stock. This abbreviation is known as the company's ticker symbol.
- **Dividends:** Dividends are the amount a company pays to its stockholders.
- **Volume:** Abbreviated VOL. This column indicates the volume of shares that were traded that day (in multiples of 100). Volume may give you an indication of the market for a company's shares.
- **Yield:** Abbreviated YLD. This column approximates the dividend yield, or the current return on invested capital. Used to compare dividend returns for firms that have different stock prices, dividend yield is calculated by dividing the current dividend by the closing stock price.
- **Price-to-earnings (P/E) ratio:** The P/E ratio compares the price per share to the earnings per share. It shows how much an investor is willing to pay for $1 of current earnings per share. The P/E ratio is calculated by dividing the price by the earnings per share.

- **Close:** The last price at which a trade was made during the trading day.
- **Net Change:** Abbreviated "net chg." This is the change between the closing price for previous day and the current day. It is measured in dollars.

Stock Symbols

Stock or ticker symbols are the abbreviations used to represent a stock or mutual fund. They are a necessary way to keep track of and find information about a security. Whenever you use a quoting service, you will be asked to type in the ticker symbol. Not all symbols correlate logically with the name of the company they represent. For example, the stock symbol for Internet America, Inc., is GEEK.OB. It's important that you learn the correct symbol for each company you invest in, and for each company you're researching for potential investment.

FACT

Cedar Fair, L.P., a publicly traded company headquartered in Sandusky, Ohio, owns and operates seven amusement parks around the United States, including Knott's Berry Farm, located near Los Angeles in Buena Park, California, and Dorney Park & Wildwater Kingdom, located near Allentown, Pennsylvania. Appropriately, the company's ticker symbol is FUN.

The NYSE and Amex use stock symbols of up to three letters for their listed companies. Companies listed on the NASDAQ exchange use four letters if the stock issued is common stock. Otherwise, they use five letters. The fifth letter has meaning. Here is a table listing the fifth letter codes:

Code	Meaning	Code	Meaning
A	Class A	N	3rd Class Preferred Shares
B	Class B	O	2nd Class Preferred Shares
C	Issuer Qualifications Exceptions	P	1st Class Preferred Shares
D	New Issue	Q	Bankruptcy Proceedings
E	Delinquent in Filings with the SEC	R	Rights
F	Foreign	S	Shares of Beneficial Interest
G	First Convertible Bond	T	With warrants or with rights
H	2nd Convertible bond	U	Units
I	3rd Convertible bond	V	When issued and when distributed
J	Voting	W	Warrants
K	Nonvoting	X	Mutual Fund
L	Miscellaneous situations	Y	American Depository Receipt (ADR)
M	4th Class Preferred Shares	Z	Miscellaneous situations

Working with an Investment Club

An investment club is a group of people who pool their money to make investments. Usually, investment clubs are organized as partnerships. Members study different investments, and the group decides what to buy or sell based on a majority vote of the members. Generally, each club member actively participates in investment decisions. Club meetings are often fun as well as educational.

For close to fifty years, the National Association of Investors Corporation (NAIC) has been helping investment clubs get up and running, and their efforts have certainly paid off. Due to the growing popularity of investing over the past several years, the NAIC has witnessed a dramatic increase in its membership. The Madison Heights, Michigan, not-for-profit organization provides members with an information-packed publication called *NAIC's Official Guide: Starting and Running a Profitable Investment Club*. The guide offers tips on the best ways to start and operate an investment club.

The organization's monthly magazine, *Better Investing,* covers a wide array of investment-related topics. In addition, members have access to sample agreements and brochures. There is a nominal annual fee per club to join the NAIC, plus a fee for each club member.

QUESTION?

Does the NAIC host any events?

The NAIC's many chapters hold regular investor's fairs to give you the chance to experience presentations from companies such as Home Depot, General Electric, AFLAC, Nokia, Intel, and many more. Visit their Web site at *www.better-investing.org* to see a schedule of events.

Overall, investment clubs can range in number from ten to twenty (or more) individuals of all ages and from all walks of life. With meetings normally held about once a month, members can include your neighbors, coworkers, friends, and relatives. Members should be able to work well together and should share similar investment philosophies. Recent NAIC statistics reveal that 67 percent of its members are female. The median age of NAIC members is fifty, and the average investment club has been operating for four and a half years.

Some of the most successful clubs witness the best results when members develop a cohesive investment strategy and stick with it. In most instances, a long-term strategy of buying and holding stocks is the best approach. Such an undertaking is a great way for new investors to get acquainted with basic investing techniques and for experienced investors to sharpen their skills. Members can share ideas and learn from each others' mistakes.

Investment clubs tend to invest in individual stocks. It is suggested that members invest a set amount on an ongoing basis, reinvest dividends along with capital gains, and invest in a variety of different types of growth stocks. Such clubs make good use of dollar-cost averaging, investing a predetermined sum of money on an ongoing basis as opposed to making an investment in one lump sum. When a stock's price declines, the investor receives more shares for the fixed investment amount. Conversely, the investor receives fewer shares for the fixed investment amount when the stock's price rises.

Chapter 7

E The Basics of Mutual Funds

Though Americans generally get credit for creating the mutual fund, the idea of pooling money for investing purposes began in Europe in the mid-1800s. However, once the idea hit the States, the faculty and staff of Harvard University created the first American pooled fund in 1893. About thirty years later, three Bostonian securities executives created the first official mutual fund. Called the Massachusetts Investors Trust, it was heckled by the investment community at the time. Little did they know how popular mutual funds would become. Currently, trillions of dollars are invested in mutual funds in the United States alone.

What Is a Mutual Fund?

A mutual fund provides an opportunity for a group of investors to work toward a common investment objective more effectively by combining their monies to leverage better results. Mutual funds are managed by financial professionals responsible for investing the money pooled by the fund's investors into specific securities (usually stocks or bonds). By investing in a mutual fund, you become a shareholder in the fund.

Mutual funds can provide a steady flow of income or can be engineered for growth in the short or long term. The success of the fund depends on the sum of its parts, which are the individual stocks or bonds within the fund's portfolio.

Just as carpooling saves money for each member of the pool by decreasing travel costs for everyone, mutual funds decrease transaction costs for individual investors. As part of a group of investors, individuals are able to make investment purchases with much lower trading costs than if they tried to do it on their own. The biggest single advantage to mutual funds, however, is diversification. Diversification, the easy accessibility of funds, and the idea that a skilled professional money manager is working to make your investment grow are the three most prominent reasons that funds have become so popular.

The History of Mutual Funds

Currently, the number of mutual funds exceeds 10,000. Consider that as recently as 1991 the number was just over 3,000 and at the end of 1996 it was listed at 6,000. As noted earlier, mutual funds have become extremely popular. Stock funds are growing as a way to play the market without having to make all the choices of when to buy and sell.

Bond funds are also growing, partly because of the complexities associated with understanding individual bonds. Bond funds are also a way to hold more bonds than the average investor could afford if buying them on an individual basis. Money market funds offer a safe alternative to bank accounts (though they are not FDIC-insured), and provide higher interest rates.

As late as the early 1950s, fewer than 1 percent of Americans owned mutual funds. The popularity of funds grew marginally in the 1960s, but possibly the largest factor in the growth of the mutual fund was the individual retirement account (IRA). Legal provisions made in 1981 allowed individuals (including those already in corporate pension plans) to contribute up to $2,000 a year tax free. Mutual funds are now mainstays in 401(k)s, IRAs, and Roth IRAs (detailed on page 202).

FACT

In 1976, John C. Bogle opened the first retail index fund, called the First Index Investment Trust. Now called the Vanguard 500 Index fund, in November of 2000 it became the largest mutual fund ever, with $100 billion in assets.

By the end of the 1980s, money market mutual funds had become a bit of cult. They offered decent returns, liquidity, and check-writing privileges. But would-be investors wanted more. Then, with computers and technology making information readily available at one's fingertips, the 1990s ushered in the age of the mutual fund. The Internet allowed the financial institutions to provide a great deal more information than they could on television commercials or in print ads. They reached out to everyone, not simply those Wall Streeters who read the financial papers. People saw how easily they could play the market and have their money spread out in various stocks as well as bonds.

Mutual Funds Today

Every financial institution worth its weight in earnings has a wide variety of funds to choose from. As of February 2005, U.S. funds held net assets of $8.125 trillion, with over 48 percent of American households owning at least one mutual fund. The number of accounts keeps growing, and there are now over 92 million individual accounts in mutual funds.

Funds today are as easy to purchase as making a phone call or a trip to your computer. Fund families (large investment firms or brokerage houses with many funds), seeing the surge in popularity and wanting to make funds easily accessible to all investors, have toll-free numbers and Web sites that make it easy for you to buy and sell mutual funds. Transactions can also be made by the old-fashioned method of snail mail.

ESSENTIAL

For those who need to put their hands on their money in a hurry and convert mutual fund shares to cash, another benefit of mutual funds is liquidity. A phone call allows you to sell your shares in the fund at its current net asset value (NAV, or posted rate per share). You should have your money in three or four business days.

Electronic trading has allowed investors to trade at all hours from the comfort of their own homes. It's not hard to find the funds rated as top ten, twenty, or fifty on your browser, as rated by some leading financial source, and then buy them online. It is also not hard to get addicted to trading and find yourself overdoing a good thing. The accessibility and ease of trading online and through toll-free numbers has landed many overzealous investors in deep trouble. Many new investors, eager to see quick profits, need to develop the patience and research skills necessary for successful long-term investing.

Diversification

The risk of investing in a mutual fund is less than that of a single stock. That's because the fund is managed professionally and because of diversification. Mutual funds offer you diversification without making you do all of the work. Funds can hold anywhere from a few select stocks to more than 100 stocks, bonds, and money market instruments. While some funds own as few as twenty or twenty-five stocks, others (like the aptly named Schwab1000) own 1,000 stocks.

The diversity minimizes much of your risk. If you invest everything in a single stock, your investment is at the total mercy of that stock price. If you buy six stocks, you assume less risk, as it is less likely that all six will go down at once. If three went down and three went up, you would be even. If you saw two dropping, you could sell them and buy something else while the others were still earning money. Mutual funds work on the same principle of safety in numbers. Although there are funds with higher and lower risks, the comfort of many mutual funds is that they limit risk by balancing higher-risk investments with lower-risk and thus safer investments. Diversity acts to your advantage as it protects you against greater swings in the market, be it the stock or bond market.

Further diversification can also come from buying more than one fund. You can also allocate your assets into different types of funds. If you buy into a few funds in different categories, you'll have that much more diversification and that much less technical risk. (It's usually not advisable to have more than six or seven mutual funds at a given time, or you can start to counterbalance your efforts to construct a strong portfolio.) For example, your portfolio might include the following:

- A more conservative bond fund
- A tech fund to cash in on a hot industry
- A more high-risk international fund
- A low-risk blue-chip fund
- A growth fund

The idea is to balance your portfolio between more and less conservative or higher- and lower-risk investments. Depending on your needs, you will diversify. One investor might have 10 percent in bond funds, 20 percent in growth, 30 percent in tech, and so on, while another has 5 percent in tech and 40 percent in blue-chip. That's why there is no one stock investment strategy that's suitable for all.

It seems odd to need to diversify your mutual funds since the job of the fund is to diversify the stocks, but it's all part of building a solid investment portfolio. Your mutual fund is the sum of many parts. Therefore, you may want another fund in your portfolio. Another significant reason for diversifying your mutual fund investments is to spread your assets out across sectors, industries, and asset classes. A fund manager, no matter how skilled, is limited by the goals and the direction set forth by the fund.

Fund Managers

As the rock stars of the financial world, successful managers of the hottest funds appear on financial talk shows. They write books and are the talk of the financial community—that is, until their hot streaks end. In the mutual fund boom of the late 1990s, the successes and failures of fund managers were a phenomenon not only in the financial world but also in the main-stream media, which began to focus its attention on these people who made (or lost) investors so much money.

FACT

Here's an impressive tidbit about mutual funds: Not a single one has gone bankrupt since 1940. This certainly can't be said for banks and other savings institutions. It's just one more reason for the popularity of these funds. No bankruptcy in over sixty years—not bad, huh?

Professional fund managers are another reason for the popularity of mutual funds in the United States. During the last quarter of the twentieth century, Americans heavily embraced the notion that if you want something done right, you should get a professional to do it for you. This is not a bad idea, particularly if you don't have the time to delve into the work of invest-ing yourself. Fund managers save you the trouble of sifting through thou-sands of potential stocks in an effort to build up your portfolio. Of course, as the number of funds grows, you will soon find yourself sifting through more funds than stocks. Nonetheless, it's the full-time job of the fund manager to select the right investments for any given fund. These managers are well versed in the intricacies of the national and international fund markets.

To assess a good fund manager, you need to look at his or her back-ground over several years. You want to look for consistency in management of the fund or previous funds. You also want to see that the fund manager is holding true to his fund's financial goals. For example, if you are looking at a more conservative growth and income fund, you don't want to find out that the fund manager is making high-risk investments and taking the fund in a different direction (known in the industry as "style drift"). Unfortunately, fund managers with roving eyes who look at and buy stocks that don't fit the fund's stated objective are more common than you might think. On the other hand, if a fund is struggling, you may appreciate a fund manager who starts drifting for the sake of keeping your investment afloat.

You should also look closely at a mutual fund's portfolio. While you may not be familiar with each and every purchase, you can ascertain whether they are following the latest trends or bucking the system. If you have heard, for example, that a certain market, such as automobiles, is taking a downturn, and the fund manager is buying heavily in that area, it will mean one of two things. Either he is buying now for an anticipated turnaround (value investing), or he is not keeping up with the market news.

ALERT!

You should also look at how the fund manager fared during the down markets of 1997 and 2001. See how quickly their funds rebounded. Did she panic and make drastic moves or hold on tight and ride out the storm? Naturally, your assessment of the manager's actions should depend on the type of fund and the particular holdings. The manager's response is worth noting, since the market does go through volatile periods.

You also need to check out changes in fund management. A new fund manager needs to show that she can work within the structure of the particular fund, holding true to the goal of that fund. Fund size and assets can matter as well. A manager who has handled a $2 billion fund successfully may not be as comfortable when dealing with $20 billion. You might also want to know whether this fund manager is working closely with a team of analysts or doing it all on her own. If the latter is the case, you could be in trouble when the manager moves to another fund and takes along her secrets.

Magazines such as *Forbes, Kiplinger's,* and *Money,* along with Morningstar.com and other online sources, will rate the mutual funds and often give you the lowdown or profile on the fund manager. It's important to look for consistency. A fund manager who has bounced from one fund to another is not a good sign if you want to hold the fund for a long time.

It is also not to your advantage to have a fund with a different manager at the helm every year.

Loads, No Loads, and Operating Costs

"Load" and "no-load" are mutual fund lingo for "with a salesperson" or "without a salesperson." A loaded fund means you are paying a commission to someone who has helped you determine which fund to purchase, either when you buy in (a front load) or when you sell (a back load). A no-load fund means you have bought the fund on your own, usually through a toll-free number. The choice is yours depending on how much help, guidance, or hand-holding you are seeking when buying mutual funds. The investor who does his homework and knows which fund is designed to meet his goals and needs can simply dial and buy without paying an additional commission.

There is certainly enough information available to support the choice of buying a no-load fund. However, if searching for the right fund is taking hours out of your potential income-earning time, or time spent enjoying your life, you may be better paying a commission with a load fund and using your time in other ways. As mentioned earlier, it's all up to you.

As is the case with everything these days, you have more than two choices. While no-loads have gained an edge on loaded funds, many companies have started offering loaded no-loads. Basically, these mean you will be paying a fee somewhere down the line for the privilege of not paying a fee. Whether the costs are for some types of special benefits, a personal finance report, or some other accompanying service, the bottom line is that loaded no-loads are not commission-free funds. There are numerous ways that companies have found to slip fees and payments into their fund business. Read the prospectus carefully. If hidden costs start popping up, you might be better off looking elsewhere. In short, no-loads by any other name are essentially loaded funds. It's to your advantage as a new investor to stick with the basics, either loads or no-loads.

Operating costs are also part of mutual funds. This is the money spent to keep the fund afloat. Along with administrative expenses, this includes advisory fees for the fund's analysts and manager. Expense ratios range from less than .25 percent to more than 2.5 percent. It is important to take note of the operating costs to determine how much of a bite they are taking out of your profits. This is an area that more savvy investors are taking note of as they compare mutual funds. In their favor, mutual funds buy in vast amounts and save you on broker fees, which would be accumulating if you were buying stocks individually.

Fees and Expenses

All this glory that is part and parcel to investing in mutual funds does not come for free. While mutual funds certainly decrease the cost of investing for the individual, there are all sorts of fees and expenses attached to becoming a shareholder in a fund. These fees can vary significantly, so it's important that you understand how to find them and understand them.

Generally listed as the expense ratio, there are several costs that shareholders will pay for services and management of the fund. While the SEC closely monitors funds to make sure they make shareholders aware of all related expenses, it's important that you understand the basics behind these fees and have a sense of what to look for on your own. After all, there are thousands of funds. While some have devised new and inventive ways to bill you, so to speak, the vast majority is fairly straightforward about where the expenses are going. International funds often have higher expense ratios than domestic funds because they are dealing with companies overseas.

A mutual fund operates like a smaller business within the structure of the larger fund family. It is an entity unto itself in that the fund does not interact with other funds under the same umbrella company. They share printed materials and costs, such as advertising the financial group, but from the perspective of the fund family, each fund is handled separately. In other words, the expense ratio you're paying for Fund A will not spill over to pay the manager of Fund B. Also, the success of one fund does not hinge upon the success of another. Often you will look down the listings of funds in one family and see some winners and losers along the way. Unlike the portfolio within a single fund, where the manager can try to dispense with the losers or at lease balance equities that are not doing well with ones that are, a fund family cannot integrate the portfolios of its different funds.

One advantage of having funds in the same family is that you can save on commissions if you want to sell your shares of one fund and move your money into another in the same fund family. You can also avoid paperwork this way, and that alone can save you lots of time.

Here's a list of fees that are generally included:

- **Service fees:** These fees are used for financial compensation of the planners, analysts, and brokers who assist customers with fund-related questions and provide information and advice regarding the fund. Accounting and legal services may also be included.
- **Administrative fees:** These are the fees associated with office staff, office space, and other fundamentals to running a business, including equipment. Sometimes these funds are absorbed into management fees. Office expenses incurred by a fund also include online support and information, check processing, auditing, record keeping, shareholders' reports, and printed matter.
- **Management fees:** This is the percentage that goes to the fund manager. This can be a flat percentage or one set up to coincide with the growth of the fund based on returns. The bigger the fund gets, in terms of assets, the lower the percentage will generally be.
- **12b-1 fee:** This fee (usually between 0.25 and 1.00 percent of annual assets) is used primarily for marketing or advertising the fund. Your fee is not just a contribution to the fund's advertising budget but will hopefully help the fund to grow. In fact, some funds report that because of advertising, their overall expense ratios have gone down as the funds have grown.

Hidden Costs

So far, this whole mutual fund thing probably sounds pretty good. There are lots of options, good return, minimized risk, and reasonable fees. But before you get too excited you should recognize that there are some costs that won't appear on the glossy surface as you explore mutual funds. Keep your eyes open for a couple of specific hidden costs.

One additional cost is that old standard: taxes. On the plus side, if you lose money on the fund, you won't be paying capital gains tax, but that's hardly a reason to celebrate. If you see a profit, you will pay taxes on dividends or on capital gains distributions paid to you while owning shares of the fund, or on your profits (capital gains) from selling your shares of the fund. You may also be subject to state taxes, depending on where you live.

You may also see capital gains based on the trading done by the fund manager, even though you haven't sold any of your shares. Buying funds late in the year is ill advised because you can be hit for higher taxes as the fund is just about to distribute its capital gains.

Fund Reports

While not quite as scintillating as the latest John Grisham novel, your mutual fund's annual or semiannual report is worth reading. This report is a tool used to measure how the fund is performing. It's probably not a great idea to peruse this report as nighttime reading—unless you're looking for a new way to combat insomnia. Nonetheless, you should find a quiet place to look over this document.

Among the most significant information within the report is the holdings of the fund. It's important to look over this list carefully to determine whether the fund manager is "style drifting." In other words, a fund that is supposed to be buying large-cap stocks may suddenly be investing in several smaller companies. It's more likely, however, that the fund may have drifted in the other direction. Small companies tend to grow—and they move from small caps to mid- or even large caps while still sitting in the same mutual funds.

Naturally, if the fund is doing well, you'll be less concerned with style drift. It's amazing how your perspective changes when looking at the holdings based on the fund's performance. What looks like a brilliant move by the fund manager in a fund that has seen a 30-percent rise doesn't look nearly as good in a fund that has seen a 10-percent drop.

Some questions may arise: Is the fund satisfying my level of risk, or is it becoming too aggressive or too conservative for me? Is the fund lacking in diversification by moving more strongly into similar stocks? The holdings will also tell you which companies the fund believes are strong. Look them over, and see if you agree. You may not know all of the companies held, but you should investigate a few.

When looking at the portfolio holdings, you want to find out this important data:

- **Familiar names:** A household name like Coca-Cola won't show up in a small-cap fund, but you are looking for smaller companies that belong in that fund. Just because you own a fund doesn't mean you no longer have to follow the activities of companies and their stocks. If you see holdings in your fund that you don't like, you can look at other funds that have shares of stocks that you feel are more promising.
- **Portfolio concentration:** Besides showing what is in the portfolio, the annual (or semiannual) report will tell you how much, or what percentage, the fund is investing in each area.
- **Performance:** Not surprisingly for funds that perform well, this information sometimes jumps off the page. It can be harder to decipher in a fund that is not performing well.

You should know how the fund has performed in the short and long term. How the fund has performed against a specific index should also be included for purposes of comparison. There should also be an explanation of *why* the fund has performed well or poorly. Which factors have made an impact on the fund? The report should describe what management has been doing and should include some indication of what they are planning to do.

The bottom line is that after reading the annual report, you should feel either confident in holding onto the fund or determined to sell your shares. (You can check out your fund's performance online as often as you like. When you're dissatisfied with performance, you can sell at that time, regardless of the last time you got a report.) If you are left feeling unsettled as to what you should do—because you do not feel you have adequate information or the report is not easily discernible—you should consult print or online sources such as Morningstar.com, *Kiplinger's,* or the *Wall Street*

Journal for a discussion of your fund. You should also call the fund or fund family and let them know you have some questions; after all, you are paying an operating fee that includes service charges, so let them serve you by providing some answers. If a fund does not help make you feel comfortable, then it's not the right investment for you. Remember, it's your money!

Fund Trading Practices

So now you're aware of the pros and cons of investing in mutual funds. There are many upsides and some negatives that each investor has to evaluate in light of his or her own investment goals. But as with all investment opportunities, there's one important question: How do you make money in mutual funds?

ESSENTIAL

Despite operating costs and commissions, mutual funds have seen some tremendous results in recent years. How long the trend will continue depends on a number of factors, including the economy, the stock market, and the number of effective fund managers, among other things.

Obviously, you will profit by selling off shares of your mutual fund at a higher net asset value (NAV) per share than that at which you bought. The fund acts as a single unit, and the total return is based on all the stocks, bonds, and other securities held. Therefore, if certain stocks do very well within the portfolio while others don't, you cannot simply sell off the lucrative investments or get rid of the losers. You have no say in the individual investments, but you can sell off your shares of the fund as a whole. There can be profits, however, in the form of capital gains when the fund manager sells off a security. While funds are constantly reinvesting money, you can actually see money from the fund as you hold onto it. Income funds dispense income from dividends paid by stocks within the portfolio or interest paid by bonds in a bond or balanced fund. If you are seeking a steady flow of income from a mutual fund, this may be the route to go.

Keeping Track

It's crucial that you stay on top of all your investment holdings. Some people become complacent when they buy into a mutual fund, thinking that the fund's professional manager is doing the job, and regular reports will provide sufficient information on the funds' performance. This is not true. You have as much obligation to know what's happening with your mutual funds as you do with any other investment option.

Financial publications, national newspapers, and local newspapers are all places to keep tabs on your mutual funds. Add to that the CNBC and online services, and it's likely that you can find all the important information on your mutual fund on a daily basis.

First and foremost, make sure you know exactly what symbol your fund goes by, and don't forget the letter following the fund. The letters primarily refer to the type of load—front load (meaning charged when you buy the fund), back load (meaning charged when you sell the fund), no load, and so on. (Refer to page 96 for a discussion of loads.) It's amazing how many people realize after several days or weeks that they either can't find their fund or have been following the wrong fund.

Once you have found your fund, you need to understand the letters and numbers that make up the mutual fund's listing. Among the many symbols and numbers, you will see information on the fund's net asset value, its past returns, and its volatility.

The net asset value (NAV) is the current price per share of the fund, or the price at which the fund is selling shares. By multiplying the number of shares you own by the fund's NAV, you can calculate the current value of your holdings. By comparing your result to your total investment in the fund, you will know how your fund is doing. For instance, if you purchased 2,000 shares in a fund from Aim at an NAV of $9 per share, your initial investment would have been $18,000. If the fund's NAV is now $11, your investment is now worth $22,000. That's a $4,000 profit (less operating costs and capital gains tax for a no-load fund, also less any sales commissions for a loaded fund).

Next, the listing will have changes, or the movement of the fund, given either by the day, week, or YTD percent (year-to-date total percentage, including reinvested dividends and capital gains). All of this will give you an idea of which direction the fund is going. This is how you can follow your fund, but it is *not* how to choose a fund. To choose a fund you need the one-, three-, five-, even ten-year totals and more information. Chasing daily returns is ill advised in stocks or mutual funds.

FACT

Some listings will include the entries "Down Market" or "Bear Market," which will indicate how the fund has performed during the downturns in the market. Again, this is information you'll want when trying to purchase a fund.

A volatility ranking will tell you how much of a roller-coaster ride you can expect. Such a rating is the "beta" of the mutual fund. (Chapter 5 discusses the beta concept in terms of stock investments.) This is not generally found in daily listings but on comparison listings of funds over time. This can ease your mind on a day-to-day basis—you see sudden drops and then realize that this fund will have its share of peaks and valleys en route (you hope) to showing solid gains.

Mutual Fund Volatility

In the world of investment risk, the good news is that mutual funds are a relatively safe bet when compared to other investment options. That said, risk varies among different funds, and funds are still subject to market fluctuations.

Mutual funds, as a rule, are not as volatile as a single stock because they are made up of a number of stocks. Even in a market crash some of the stocks will stay afloat, although the fund's per-share price (its NAV) will drop. The balance tends to offset losers with winners, particularly since the market has always fared well over time. The more aggressive and risky the fund, the more volatile it will be. Don't be fooled by short-term pluses and minuses. Once you have looked at the track record of a mutual fund and have seen that the fund you've chosen has performed well over one, three, and five years, you should anticipate investing for at least three to five years.

Greater risk means greater volatility. It also means you need more perseverance, as most funds will recover from most losses. If, however, your fund is experiencing volatility because of a change in managers or the direction the fund is taking, you may want to investigate more thoroughly. Who is at the helm of the ship, and what direction is the mutual fund taking? There are several reasons a fund may be volatile, including fluctuations in the stock market, changing interest rates (particularly pertaining to bonds), foreign currency rates, and fund management. Also, a fund that is actively buying and selling more heavily will often be more volatile. Check to see if similar funds in the same category are experiencing similar volatility. Returning to the notion that a rising tide raises all ships, you may simply find that the volatility of your fund is typical for that type of fund at the present time. If, however, your fund is acting differently from similar funds, look more closely at the management.

In general, whatever the reason, short-term volatility is not at all uncommon for mutual funds. While you can lose money, the odds are strongly in your favor that the fund will bounce back if you hold onto it over time, particularly if it is a domestic-based equity fund. Don't get impatient when the market takes a turn for the worse; an upsurge may be right around the corner.

Chapter 8

Stock Mutual Funds

The hottest and most talked-about mutual funds on the market are stock (or equity) funds. These are primarily made up (at least 75 or 80 percent) of individual stocks. Your potential profit is the result of having a fund manager who has accumulated more winners than losers in the funds—and more shares of the winners. The stocks comprising the fund are most often common stocks, and the fund managers purchase them based on potential earnings of companies, while looking at the issuer's management, track record, and financial condition.

Benefits and Choices of Mutual Fund Stock Investing

Mutual fund investing needn't be complicated, and the benefits are many. For starters, mutual funds offer you the chance to pool your money with other like-minded investors and avail yourself of the services of a top-notch mutual fund manager. This person is usually an expert in the field or sector you are investing in.

Then there is the "break in" factor. In short, investing in mutual funds is cheap—quite often you can invest in a fund for as little as $25 or $50, giving the reluctant or procrastinators among us no good reason not to invest in growth-driven mutual funds. Add to the mix flexibility, choice, ease of management, and generally positive performance from stock mutual funds over the years, and you begin to see why these are so popular.

In an age where there are numerous types of Coca-Cola—Classic, Diet, Cherry, Caffeine-Free, Caffeine-Free Diet, and so on—it should not be surprising that there is also a wealth of mutual fund categories. As the market continues to grow, more and more types of funds are created, which adds further confusion. The remainder of this chapter explores some of the many types of stock funds.

When looking at a stock fund (or any fund), you first want to know the overall goal. Does it aim for long-term growth or short-term aggressive growth? Before purchasing a fund, you should ask to look at a listing of the stocks currently owned so you can see if the fund managers are indeed following the plan of action they have listed as their goal.

Growth Funds

A growth fund is less concerned with the current price of a stock and more concerned that the sales and earnings of the company will grow (in which case the stock price should rise). The idea is not the traditional "Buy low, sell high," but "Buy at whatever price and watch the company build momentum, get on a roll, and grow." Growth investors seek out companies that have tremendous potential, based perhaps on new products, unique services, or excellent management. In recent years, growth funds have outperformed value funds, but that has not been the case in the past. Long-term growth funds seek to capitalize on larger, steadily growing companies (like Microsoft). Aggressive growth funds involve smaller companies that are taking off fast, like Amazon.com.

Aggressive Growth Funds

Also known as capital appreciation funds, these are the funds that generate the most press. When they go well, they go very well. Some of these have, of late, produced tremendous results. For example, the UltraOTC Pro Fund saw a return of 185.3 percent in 1998. However, investors should know that things in this volatile category can turn around very fast. Aggressive growth funds look for companies poised to grow in the short term, which is why they are riskier investments. You'll find many stocks recently included in aggressive growth funds on the NASDAQ, such as Starbucks and Intel.

Growth and Income Funds

You might also choose to go with a fund that specifically seeks out companies whose stock is not only expected to grow but pay dividends. Such a fund provides steady income, which is attractive to anyone who likes to maintain cash flow even during major dips in the market. A growth and income fund can also work very well for an individual who may be retiring but still wants to have money in the market. Such a fund will provide cash toward living expenses while allowing the investor to maintain some capital. There are also straight income funds, which are more conservative by nature, seeking as their primary objective to pay you dividends from consistently well-performing (usually major) companies. One of the nicest aspects of an income fund is that the companies that pay dividends, hence those in the portfolio, are usually not affected greatly by downturns in the market.

Value and Sector Funds

A value mutual fund invests in stocks that are undervalued. These are companies that—for one reason or another—are struggling, and while the stock prices are low, the actual value of the company may be much higher. Sometimes it's a matter of too much market competition; in other cases it's a company that is lagging behind in the latest technology or has not made a major impact of late. However, if the P/E ratio and book value of the stocks in the portfolio are good, the fund can be worthwhile. Although in recent years value funds have been outperformed by growth funds, they adhere to the old adage: "Buy low, sell high." A stock that is valued at $40 but selling at $20 allows you more room for error, even if the stock never reaches the $40 mark. Even at $30 per share you would still come out ahead.

Sector funds diversify, but only in one sector. Rather than spread your investment around among various types of industries, they choose stocks from one particular industry, such as oil, health, utilities, or technology. This lets you play a variety of stocks in one industrial arena. Naturally, the risk lies in whether the time is right for that particular market. Thus, the risk is higher. Tech stocks in recent years would have been an excellent choice for a sector fund as some have seen huge returns. Certain industries, such as utilities or companies in the food industry, will be less volatile and more consistent than others that are more cyclical.

Like market timing, the idea behind buying a sector fund is to select an industry that you foresee taking off in the next few years. For example, new health-related technologies have people looking at stock in companies doing new and innovative things in medicine. Internet sector funds may also generate more attention, but be careful that an overabundance of Internet providers doesn't bring prices back down to earth. A sector fund can give you a bumpy ride if you are planning to stay there for the long haul. Often such a fund works best as part of a larger portfolio that diversifies across industries and sectors.

International and Global Funds

Funds categorized as "Europe" or "Japan" invest overseas in one of, or a wide mix of, the global markets. Many international funds spread your investment around, buying into markets worldwide, while others look at the economic potential of one country. International specialized funds have not fared well over the past three or even five years. This doesn't mean there are not some winners, primarily the European funds in recent years. Overall, however, big gains have not been seen in this arena of late.

FACT

Morgan Stanley predicts foreign stocks will outperform domestic ones by 1.7 percentage points annually over the next ten years. According to global strategist Barton M. Biggs, "The return numbers we derive are not exactly scintillating, but international markets do better than the United States."

Usually not the place for a beginning investor, international specialized funds can be risky because of the high volatility of many overseas markets. Unless you are quite familiar with a foreign market—perhaps you've spent time in that part of the world and know something about the future economics of the country—these funds may be best left to the more daring and experienced investor. Besides, other funds may already be investing a small portion into overseas investments, thus dabbling in the arena and letting you have some foreign diversification.

Changes in currency and politics make it hard to assess, even for fund managers, what the future investing climate will be on a global basis. An investor certainly may not do well with an international fund. If you look at a market such as Asia or Brazil and have time to wait for it to turn around, you might get into a fund at a very low price (or get a great discount on a closed-end fund, which we describe later in this chapter).

Index and Balanced Funds

Index funds are passively managed funds that try to match the performance of a particular index. The investment objective of the fund is to mirror an index, the most popular of which is the S&P 500. From 1987 through 1997, the S&P 500 performed better than 81 percent of general equity funds. However, from 2001 through 2004, the S&P 500 trailed more than half of actively managed funds.

While index funds may seem like an easy way out, they are really an easy way to stick with a successful benchmark that everyone uses. They allow you to be in various sectors and to invest in both growth and value stocks, giving you maximum diversification. If the S&P 500 is the standard, why not go with it? After all, your goal is to make money. Index funds have lower costs since they don't involve a lot of transactions. Also, there is not an amount going to the management of the fund (as they are not managed funds).

ESSENTIAL

Vanguard founder and indexing guru John Bogle claims that index funds will beat 70 percent of managed funds over time. If this claim is true, that means 30 percent, or nearly one in three active funds, will out-perform the index.

Balanced funds, logically enough, are characterized by their balanced approach to investing. They derive capital gains from a mixed bag of investments, primarily consisting of stocks and bonds. This is ideal for those investors who do not want to allocate their own portfolios. Balanced funds provide maximum diversity and allow their managers to balance more volatile investments with safer, low-risk investments such as bonds. They are usually designed for the more-conservative investor who does not want to go too heavily into equities. Naturally, since this fund can have a wide range of investments, it is important to look over the fund's portfolio and get an idea of what makes up the balance in your balanced fund. The combination of good returns and nice yields makes these funds worthy of your attention.

Asset Allocation Funds

Like a balanced fund, an asset allocation fund maximizes diversification. The fund is managed to encompass a broad range of investment vehicles and asset classes. If managed correctly, an asset allocation fund will include a mix of stocks, bonds, and short-term instruments and distribute the percentage of holdings in each area according to which is providing better returns.

Whereas a balanced fund tries to maintain a balance between stocks and bonds, an asset allocation fund (depending on market conditions) can be 75 percent stocks one year and 75 percent bonds the next (say, if the economy experiences a bear market). Factoring in each type of investment, the fund manager has a wide range of choices across asset groups. In a broad sense, this is a manner of market timing. These fund managers have more leeway, as they are not locked into a set percentage allocated to one type of investment.

Socially Responsible Funds

The identity of these funds depends largely on the fund manager's definition of social responsibility. Some funds steer clear of products that use animal testing; many do not invest in companies involved with the defense industry, guns, or tobacco; others concern themselves with child labor issues. Some funds use all of the above or other criteria. You need to match those investing criteria with what you consider to be socially responsible and find funds that are earning money. They are out there, but they require that you take time to look beyond the marketing and the numbers of a company.

ALERT!

When it comes to socially responsible funds, the intentions are good and the funds are profitable. However, exactly how closely any of these funds stick to their overall criteria is hard to judge, even with a concerted effort. While a company may clearly not be manufacturing weapons, it may be inadvertently polluting the environment.

Several funds are trying to make an effort to seek out the less socially offensive aspects of business and society in general. Dreyfus Third Century Fund and PAX World are two of the most successful, best-known funds in this area. They are looking for protection of the environment and natural resources, occupational health and safety, life supportive goods and services, and companies that do not sell liquor, firearms, or tobacco products.

Large-Cap, Mid-Cap, and Small-Cap Funds

In the world of mutual funds, "cap" means "capital," which indicates the size of a company. Large-cap funds invest in the major corporations; small-cap funds seek out smaller, often growing companies; and the investments of mid-cap funds are somewhere in between. Usually, the larger, more established companies present less risk and, therefore, tend to make safer investments. Small-cap stocks can take off and often have fared better (though they certainly experience down periods as well), but there is a greater risk since these companies are trying to establish themselves. While some small-cap companies have become huge quickly, others have moved along slowly or vanished into oblivion.

QUESTION?

What is a mega fund?

This is a fund that buys into other funds. Like a big fish eating smaller fish, it looks at the smaller funds and lets you diversify your diversification. As the number of mutual funds grows by leaps and bounds, you may see more mega funds buying mutual funds much the way mutual funds select from the thousands of stocks at their disposal.

Small-cap stocks can sometimes be deceiving. A company that starts out small and continues to grow is ultimately no longer a small-cap company. Yet it still may remain in the fund. After all, why throw out your ace pitcher even though he's no longer playing in the Little League? E*TRADE was a small-cap company found in many small-cap funds, but as it grew and brought the funds high returns, fund managers enjoyed reaping the rewards (as did those investing in the fund), so it stayed.

Investing in different types of cap funds primarily serves to diversify your investments. You don't want companies that are all the same size because success does go in cycles. In 1998, large-cap funds sitting with Coca-Cola, General Electric, IBM, and other giant companies performed better than the small-cap mutual funds. One of the possible reasons is the tremendous growth in investing to a much wider sector of the population. No longer are yuppies and Wall Streeters the only ones seeking out stocks and funds. As more and more people get into the stock market and buy into funds from their home computers, they tend to be more comfortable—at least in the beginning—buying stock in larger, more familiar companies. There's nothing wrong with this. After all, unless you've taken the time to sufficiently study some new, small-but-growing plumbing supply company, you too might lean toward the more familiar Wal-Mart or Disney.

Some small-cap companies, such as those in the technical sector, are also very well known to a very literate computer population, which is why a company like Intel or Dell Computer can also shine. As the newer online investors become savvier, they too will branch out from safer, more familiar territory and explore the many growing companies.

Closed-End Mutual Funds

As opposed to being another separate fund category, closed-end funds (CEFs) are a broader grouping of mutual funds that include several fund categories you can buy into. CEFs are unique in several respects. While most mutual funds are open-end, meaning they will continue offering shares as long as they have buyers, closed-end mutual funds have a fixed amount of shares that they can sell to investors. A CEF is publicly traded. An initial public offering (IPO), like the offering to introduce a new stock to the public, is where the CEF begins. The shares then trade like stocks on the Amex or NYSE. Since these funds require you to participate in an IPO, they are bought through brokerage houses, meaning there will be a commission.

FACT

Closed-end funds differ from their open-end counterparts in that by selling a specific number of shares, they do not keep growing indefinitely as more investors put money into the fund. Like open-end funds, they have a fund manager who buys and sells stocks, but the structure and limits of the fund dictate how many shares there are to sell and at what price.

Another distinct feature of closed-end funds is that unlike an open-end fund, in which you buy or sell your shares with the fund directly, with a CEF you buy and sell shares with other investors. If there is a greater demand for the shares, the market price rises and you make a profit, called a premium, when you sell. The premium is equal to the difference between the market price and the fund's net asset value. (The NAV is the price of the fund, like open-end mutual funds, which is based on the holdings in the portfolio.) Conversely, you can also sell a CEF at a lower price.

Building Your Own Mutual Fund with Personal Portfolios

Did you know that you can build your own mutual fund, thus giving you even more control over your financial future? With personal portfolios, you can. Mind you, personal portfolios should only be driven by experienced investors who know their way around a prospectus or a balance sheet. If you fall into that category, then personal portfolios are certainly worth a look.

Personal portfolios combine some of the best qualities of mutual funds with the trading ease of a discount brokerage. Folios, as they're commonly called by those in the know, essentially let you build your own mutual fund, minus the usual limitations. You get to choose all the stocks, you decide when to buy and sell, you directly manage the investments, etc. In short, you get diversification and complete control.

Building Your Folio

Once you've decided to create your own personal portfolio, you'll buy its initial holdings in one fell swoop. Typically, your folio holds one to fifty stocks (with some companies allowing even more), either equally weighted or in specified percentages. If you're not quite comfortable making those choices yourself, you can choose a prepackaged model to start and wait until you're ready before making changes. You'll have literally thousands of stocks to choose from, including most of those traded on the major exchanges. If you want to include a stock outside your folio company's selection, you can usually still get it—for an extra fee, of course. Most folio companies let you make trades at least daily, allowing you to take advantage of sudden turns in the markets. You can track your holdings online, add or withdraw funds, even change your allocations without doing more than clicking your mouse.

Where Do You Stand?

Although folios may seem like a magical answer to the woes of mutual fund investing, they are not necessarily a better choice for everyone. If you're a new investor, you may not yet be experienced enough to successfully (or calmly) manage an entire portfolio. Or you simply may not have the time and commitment it takes to track your investments on a daily basis. If you have a relatively small amount of money to invest (less than $2,000), the folio fees may come out to a higher percentage of your holdings than a no-load mutual fund. If any of these instances describes your situation, you may be best off starting with an index fund; once you've gained confidence in your investing skills, you can always switch your stash into a personal portfolio.

On the other extreme, if your style calls for active trading—even opening and closing positions several times a day—a personal portfolio could hold you back. In fact, most don't allow more than single daily trades, and in some cases those trades won't take place in real time but rather through daily trading windows. For risk-loving, highly active traders, an online discount brokerage account may be a better choice.

Should you fall somewhere in between these two, personal portfolios just make the ideal fit for your investing personality. If you want more control than you'd get with a mutual fund without giving up diversification, consider looking more closely into personal portfolios. They may be able to give you the best of both worlds.

Chapter 9

E Choosing the Right Fund Combination

There's an old joke that the key to success is setting aside eight hours a day for work and eight hours a day for sleep and making sure they are not the same hours. This is especially true with your investments. Investment gurus agree that finding the right mix of funds for you is a combination of feeling comfortable with your investment goals and tolerance for risk, and finding funds that meet those objectives and limitations. If you're losing sleep over your investments, something isn't right.

Risk Tolerance and Your Fund Portfolio

Chapter 3 directed you to think long and hard about your personal tolerance for risk in your investment strategy. By now, you have decided whether you are a conservative, moderate, or aggressive investor. Now it's time to apply what you've discovered about your risk tolerance to your fund portfolio objectives.

A fund's beta is the measure that compares a mutual fund's volatility with that of a benchmark (usually the S&P 500). The beta should give some sense of how far you can expect a fund to fall when the market takes a dive, or how high it might climb if the bull is running hard. A fund with a beta of greater than 1 is considered more volatile than the market. A beta of less than 1 means less volatility than the market.

Identifying individual risk tolerance is one of the basic factors in determining your optimum investment strategy for a mutual fund portfolio. Regardless of whether a strategy applies to a total portfolio, a portion of a portfolio, or a qualified retirement plan, risk tolerance can affect both asset allocation and the selection of fund categories: small company growth, global, growth and income, corporate bond, government bond, and so on.

Risk in mutual funds usually refers to the fluctuations in the price of a fund, as opposed to the dividend risk and market risk associated with stocks. As risk increases, both price volatility and total return potential increase proportionately. As risk decreases, price volatility and total return potential decrease proportionately.

If you've decided that you have a conservative level of risk tolerance, you will accept lower returns on your investments in order to minimize price volatility. If you're an aggressive investor, you'll seek out the highest returns regardless of price volatility.

Regardless of your risk tolerance level, you can achieve your investment goals with mutual funds—whether they're categorized as growth, balance, or income—as long as you keep your money invested over the long term. The shorter your investment, the fewer options are available to you in the mutual fund market that will allow you to achieve your end goals.

Risk tolerance can be the most important element in determining mutual fund selections. Two investors with the exact same investment objectives and investment capital will enter into two dramatically different portfolio scenarios if they have different tolerances for risk.

Using Diversification to Minimize Risk

Diversification in an investment portfolio is absolutely necessary to achieve a well-rounded investment strategy. Ideally, diversification spreads an investment portfolio among different fund categories to achieve not only a variety of objectives, but also a reduction in overall risk.

Different fund types (growth, growth and income, corporate bond, etc.) offer distinct risk/return objectives. Diversification increases as the combination of different risk/return objectives increases. Here are some guidelines to help you master the diversification process:

- **Define your investment objectives.** Your personal time horizon, return objectives, risk tolerance, and portfolio amount all contribute to the focal point for your investment strategy. If your selected funds accurately represent your objectives, you have an effective investment plan.
- **Choose quality over quantity.** What is important is how distinct your funds are and how they fit your investment strategy, not how many funds you own. Don't think of diversification as a challenge to buy as many funds as possible or you'll end up with a portfolio that does not match your strategy.
- **Value fund category above fund style.** A fund category defines its objectives; the fund's style is the method used to pursue those objectives.

- **Avoid duplication.** It is a waste of your investment monies to own multiple funds with identical objectives. It's best to own just one fund in any particular fund category.
- **Fewer is better.** Use the fewest funds possible to accomplish your goals. Most funds are comprised of fifty to 150 separate stocks or bonds, so you do not need to buy a huge number of funds to meet your diversification objectives.

Regardless of the number of funds in your portfolio, the key to effective diversification is to make sure that each fund serves a distinct purpose toward meeting your investment strategy.

Investing for Your Family

It's important that your investing strategies be tailored to your family situation, whether you're investing as a family or as a couple. While children generally do not have a say in the family's investments as they grow up, explaining that Mommy and Daddy own a very tiny piece of Disney through shares of stock is a way of teaching them about money and, in time, about investing. Investing is a way of building toward a brighter future for your children. It can open the door to a college education as well as give them some financial backing to pursue their own goals and dreams. It also teaches them by example that saving money can bring you more money.

FACT

The Internet has democratized Wall Street. Online features have opened up a plethora of information to retail investors that was previously only accessible by professionals. There's easier communication between IPOs and shareholders, and investors can access the entirety of their account, from research to portfolio—all at the click of a mouse.

Couples often find that money is their most significant cause of discord. In fact, it is listed in survey after survey as the top reason couples fight or break up. Money can be, and is, very easily equated with power—and that can spell trouble in a relationship. If one person uses his or her income or savings as a means of control, the other party can, and often will, become disenchanted. For other couples, money is a source of pressure or tension if one party does not feel the other is earning enough. When it comes to investing, the problem that often arises is lack of full disclosure, when one party makes investment decisions without telling the other.

The road to harmonious investing in a relationship is an open line of communication, starting with determining your goals and dreams as a couple. If one person has a greater aversion to risk than the other, this too must be discussed, and a compromise needs to be reached. The handling of finances in the home also needs to be addressed. One couple may be satisfied with letting one party make the investment decisions, while another couple might discuss all money matters, including investments. It's important that no matter what approach a couple takes, it is discussed and established early on in the relationship. Communication and honesty are important in all relationships and especially when it comes to money—which is often at the root of many other problems.

Your Lifelong Fund Strategy

Everyone's attitude toward investing is different, and people have very distinct long-term financial goals that they are trying to achieve with their portfolios. One investor might be looking solely at producing maximum retirement income, while another may be focused on how to send his six kids through college. Even so, most investors share some common situations throughout their lives. Where you are in your life cycle certainly affects how you invest for retirement, but other life stages aren't so closely related to age.

Let's say you're forty and expecting your first child. You'll need to decide how to balance your finances to account for the additional expenses of a baby. Perhaps you'll need to supplement your income with income-producing investments. Moreover, your child will be entering college at about the time you're ready to retire! In these circumstances, your growth and income needs most certainly will change, and maybe your risk tolerance will too.

Major Events

The following are some major life events that most people share, along with some investment decisions that you may want to consider when thinking about your fund portfolio:

Getting your first "real" job . . .

- Start a savings account to build a cash reserve.
- Start a retirement fund and make regular monthly contributions, no matter how small.
- Start to think about long-term financial goals.

Every time you get a raise . . .

- Increase your contribution to your company-sponsored retirement plan.
- Invest after-tax dollars in municipal bonds that offer tax-exempt interest.
- Increase your cash reserves.
- Re-evaluate your financial position to determine how much of your income you can afford to invest. Invest more whenever possible.

When you get married . . .

- Determine your new investment contributions and allocations, taking into account your combined income and expenses.

When you buy your first house . . .

- Invest some of your nonretirement savings in a short-term investment specifically for funding your down payment, closing, and moving costs.

When you have a baby . . .

- Increase your cash reserves.
- Increase your life insurance.
- Start a college fund.

When you change jobs . . .

- Review your investment strategy and asset allocation to accommodate a new salary and a different benefits package.
- Consider your distribution options for your company's retirement savings or pension plan. You may want to roll money over into a new plan or IRA.

When all your children move out of the house . . .

- Boost your retirement savings contributions.

When you reach fifty-five (or near your target retirement age) . . .

- Review your retirement fund asset allocation to accommodate the shorter time frame for your investments.
- Continue saving for retirement.

When you retire . . .

- Carefully study the options you may have for taking money from your company retirement plan. Discuss your alternatives with your financial advisor.
- Review your combined potential income after retirement.
- Reallocate your investments to provide the income you need while still providing for some growth in capital to help beat inflation and fund your later years.

ALERT!

Many funds allow an exchange of shares for the shares of another fund managed by the same advisor. Look at the first part of the fee table to find out if there's an exchange fee for your fund—you might be able to make a move that would benefit your portfolio for free.

Building your mutual fund portfolio is a long process. The sooner you start, the better off you'll be in the long run. It's best to start investing as soon as you start earning money, even if it's only $10 a paycheck. The discipline and skills you learn will benefit you for the rest of your life. But no matter how old you are when you start thinking seriously about your investment strategy and how mutual funds fit into it, it's never too late to begin.

Past Performance

Judging past performance of a fund can be trickier than it might seem by glancing at five- and ten-year returns. Sectors or industries that are in vogue during one period may not be during the next. One spectacular year of 90-percent growth, followed by four years of 10-percent growth, will average 26-percent growth per year. This average would not be a good indicator of how that fund is performing at the end of the fifth year, when you are thinking about buying. Also, a sector that has not fared well over a stretch of time may be on the upswing due to new products, consumer needs, or public awareness (as with the socially responsible stocks). This won't show up in past performance.

The same holds true for the large- and small-cap companies. A fund that invests in small companies will not see large returns when the trend leans toward the large corporations, as it did in the late 1990s. The best you can do is look at each measure of past performance, read up on future expectations, and try to make an informed decision. Remember this: Long-term five- and ten-year returns are important, but they are only part of the larger picture.

ESSENTIAL

A fund's past performance is not as important as you might think. Advertisements, rankings, and ratings tell you how well a fund has performed in the past, but studies show the future is often different. This year's number-one fund can easily become next year's below-average fund.

Over the long-term, the success (or failure) of your investment in a fund will also depend on factors such as these:

- The fund's sales charges, fees, and expenses
- The taxes you may have to pay when you receive a distribution

- The age and size of the fund
- The fund's risks and volatility
- Recent changes in fund operations

As for selecting a fund family, it is often suggested that you look for one that has been around a while, unless you're going with an emerging industry such as tech stocks, in which the newer fund families may all have been around for about the same length of time. The better-established fund families can show you ten-year returns, which you can compare against comparable funds in other fund families. They can also give you an indication of how the fund has fared during the bear markets and how long it took them to recover. Naturally some of this will depend on the fund manager, but you have a better chance of finding a fund manager with ten years of experience at the helm of a fund at an older, more-established company. Look at the ten-year returns and see if the same fund manager was there over that time period. If you look at ten-year returns and see that the current manager has only been on board for three years, those ten-year returns won't mean as much. It's like looking at the last ten years of a baseball team that only acquired its superstars in the past three years; management experience makes a big difference.

Additionally, you should compare the mutual fund that interests you with other comparable funds. If the fund you like had a 10-percent return last year and other similar funds were also around 10 percent, then the fund is performing as expected. However, if the fund is bringing in 10 percent, and comparable funds in the same category are bringing in 12 and 15 percent, you can do better without changing your goals or choosing a more (or less) risky fund. All you have to do is find another fund in the same category.

Once you finally make a decision, expect to be in the fund for at least one year, usually five or more. Mutual funds are not generally thought of as a short-term investment, but sometimes market conditions can dictate change earlier than you had planned. If you've invested in a fund that was on the upswing, and now it's heading back down (or "correcting"), you may be better off selling before share prices drop lower. You'll almost always have the opportunity to revisit the fund after it stabilizes, when you'll have a chance to benefit from the next round of growth.

Reading the Prospectus

Examining a mutual fund's prospectus will most likely not be the highlight of your week, even if returns are spectacularly high. A prospectus can be dense and wordy, even hard to decipher, with little consideration for the information needs of the average investor. Important information is in there, somewhere, but it can be hard to find in the midst of the legal jargon. In this highly competitive market, however, some funds are actually trying to soften the legalese in which the fund's prospectus is written. In fact, many now publish easy-to-read newsletters to supplement the information in the prospectus—or at least translate some of it. However you get it done, it's to your advantage to read the prospectus with an eye for specific areas of importance. There are certain details that deserve particular attention. (Obtaining a prospectus, by the way, should be as easy as calling the fund's toll-free number.)

The Fund's Objective

The fund should have a clear statement of the objective. Is it aggressive growth? Current income? While it may be far more clear-cut in bond funds, a fund's objective is not always as obvious when reading the prospectus of a stock fund. If the objective is unclear, the mutual fund manager has more leeway. It also means your intentions in choosing that particular fund may not be carried out. If the fund objective is not clear, either seek out a fund that is more clearly defined, ask someone in the fund's investment information department, or follow the old rule of thumb and do your homework. Look up the fund's current holdings.

ESSENTIAL

One of the most common errors investors make when buying mutual funds is simply buying at the wrong time. Don't invest in a mutual fund before it makes its annual capital gains distribution—even if you buy the fund just one day before gains are distributed, you'll owe taxes as if you owned the fund all year.

The Investment Risks

The mutual fund prospectus should discuss the level of risks the fund will take in conjunction with its objective. Stock funds should discuss the types of stocks they are buying. Are they talking about speculation? Are they telling you about the volatility of particular stocks? Look at the warnings they're giving you. Are they telling you about the currency and political risks involved with their international holdings?

The prospectus should specify the risks associated with its portfolio. As an investor, you should be aware of the risks of investing and how those risks mesh with your risk tolerance. To make the best possible investment choices, it's important to understand how different investments perform under different economic scenarios. For example, aggressive growth stock funds typically perform best as the market is emerging from a long downward trend. Bond funds, on the other hand, often do well during periods of slow growth, as interest rates fall and bond prices climb. By combining your knowledge with the information in the prospectus, you'll be able to make better, and better-informed, investment choices.

Investment Breakdown

The fund should clearly lay out the percentage of holdings they are committed to in each asset group. They should say, for example, that the management is required to hold at least 70 percent of U.S. bonds, or 80 percent in common stocks, or no more than 20 percent in international investments. The breakdown and parameters of the fund give you an idea where your money will be invested. Other types of investments, such as cash instruments, may also be included.

A fee table should outline all the fees associated with that fund. Read them carefully, and make sure you are left with no surprises. Operating costs, loads, and any other fees should all be included.

Financial History

A prospectus will also give you the history of that mutual fund. The financial information should provide the per-share results for the life of the fund—or for funds that have been around for a long time, at least the past ten years. You can gauge the annual total return of the fund on an annual basis. You can also look at the year-end net asset values, the fund's expense ratio, and any other information that will help you gauge how the fund has performed over time. You can check on dividend payments, if it is an income fund, or see the types of holdings the fund has sold and purchased.

Building Your Fund Profile

If you've targeted a fund that looks appealing to you, you need to build a profile for the fund so that you can make the best decision when it comes time to pull the trigger and buy. You should be able to construct an accurate profile of your fund from the prospectus or one of the leading financial magazines (or both). This process simply involves identifying the key features of the fund. Many of the leading financial magazines do this all the time, but rather than waiting for them to highlight the fund you're interested in, you can do it yourself. Here's an example of such a profile:

- **Name:** ABCD Fictitious Investment Fund
- **Symbol:** ABCDIF
- **Category:** Small-cap, aggressive growth
- **Assets:** $21.5 million
- **Expense ratio:** 2 percent
- **Load fund?** No
- **Minimum investment:** $500
- **Fund manager:** James B. James
- **Tenure:** 3 years
- **The fund generally has a minimum of 70 percent of its assets in small-cap companies, with market capitalization under $250 million. 10 percent of the investments may be in foreign securities.**
- **Composition as of 4/15/05:**
    Domestic stocks: 87 percent
    Foreign securities: 8 percent
    Cash: 5 percent

- **Sector breakdown:**
  Technologies: 41.3 percent
  Financials: 19.7 percent
  Services: 21.5 percent
  Retail: 10.0 percent
  Health: 7.5 percent

Add to these statistics the fund's three-month rate of return plus its one-, three-, and five-year rate of returns, and you have a basic idea of what can be put together to profile a specific mutual fund. You can then examine the individual segments.

ALERT!

Liquidity is another benefit of mutual funds. Funds can be sold on any business day at that day's closing price—or at the following day's close if the sell order is placed after the market closes.

You might, for example, want to look more closely at the track record of the fund manager. If the direction and category of the fund appeals to you, you may want to look at the specific stocks held by the fund to see their P/E ratio and performance in recent months and recent years. Essentially, the prospectus will help you determine your level of interest in the fund. Building a profile, or reading a profile in one of the leading financial publications, will allow you to organize the vital information and determine what additional details you may want to learn about the fund.

Six Fund Investment Strategies You Can Swear By

As you head into the world of mutual funds, here are six strategies that will help steer you through the murky depths of what can sometimes be a confusing investment genre. Don't let yourself become overwhelmed; simply take your time and cover your bases.

- **Start early.** There's no substitute for getting a good start on your financial future. All the studies on the subject conclude that the earlier you get going with your investment strategy, the more money you'll have in retirement. That's because the earlier you start, the earlier compound interest goes to work for you.

- **Max out.** The more money you invest, the faster you'll become a successful investor. Put as much money as you can possibly afford into your investment plan, even if it means sacrificing some of life's luxuries.

- **Learning is earning.** Knowing enough about your investments to become the master of your financial future is priceless. Read all you can on finance and investments, and make sure you read every word of the prospectuses that come your way from the mutual fund each year. The payoff for spending an hour or two per week boning up on the ways of Wall Street is potentially huge. Don't be left behind.

- **Be aggressive.** Prudence is the proper course if you're an airplane pilot or a brain surgeon, but it's a drawback for investors. Studies show that to beat inflation and to make your money grow faster, a good chunk of your plan should be earmarked for higher-performing stock funds. That doesn't mean you should be reckless. But if you stick to conservative investments like bonds or bank savings accounts, your chances of developing a successful investment portfolio will be low to nonexistent.

- **Keep the money working.** Don't be tempted to take money out of your investments or borrow against them in order to meet short-term financial crises at home. It's important that the money you've invested be allowed to do its job over time so that you can meet your long-term financial objectives. If you hit a financial stumbling block, try to find other ways to get over it before you even think about tapping your investment monies. The government wants you to keep that money invested, and they've set up expensive traps if you don't.

- **Keep an eye on the market.** Don't ignore market trends as you're evaluating your holdings or making new investment choices. No matter how well a fund is managed, or how well it's performed in the past, changes in the overall geopolitical and economic climate can turn the markets upside down. Wise investors keep an eye on the overall trend of the markets, and accordingly on their investments.

Chapter 10

Tracking Your Fund's Performance

An airline captain who has a plane, fuel, and passengers but no itinerary or destination won't know when and where to land. Similarly, you might have all the components of a successful mutual fund portfolio, but if you don't have a plan to track where you're going and where you've been, you'll find yourself flying around in search of a resting place. Tracking your fund's performance isn't difficult; it just takes dedication and time. By understanding economic indicators and knowing when to act, you can retain control over your funds.

How to Keep Tabs on Your Portfolio

You got into this investing game to make your money work for you. In a way, your investment money has become your employee, and that makes you the boss. And like any good manager, you'll want to keep a close watch on how your employee, your money, is doing.

ALERT!

Watch out for unauthorized trades in your account. If you get a confirmation slip for a transaction that you didn't approve beforehand, call your broker. It may have been a mistake. If it happens more than once, or if your broker refuses to correct it, call the SEC or your state securities regulator.

Some people like to look at the stock quotations every day to see how their investments have done. That's probably too often. You may get too caught up in the ups and downs of the trading value of your investment, and sell when its value goes down temporarily—even though the performance of the company is still stellar. Remember, you need to be in this game for the long haul.

It's not enough to simply check an investment's performance. You should compare that performance against an index of similar investments over the same period of time. You should also compare the fees and commissions that you're paying to what other investment professionals charge. And while monitoring performance regularly is one part of the role of a good investor, you also need to pay close attention every time you make a decision to put some of your hard-earned cash into another investment.

Every time you buy or sell an investment, you will receive a confirmation slip from your broker. Make sure each trade was completed according to your instructions. Make sure the buying or selling price was what your broker quoted. And make sure the commissions or fees are what your broker said they would be.

Keeping tabs on your portfolio depends at least in part on how you've decided to structure your investments. Regardless of the kind of portfolio you've decided to create, monitoring the rising and falling prices of stocks is an essential part of being a successful investor or stock trader.

At the minimum, fund-based investors should check performance, costs, and fees once or twice a year, and re-examine their contribution schedule. Investors in individual shares should keep a much closer eye on the financial pages, but they probably don't need to look every day unless they are actively trading.

To help keep track of your investments and trends in the market, you can subscribe to the *Wall Street Journal* or *Barron's*. Both are available in print and on the Internet (at *www.wsj.com* and *www.barrons. com*). Publications like these will provide you with specific data related to your investments, and they will also help keep you on top of news and events that might affect your portfolio.

The longer your time commitment to your investment portfolio, and the broader the range of your investments, the less active you'll have to be in monitoring them. If you've decided (against the best recommendations of this book) to place all your investment eggs in one basket, however, you really have to watch that basket very closely.

Ten Tips to Keep Track of Your Investments

Whether you work with a broker or advisor or you trade on your own, you should always monitor your investments. By keeping an eye on your investments, you can prevent minor mistakes from turning into big problems. Mastering the following pointers will allow you to be the commander of your investment ship:

- **Verify every document you get pertaining to your investments.** If you find an error, contact the sender (be it mutual fund company, stockbroker, or investment advisor) immediately, and request a written correction confirmation.

- **When you talk with your financial advisor, either in person or over the phone, make some notes of your discussion.** Be sure to jot down any actions you've authorized so you'll have a record of the conversation in case problems crop up.

- **Make sure that all account paperwork, especially the trade-related, is sent directly to you and not first to your financial advisor.** If the paper trail is too cumbersome for you to follow, have the papers sent (or bring them) to someone you trust who is not connected with the account: your accountant, a competent relative, or your family attorney, for example.

- **If you don't get account statements or confirmations, follow up.** You have a right to this information. If you are not receiving these documents on a regular basis, that could be a sign of trouble.

- **When something unexpected shows up on your investment account, address it right away.** If there's a transaction that doesn't make sense, call your advisor and ask about it at once.

- **Even if you don't trade online, consider getting online access to your account.** Online access to your account allows you to review your account whenever you want. You can verify information that you received from your broker or advisor or in your confirmations or account statements. You also may be able to request that your confirmations and account statements be sent to you via e-mail.

- **Do not make checks or other payments payable to your broker, advisor, or another individual for an investment.** In most cases, money should only be sent to your brokerage firm, its clearing firm, or another financial institution.

- **Meet with your broker and visit the firm, if possible.** Investments are a major financial undertaking and should be afforded the same degree of investigation and caution as any other major purchase you might make.

- **Know your investments.** Don't rely on canned information from someone else—do your own research. The materials are out there, and easily available; all you have to do is read them. Before you make a trading decision, check out the following documents: annual reports (Form 10-K), quarterly reports (Form 10-Q), prospectuses, independent research reports, and even the company Web site.

- **Periodically review your portfolio.** Make sure the pieces that comprise your portfolio still meet your investment objectives. Also make sure you understand and are comfortable with the risks, costs, and liquidity of your investments. As part of this review, you may want to check the information that is on file at your brokerage firm regarding your accounts. You have a right to know what is on file about you.

What to Do If You Have a Problem

If you believe you have been wronged or you see a mistake in your account, act quickly. Immediately question any transaction or entry that you do not understand or did not authorize. Don't be timid or ashamed to complain. The securities industry needs your help so it can operate successfully.

If you think it's a minor mistake, talk to your broker. This may be the fastest way to resolve the problem. If you can't resolve the problem with your broker, or you believe your broker engaged in unauthorized transactions or other serious misconduct, report the matter to the firm's management or compliance department in writing. If you and your firm still can't resolve the problem, contact the SEC at ✐*www.sec.gov.* You can file a complaint using their online complaint form.

Remember that the stock market is often in flux and can be extremely volatile depending on the financial happenings in the world. A smart investor looks forward three years in his or her investment strategy, keeping in mind that quick turnaround on investments is not only improbable but sometimes dangerous.

Economic Indicators: Part I

An investor who doesn't understand economic indicators is like a tourist trying to navigate a foreign country without a map. Sooner or later you'll get lost, and it might take you a while to find your way again. It makes sense for investors in the stock market to have a thorough understanding of how the economy works and how economic activity is measured. The four indicators covered in this section are business inventories, gross domestic product (GDP), consumer price index (CPI), and job growth.

Business Inventories

As a monthly running total of how well companies are selling their products, business inventories are like a big neon sign to economists and investors alike. The business inventory data are collected from three sources: the manufacturing, merchant wholesalers, and retail reports. Retail inventories are the most volatile component of inventories and can cause major swings. A sudden fall in inventories may show the onset of expansion, and a sudden accumulation of inventories may signify falling demand and hence onset of recession.

Gross Domestic Product

The gross domestic product (GDP) is the most important economic indicator published. Providing the broadest measure of economic activity, the GDP is considered the nation's report card. The four major components of the GDP are consumption, investment, government purchases, and net exports. As the barometer of the nation's total output of goods and services, the GDP is the broadest of the nation's economic measures.

Consumer Price Index (CPI)

The consumer price index (CPI) is considered the most important measure of inflation. It compares prices for a fixed list of goods and services to a base period. Currently, the base period, which equals 100, is the average prices from 1982 to 1984. Unlike other measures of inflation that only cover domestically produced goods, the CPI covers imported goods, which are becoming increasingly important to the U.S. economy.

Job Growth

Except for the GDP, the government's employment report is the most significant economic indicator reported. It sets the tone for the entire investing month, providing information on employment, the average workweek, hourly earnings, and the unemployment rate. Consumers feel more at ease when the job market is expanding. But when job growth contracts to 100,000 or less month to month, watch out—the economy could be headed for a slowdown.

Economic Indicators: Part II

Economic indicators are key statistics that show where the economy is headed by monitoring inflation. Inflation highly influences the level of interest rates, which impact the stability of the economy. While you don't need a degree in economics to be a good investor, you need to understand how the economy can impact your portfolio. Four other important economic indicators are consumer confidence, the unemployment index, housing starts, and the producer price index.

Consumer Confidence

The Conference Board maintains this index of consumer sentiment based on monthly interviews with 5,000 households. The consumer confidence index dropped drastically after the terrorist attacks of September 11, 2001. Now, in spring 2005, the index remains fairly steady, meaning that consumers are maintaining buying patterns, despite rising gasoline prices and interest rates. In bad times or good, consumer confidence serves as a reflection of the nation's financial health. Sometimes the consumer worries about inflation more than unemployment, and at other times the reverse is true. Consumer confidence is far more important to the financial markets during times of national crisis or panic—such as after the 1987 stock market crash, before and during the Persian Gulf Wars, after oil shocks, during recessions, and so forth.

Unemployment Index

The government's employment report covers information on payroll jobs, including employment, average workweek, hourly earnings, and unemployment. Unlike the jobs data, which is a coincident indicator of economic activity—it changes direction at the same time as the economy—the unemployment rate is a lagging indicator. It rises or falls following a change in economic activity. Consequently, it is of far less significance to economists and investors.

In its favor, and unlike the payroll jobs data, the unemployment rate is not subject to change. During the past year, the unemployment rate has gradually declined. Recently, it has been running at levels below what economists believe to be the natural rate, or that rate at which sustained unemployment can exist without rekindling inflation. The natural rate has been pegged at 5.5 percent. Consequently, four months at levels as low as 5.1 percent have many investors and economists concerned that inflation is just around the corner.

Housing Starts

This indicator tracks how many new single-family homes or buildings were constructed throughout the month. For the survey, each house and every single apartment are counted as one housing start, meaning a building with 200 apartments would be counted as 200 housing starts. The figures include all private and publicly owned units with the exception of mobile homes, which are not counted.

Most of the housing start data is collected through applications and permits for building homes. The housing start data is offered in an unadjusted and a seasonally adjusted format. According to the U.S. Census Bureau, the housing industry represents over 25 percent of investment dollars and a 5-percent value of the overall economy. Declining housing starts show a slowing economy, while increases in housing activity can pull the economy out of a downturn.

FACT

The index of leading economic indicators (LEI) is intended to predict future economic activity. Typically, three consecutive monthly LEI changes in the same direction suggest a turning point in the economy. For example, consecutive negative readings would indicate a possible recession.

Producer Price Index

The producer price index (PPI) is a basket of various indices covering a wide range of areas affecting domestic producers. The PPI includes industries such as goods manufacturing, fishing, agriculture, and other commodities. Each month, approximately 100,000 prices are collected from 30,000 production and manufacturing firms. There are three primary areas that make up the PPI. These are industry-based, commodity-based, stage-of-processing goods. Other good barometers of economic growth include retail sales, employee cost index, factory purchase orders, and new and existing home sales.

The Value of Asset Allocation

In Chapter 3, you read about the concept of asset allocation in relation to your entire investment outlook. Asset allocation also has a place in your thinking regarding your mutual funds portfolio. Asset allocation works on the principle that not all investments behave the same way at the same time. Some, such as equities or equity mutual funds, have greater short-term price fluctuations; others, such as guaranteed investment certificates (GICs) and money market mutual funds, are generally more stable. More volatile investments, however, offer the potential for greater long-term gains.

Financial markets also vary in performance cycles. If North American stock markets are on the rise, those in other areas of the world may be in decline. In times of dropping interest rates, shorter-term bonds generally outperform longer-term bonds. Moreover, when stock markets are strong, bond markets may be weak.

Through asset allocation, you can use these variations in the performance of different mutual funds to your benefit. Asset allocation ensures that your portfolio is diversified, so you reduce the degree of short-term fluctuations while maintaining the potential for long-term returns. You can also reduce the risks associated with putting all your eggs in one basket.

Once you've devised an asset allocation strategy, you can adjust it to meet your changing financial goals as you develop and rethink your mutual fund portfolio strategy. For example, when you're younger you may want to concentrate higher-risk funds that yield higher returns for greater wealth. When you approach retirement, you may wish to preserve the wealth you've accumulated through a greater concentration of lower-risk funds.

The cornerstones of asset allocation are the same whether you are applying them to stocks, bonds or mutual funds—selecting certain types of investments and then determining how much to invest. Anywhere on Wall Street, or Main Street for that matter, the goal of asset allocation is to achieve the best possible return while reducing the risk. When establishing an asset allocation strategy, try these simple steps:

- Think about how long you'll be investing.
- Decide how much risk you can take.
- Pick a target mix that's right for you.
- Select investments that will help you achieve that mix.
- Adjust your investments gradually. Start with your future deferrals to match your asset mix, and gradually redirect existing balances to fit into your overall plan.

When to Sell

The single most important reason for selling a fund is an echo of the reason for buying it—your investment goal. Even the best performing fund can and should end up on the selling block if it does not meet your investment needs. Just as you should make your buying decisions solely on the basis of how they contribute to your long-term financial goal, your selling decisions should be made the same way.

ESSENTIAL

Someone approaching retirement might want to sell aggressive funds and buy more conservative investments. Or perhaps it's time to sell a fund simply because you need the cash for some other pursuit.

Several other factors can help you determine when it's time to sell a fund—a fund's unsuitability for your portfolio, deteriorating performance, a change in the style or allocation of the fund, a change in management, or inefficient service. Taxes can provide another motive for selling a fund. Taking a loss on a fund and switching to another may allow the government to share in the loss through an income tax deduction.

And, of course, there's the good-night's-sleep factor. You may need or want to sell when you just can't take it anymore. The point of investing is meeting financial goals, not developing ulcers. If your fund is so volatile that not even the visions of your brand-new vacation home calm you down, then by all means sell—as long as you're sure you will never buy the fund back again.

You should also sell a fund that is doing badly because it is not sticking to any real style. Keep your eyes open when you look at your funds. Are they still doing what they said they would do? If not, you should sell, and you should also question whether the investment concept you bought into is worth buying into again.

Does Dollar-Cost Averaging Really Work?

One strategy that can work well with mutual funds is dollar-cost averaging. Essentially, this is where you invest a fixed sum of money into the mutual fund on a regular basis regardless of where the market stands. Retirement plans and 401(k) plans are generally built on this principle, except they have restrictions on the withdrawal end. Following a regular investment schedule, whether it's weekly, monthly, or bimonthly, you are not trying to time the stocks in the fund's portfolio.

Frequently, an investor will decide to have the same amount of money automatically withdrawn from his or her account and invested into the mutual fund on a consistent weekly, or monthly, basis—not unlike a 401(k) or retirement plan. Over time, a fixed amount invested regularly, as opposed to buying a fixed number of shares, will reduce your average cost per share over time. In essence you are buying more shares when the prices are low and fewer shares when the prices are high, all by putting in the same amount.

Dollar-cost averaging also eliminates the popular "timing the market" game played by the professionals—sometimes for better and sometimes for worse. As we discussed in Chapter 3, market timing essentially means trying to determine the peaks and valleys of the market and buy and sell accordingly. This is usually not advised for beginning investors. The volatility of the market in recent years has made this method particularly difficult. Fund managers, however, spend a great deal of time trying to time the market—with varying results.

Dollar-cost averaging can be emotionally difficult for one reason. By investing on a regular basis, you will also be investing during bear markets. Direct deposit makes this a little easier. It's also easier with mutual funds, where you know that a good fund manager should be setting up the portfolio with stocks that will best recover from a market downturn, rather than with one stock, which could take longer to rebound.

Chapter 11
Bond Basics

Bonds are like the geeky cousins of the hip and trendy stocks and mutual funds you've already learned about. However, bonds are part of a completely different asset class, and the two often move in different directions. Like the stock market, the bond market is heavily influenced by global economic and political trends—but to a much higher degree. In fact, the world bond market is considerably larger and more influential than the stock market, and much of the world economy depends on international bond trading.

What Are Bonds?

Bonds are essentially a manner in which you loan a company, municipality, the government, or a foreign government money to be paid back at a set date in the future. Bonds can be bought directly as new issues from the government, from a municipality, or from a company. They can also be bought from bond traders, brokers, or dealers (as they're called) on the secondary market. The bond market will dictate how easily you can buy or sell and at what price.

For lending them the money, the borrower (or issuer of the bond) agrees to pay you a rate of interest. Bonds are sold in specific increments and can be bought on a short-term basis (up to five years), intermediate-term basis (generally seven to ten years), or a long-term basis (usually around twenty to thirty years). Longer-term bonds typically will pay higher yields—averaging higher than 6 percent over the last fifty years—than short-term bonds. Over the time you hold a bond, its yields will fluctuate more with changes in interest rates, which primarily matters if you are trying to sell a bond.

Because they often move in the opposite direction of the stock market, bonds can be a key component in both the risk-reducing diversification and asset allocation strategies essential for good portfolio management. While bonds typically don't function as a complete substitute for stocks, they do make a strong complement, in addition to providing steady interest income to investors.

A bond will have a date of final maturity, which is the date at which the bond will return your principal, or initial investment. Some types of bonds can be called earlier, which means that the lender pays you back at an earlier date. A $5,000 bond is therefore worth $5,000 upon maturity as long as the issuer does not default on the payment. The interest you receive while holding the bond is your perk, so to speak, for lending the money. Interest is usually paid semiannually or annually, and it compounds at different rates.

As a bondholder, unlike a stockholder, you are not taking part in the success or failure of the company. Shares of stock will rise and fall in conjunction with how the company is doing. In the case of bonds, you will receive interest on your loan (from the bond issuer) and get your principal back at the date of maturity, regardless of how well a company is doing—unless, of course, they go bankrupt. Bonds are therefore referred to as fixed-income investments because you know how much you will get back—unless you sell, in which case the market determines the price.

ALERT!

Some of the key variables to look at when deciding whether to invest in bonds are their maturity, redemption features, credit quality, interest rate, price, yield, and potential tax benefits. Together, these factors help determine the value of a bond investment and how well it matches your personal investment goals.

As a general rule, bonds are considered less risky than stocks and are therefore considered a more conservative investment, particularly when you discuss U.S. government bonds. Bonds also provide a higher rate of interest than you'll receive from a bank account or CD, and this, along with a steady flow of income, usually makes them attractive, safe investments.

There are drawbacks and risks inherent to bonds, which will also be discussed in more detail later. The most basic is that an issuer may default. You can also lose money in bonds if you are forced to sell for purposes of liquidation when interest rates are high. As returns go, you may not see the type of high returns from bond investments that you can see from (more risky) equity mutual funds or from a hot stock.

The Value of Bonds in Your Portfolio

Allocating some bonds or bond mutual funds to your investment portfolio is a good idea, especially if you have a lower tolerance for risk. For investors of every kind, bonds offer a wide variety of benefits.

Bonds can help to stabilize a portfolio by helping to offset the investor's exposure to the volatility of the stock market. Bonds inherently have a different risk and return character than stocks, so they will necessarily behave differently when the markets move. Also, bonds generally provide a scheduled stream of interest payments (except zero coupon bonds, which pay their interest at maturity). This attractive feature helps to meet expected current income needs or specific future expenditures such as college tuition or retirement income. Callable bonds and pass-through securities have less predictability, but investors are compensated for the uncertainty in the form of higher yields.

ALERT!

Many brokers and mutual fund companies offer bond investment calculators you can use yourself on the Internet to decide whether a bond will benefit your tax situation. This is a far superior option to guessing whether a bond is right for you and doing the math in your head.

Unlike stocks, bonds are designed to return the original investment, or principal, to the investor at a future maturity date. This preservation of capital provides stability to a portfolio and balances the growth/risk aspect of stocks. You can still lose your principal investment if you sell your bonds before maturity at a price lower than your purchase price, or if the borrower defaults on payment. By choosing high-credit-quality bonds, you can limit your exposure to default risk.

Another noteworthy benefit is that some bonds offer special tax advantages. There is no state or local income tax on the interest from U.S. Treasury bonds. There is no federal tax on the interest from most municipal bonds, and in some places, no state or local income tax, either. A good broker or tax advisor can help you determine which bonds are best for you.

Stocks Versus Bonds: Performance and Security

Stocks and bonds differ dramatically in their structures, payouts, returns, and risks. It's important to recognize that in a truly balanced portfolio, using the integral value and risk of stocks and bonds to balance each other can create stability through diversification. Unlike bonds, which are a form of debt that requires repayment with interest, stocks are a form of ownership, the value of which is based entirely on a company's growth. As a rule, investors in stocks are given no guarantees about the likelihood of seeing the return of their initial investment. Your stock investment's value is almost entirely dependent on the increasing profits of the company, which will hopefully generate a rising stock price.

Stocks are subject to many kinds of market fluctuations, including fluctuations in earnings and fluctuations in interest rates. Bond prices, while also affected by earnings (as with corporate bonds), are often affected to a much stronger degree by fluctuations in interest rates. (This is true even though the bond market itself often takes the lead in setting those rates.) And both types of securities are subject to influences like terrorism, politics, and fraud.

E ALERT!

Historically, the average return on bonds, particularly on treasury bonds, is very low compared to the return on stocks. But this is not always the case. Some analysts predict that bond performance may outpace stock performance over the next ten years. According to an article entitled "The Death of the Risk Premium: Consequences of the 1990s," by Arnott and Ryan, stocks could underperform bonds in the decades ahead by about 0.9 percent a year.

So which security is better? The answer is simple: both and neither. Stocks and bonds can be equally valuable in your portfolio depending on your investment goals and willingness to take risk. If you want to reduce part of your risk, some types of bonds (like U.S. Treasury bonds) can help further that goal. The downside is that you'll usually get a lower return in exchange for the reduction in risk level, although there have been times (such as during the bear market of 2000 to 2003) when bond returns have been superior. And some types of bonds—like junk bonds—can offer stock-like returns because they come with much higher inherent risk.

For most investors, a combination of stocks and bonds is the best situation. By diversifying your investments and putting some money into both stocks *and* bonds, you ensure some safety while leaving opportunity for above-average returns in your stock investments.

What is interest like with bonds?
A fixed interest rate is common, though you can also have interest paid at a floating rate, which changes with the economy. Zero coupon bonds pay no ongoing interest. They are sold at a deep discount and redeemed at full value, causing them to build up, through compounding interest, to their face value (the value stated on the bond to be paid at maturity).

Bond Yields

There are two types of yields that you need to be aware of with a bond: current yield and yield to maturity. It is important to understand both types of yields and how they affect the value of your bonds.

Current Yield

Current yield is the yield you receive annually based on the dollar amount you paid for the bond. A $2,000 bond bought at par value (at $2,000) receiving 6-percent interest would earn a current yield of 6 percent. The current yield will differ if you buy the bond at a price that is higher or lower than par. For example, if you bought a $2,000 bond with a rate of 6 percent at $1,800, you are paying less than par, buying the bond at a discount. Your yield would be higher: 6.67 percent. Multiply the $2,000 by .06 (interest rate in decimals), and you get 120. Now divide that by $1,800, which you paid for the bond to get .067 or 6.7 percent. Add that to the current interest of 6 percent to account for the $200 discount.

Yield to Maturity

Generally considered the more meaningful number to look at, yield to maturity is the total amount you will see as a return on the bond from the time you buy it until it reaches maturity. This includes interest over the life of the bond, plus any gain or loss you may incur based on whether you purchased the bond above or below par, excluding taxes. Taking the term of the bond, the cost at which you purchased it, and the yield into account, your broker will be able to calculate the yield to maturity. Usually this calculation will factor in the coupons or interest payments being reinvested at the same rate.

Yield to maturity will make it easier to compare various bonds. Unlike stocks, which are bought at a specific price per share, various factors will come into play when buying a bond, including term of maturity, rate of interest, price you paid for the bond, and so on. The idea is to find out how well the bond will perform for you.

Bond Credit Risks

As is the case with all investments, there is some degree of risk involved in bonds. There are several types of risks that pertain specifically to bonds. Here are three of the most significant risks and how they affect the bond market. Other less common risks also exist, like Call risk, which means the issuer can buy you out of your investment before maturity. (That can happen when rates drop, and they want to call in high interest bonds so they can issue new ones at the new lower rate.) And since risks like these are less common, especially in a period of rising interest rates, we'll concentrate mainly on the three big risk factors discussed next.

Credit Risk

This is the risk that the company issuing the bond could default, resulting in the loss of your principal investment. This is why bonds are rated (as discussed on page 151). Government bonds don't have this risk and therefore need not be graded; they are simply safe investments. As a potential investor, you need to compare the risk and the yield, or return, you will get from different grades of bonds. If, for example, you will do almost as well with a tax-exempt municipal bond after taxes than you will do with a lower-grade bond, take the safer route. Buying riskier bonds, or lower-grade bonds, is only worthwhile if you will potentially see returns that merit taking that credit risk.

Buy bonds based on your needs and financial situation. Don't fall victim to "what if" risk, which is planning to buy a particular bond with the intention of holding it to maturity, and then altering your purchase plans because brokers (who make their living buying and selling) ask, "But what if you need to sell the bond?" Buying just in case you need to sell—as opposed to buying because you want to hold—is defensive buying, and in the long run you may regret your decision.

Interest-Rate Risk

If you are holding the bond to maturity, interest-rate risk is not significant, since without selling you cannot be particularly affected by changing interest rates. However, if you are selling a bond, you need to concern yourself with the rate of interest that—as mentioned earlier—ties in with the yield of the bond.

The longer the maturity of the bond, the more volatile the price will be with a change in yield. You will better manage interest-rate risk by buying shorter maturities and rolling them over. However, if you are looking for higher returns over a longer period of time, you should go with the longer-term bond and hope you do not have to sell it.

Many financial brokers talk a great deal about the interest fluctuations on bonds. This is because they are in the business of buying and selling them. Many bond owners, however, tuck bonds away for years and enjoy the income generated. Therefore, before worrying greatly about the interest-rate fluctuations making your bond more or less valuable in the secondary market, decide what your plan is. Are you buying bonds to sell them or to hold them to maturity? If you consider yourself financially sound, and are simply looking to purchase a long-term bond for a future goal, with every intention of holding it to maturity (and subsequently enjoying the higher yield), then by all means go with your plan. Even if you are forced to sell a fifteen-year bond twelve years toward maturity, and you take a loss on the price, you will have still enjoyed higher yields than you would have with short-term bonds.

Income Risk

This is a double risk: first that should you sell, you won't get the full value (or par); and second that inflation will surpass the rate of income you are receiving from the bond (known as inflation risk.) If you are reinvesting your interest income, you also will see less income. However, you will be building your investments.

The best way to manage income risk is, once again, to stagger or ladder your bonds so that you can pick up the higher interest rates along the way (as well as the lower ones). Inflation risk can be combated by simply re-evaluating your asset allocation and possibly moving to an investment that is higher than the inflation rate until the rate drops. If you already have an income-producing bond paying a rate of 3.9 percent and inflation has gone up to 4.1 percent, you can reinvest the income in a higher-yield (perhaps slightly riskier) vehicle. An equity fund will more likely beat the inflation rate.

Bond Ratings

Corporate bonds and some municipal bonds are rated by financial analysts at Standard & Poor's (S&P) and Moody's, among others. They are rated to give you an idea of how sound the issuer of the bond actually is as a company, municipality, or corporation. The ratings are, therefore, a report card of sorts on the company issuing the bond. Analysts look at the track record and financial situation of the company, the rate of income, and the degree of risk associated with the bond. All of this information is put together, and the bonds are graded.

A high rating or grade of AAA (or Aaa, depending on which rating system you are looking at) goes to the highest quality bond. This means you are dealing with a sound financial corporation or municipality. Generally, bonds rated AAA, AA, A, or BBB (Aaa, Aa, A, or Bbb in Moody's system) are considered high-quality bonds. BB or B bonds are more questionable because the companies are lacking some of the characteristics of the top-level corporations. Anything below B, such as C- or D-level bonds, are considered low-grade or junk bonds. Obviously they are investments in companies that have a much greater chance of defaulting on the bond. These companies, however, may also be new emerging entities that at some point in time may be the next Disney. If you pick the right rising company, a junk or high-yield bond can be very successful. But the risks are high.

Bond ratings from an issuer can change over time. A company issuing BBB bonds may become a much more stable fixture as a largely successful company, and their bonds may be A-rated next time they are graded. Like report cards, bonds are graded periodically. Depending on the company's stability—among other factors—the grade of a bond can change. It's a good idea to keep tabs on the grades of the bonds you own for the purpose of potential resale, as the grade does affect the bond's marketability.

How Are Bonds Priced?

So you want to sell a bond or buy one on the bond market. First, you need to know the latest in bond prices. For this information you can go online, to a financial newspaper such as the *Wall Street Journal* or *Barron's,* or to the financial section of *USA Today* or your local paper. Bond prices do fluctuate, so the price you see quoted may change several times throughout the next business day.

Since there are far too many bonds to list—1.5 million in just the municipal bond market alone—there is no single complete listing. A single listing would not be practical, as many bondholders hang onto their bonds until maturity. Therefore, the listings you will see are benchmarks from which you can determine a fair price. Interest rates play a role on bonds in a broad sense. Fixed-income securities, as a rule, will therefore be affected similarly.

In the bond listings you will find key information for treasury, municipal, corporate, and mortgage bonds. The numbers you will see listed may vary in format from paper to paper, but will essentially they look like the following:

- **Rate 6½ percent:** This is the yield that the bond is paying.
- **Maturity March, 06:** This is the date of final maturity—in this case, March of 2006.
- **Bid 103:12:** This means a buyer is offering a bid of $1033.75 on a $1,000 bond, or a profit of just over 3 percent to the bondholder who bought the bond at a par, or face value, of $1,000. The numbers before the colon represent the percent of par value of the bond (in

this case, 103% of $1,000 is $1,030). The numbers after the colon are measured in 32nds of $10 (here, 12/32 gives you $3.75 to add to that $1,030). This math works the same way for both the bid and ask.

- **Ask 104.0:** This is the seller's lowest asking price, in this case $1040.00.

You might also see an Ask/Yield entry, which gives you the bond's yield to maturity based on the asking price. This means how much the buyer will earn on the investment based on interest rate, plus how much he or she paid for the bond. A buyer who bought the bond at more than the face value will receive a lower yield-to-maturity value. The opposite is true if the bond was purchased at a discount, which means it was purchased for less than par.

Bond trading is brisk, so the price you see in the paper is likely to change by the time you make your decision to buy or sell. The price will also be affected by which broker can get you the best price on a particular bond. Don't forget that the dealers set their prices to allow for a spread, or some money for themselves on the transaction.

How to Buy Bonds

Bonds are almost always purchased through brokers and brokerage houses. All the major brokerage houses handle bonds and can get you the best bond rates. They sell bonds that are already on the market and inform you about new issues. This is true for corporate and municipal bonds as well certain types of government bonds, such as treasury bonds. The government also sells treasury bonds through the U.S. Treasury Department as well as savings bonds, which brokers do not handle. Savings bonds can also be purchased through some banks.

Importance of Interest Rates

If you own a bond with a fixed interest rate and plan to hold it to maturity, you need not worry about the fluctuations in the interest rate unless you are forced to sell. When you want to buy or sell a bond, it's important that you follow interest rates. Interest rates vary based on a number of factors, including the inflation rate, exchange rates, economic conditions, supply and demand of credit, actions of the Federal Reserve, and on the activity of the bond market itself. As interest rates move up and down, bond prices adjust in the opposite direction; this causes the yield (that is, the return on your investment) to fall in line with the new prevailing interest rate. By affecting bond yields via trading, the bond market thus impacts the current market interest rate.

ALERT!

While the stock market sees consistent gains for long-term players, the volatility can be too much for some investors. During particularly volatile periods, more investors look to the bond market. Also, as more people reinvest money from plans like 401(k)s and pension plans, bonds become attractive places in which to invest. They offer income as well as greater security than equities.

The simplest rule of thumb to remember when dealing in the bond market is that bond prices will react the opposite way to interest rates. Lower interest rates mean higher bond prices, and higher interest rates mean lower bond prices. The phrase "You're only as good as those around you" might explain how this works. A marvelous young actor is less sought out when the cast around him is full of headliners. Inversely, the same talented actor shines when performing with a group of amateurs. The bond market works the same way. Your bond paying 8 percent is sought out when interest rates drop and other bonds are paying 6 percent. However, when interest rates rise, and they are all paying 10 percent, suddenly your bond is not sought out and is therefore harder to sell and less valuable. Therefore, the old concept of supply and demand will be a major factor in your selling a bond.

Since the rate is generally locked in when you purchase it, the bond becomes more or less valuable as the interest rate moves. The bond's current yield (the current percent of interest you are receiving) versus the rising and falling interest rate will determine the bond's volatility. Shorter-term bonds (with less than five years to maturity) come due more quickly and are usually less affected by interest rate movement; therefore, they usually pay lower yields. Longer-term bonds will be subject to greater interest rate fluctuation because there is more time until your bond matures. Therefore, bonds with longer maturities usually offer higher yields than shorter-term bonds because they are subject to a greater degree of risk in the bond market. Long-term bonds are considered to be those that mature in twelve years or more.

Yield Curve

The interplay of short-term and long-term interest rates is depicted by the yield curve, a graph that maps out the connection between bond yields and time to maturity. Understanding the yield curve can help you when you're trying to decide which bond to purchase; the curve allows you to compare prices among bonds with differing features (different coupon rates, different maturities, even different credit ratings). Most of the time, the yield curve looks normal (or "steep"), meaning it curves upward and to the right—short-term bonds have lower interest rates, and the rate climbs steadily as the time to maturity lengthens. Occasionally, though, the yield curve is flat or inverted. A flat yield curve, where rates are similar across the board, typically signals an impending slowdown in the economy. Short-term rates increase as long-term rates fall, equalizing the two. An inverted yield curve, where short-term rates are higher than long-term rates, signals a recession on the horizon as investors prepare for a dip in overall interest rates.

Bond Popularity

While adding bonds to a portfolio has typically been considered a conservative move, there are other reasons why bond investments are gaining momentum. Today, with baby boomers approaching their fifties and seeing higher levels of income, the bond market is looking brighter as a place to avoid paying higher taxes. Municipal bonds and municipal bond funds are generating attention with this very investment-conscious and savvy level of investor. Baby-boomer bracket watchers are investors keeping an eye on their tax bracket and looking more closely at municipal bonds. They provide a way to manage tax risk within the area of bonds or while allocating overall investments. Many equity investors are interested in putting a percentage of their portfolio into bonds, and tax-exempt bonds are inviting.

On the other side of the equation are a larger number of retirement plans than ever before, with IRAs and 401(k)s also being utilized by the higher-income baby boomer set. This points to a segment of these portfolios going to taxable, generally corporate, bond funds. The low-expense costs are making these funds even more attractive, with some seeing 8- and 9-percent yields against 0.25 percent in expenses. Suffice to say, the future of the bond market looks promising, particularly with inflation being low.

Chapter 12

Types of Bonds

B y now you've likely figured out that diversification is as important to your investment
portfolio as the money that you invest in it. You'll
continue to learn more about this as you read
about the bond market. Stocks and mutual funds
provide investors with a wide variety of options
to choose from, and the bond market is no different. As discussed in Chapter 11, bonds offer
yet another means to bring diversity into your
investment life. It's important that you understand the different types of bonds available to
you, and their inherent risks and benefits.

Overview of Bond Categories

There are a variety of types of bonds, ranging from government-issue to the more speculative and even foreign company and government bonds. They have different risk and investment characteristics, can create different tax situations, and may be used in a variety of ways to hedge stock exposure in a portfolio or to create an income stream for an investor who needs it. That's why it's so important to understand the critical role that bonds can play in helping you to create wealth.

FACT

Among the different types of bonds investors can choose from are U.S. government securities, municipal bonds, corporate bonds, mortgage-backed securities, and high-yield bonds. These all have their own benefits, and some may suit your investment plans better than others.

Investors use bonds to receive interest income or to preserve and accumulate capital. It's usually easy to predict principal repayment with bonds, and interest payments come in steadily. For example, investors who seek current income will most likely be interested in bonds that have a fixed interest rate until maturity and that pay interest semiannually.

But investors saving for retirement, or for a child's education or a similar capital accumulation goal, should probably invest in zero coupon bonds. You won't get regular interest payments with these bonds. Instead, you buy these bonds at a price much lower than their face value. You then receive one lump payment, representing the purchase price plus earned interest, compounded semiannually at the original interest rate, upon the bond's maturity.

The types of bonds you select to help you balance your portfolio should be based on your long-term investment goals. The rest of this chapter is aimed at helping you find the right bonds for your needs.

Corporate Bonds

Unlike buying shares of stock, which means you own a piece of a company, buying corporate bonds (or corporates, as they're also known) means you are lending the company some money for a specified amount of time and at a specific rate of interest. While corporate bonds are more risky than government or municipal bonds, long-term corporate bonds have outperformed their government and municipal counterparts over the past fifty years.

Unlike the U.S. government, however, companies can—and do—go bankrupt, which can turn your well-intentioned bond certificates into wall-paper. K-mart, United Airlines, and Enron are all examples of large companies that have declared bankruptcy in recent years. Therefore, the risk of default comes into play with corporate bonds. The rating system, described in Chapter 11, will guide you to the more secure bonds issued by the more stable companies.

You can buy up to $15,000 of U.S. savings bonds each year, from banks or through payroll deductions. They're really cheap—you can invest as little as $25 and get a guaranteed rate of interest if you hold them until they mature. And there's no commission and no state or local tax on the interest.

Corporates are generally issued in multiples of either $1,000 or $5,000. While your money is put to use for anything from new office facilities to new technology and equipment, you are paid interest annually or semiannually. Corporate bonds pay higher yields at maturity than various other bonds—though the income you receive is taxable at both the federal and state level.

If you plan to hold onto the bond until it reaches maturity, and you are receiving a good rate or return for doing so, you should not worry about selling in the secondary market. The only ways in which you will not see your principal returned upon maturity is if the bond is called, has a sinking-fund provision, or the company defaults. The following sections provide more information about those terms.

Bond Calls

A call means the bonds are recalled when the issuer wants to issue new bonds at a lower interest rate. A bond that can be called will have what is known as a call provision, letting you know exactly when the issuer can, if they so choose, call in their bond. A fifteen-year bond might say, for example, that it is callable after eight years. A called bond usually means that if you choose to reinvest in another bond, it will generally be at a lower rate. The problem with a bond being called is that to reinvest, you will usually be looking at lower rates. Since the call will change the mathematics, your yield to maturity won't be the same if the bond is called.

Sinking-Fund Provision

This means essentially that earnings within the company are being used to retire a certain number of bonds annually. The bonds will indicate clearly that they have such a feature. Each year where enough cash is available, a portion of the bonds will be retired, and those are usually chosen by lottery. Whether the bonds you're holding are selected is merely the luck of the draw. Unlike a call provision, you may not see anything above the face value when the issuer retires the bond. On the other hand, since the company uses money to repay debts, these bonds likely won't default, making them a lower-risk investment.

There are a few other reasons why bonds can be called early, and those are written into the bond provisions when you purchase them. As is the case when you buy any investment, you need to read everything carefully when buying bonds. There are numerous possibilities when it comes to bonds and bond provisions. Again, read all bond provisions very carefully before purchasing.

U.S. Treasury Securities

If the thought of watching a stock tumble in value makes you queasy, or if you have the need to invest in really safe cash equivalents, consider U.S. treasury bonds. Uncle Sam's gift to U.S. investors, the treasury market offers a safe haven to battered stock investors looking for short- or long-term relief.

Treasuries, as these bonds are known, are predictable and lower yielding on average than stocks, but they are also far more secure. Generally, federal taxes must be paid on the interest, but the interest is free from state and local taxes. Treasuries are also backed by the full faith and credit of the U.S. government.

What makes treasuries so valuable? They are liquid investments and can be sold for cash. Treasuries are also easy to sell because of the enormous size of the government bond market. The treasury market is the world's largest securities market. Its average trading volume exceeds $250 billion daily. Treasuries are also good hedges against interest rate fluctuations. Investors who buy them lock in a fixed, annual rate of return that holds firm even if rates change during the life of the bond.

There are three basic varieties of treasuries:

- **Treasury bills (T-bills) offer the fastest rate of return.** They are sold in four-, thirteen- or twenty-six-week maturities, and you must have a minimum of $1,000 to buy a T-bill.
- **Treasury notes mature in two, three, five, and ten-year increments and can be purchased in $1,000 increments, with a minimum $1,000 investment.**
- **Treasury bonds, which range between ten- and thirty-year maturities, can be purchased for as little as $1,000.** Financial planners generally recommend these bonds for people whose money can be parked for long periods. However, the U.S. government is no longer issuing thirty-year bonds (at least for now); the only way to purchase such a bond now is on the open market, with whatever amount of time is remaining until maturity.

ESSENTIAL

If you want to avoid paying commissions or fees to a bank or broker in order to buy treasuries, Uncle Sam's TreasuryDirect program may be your best bet. Investors can get more information about the TreasuryDirect program from the Bureau of the Public Debt's Web site, at *www.treasurydirect.gov.*

High-Yield Bonds

Known in the financial world by their official name, "high-yield bonds," but known to many investors as junk bonds, these bonds can provide a higher rate of return or higher yield than most other bonds. Junk bonds are risky investments, as investors saw in the 1980s debacles involving Ivan Boesky and Michael Milken. These two infamous financiers brought an awareness of junk bonds to the mainstream when their use of this risky debt to finance other endeavors came crashing down. The "junk bond kings" issued debt with nothing backing it up. When it came time to pay up, the money just wasn't there, and investors were left holding worthless pieces of paper—hence the term "junk bonds."

High-yield bonds are bonds that didn't make the grade. They are issued by companies that are growing, reorganizing, or are considered a more risky investment in terms of the possibility of defaulting on the bond, for whatever reason. Often these bonds are issued when companies are merging and have debts to pay in such a transaction. They are used as a method of financing such acquisitions.

The risks of high-yield or junk bonds include a risk of default and a risk of the market value of such a bond dropping quickly. Since the companies that issue these bonds are not as secure as those issuing high-grade bonds, their stock prices may drop, bringing the market value of the bond down with it. This will mean that trading such a bond will become very difficult, therefore eliminating your liquidity.

FACT

Before the 1980s, most junk bonds resulted when investment-grade issuers experienced a decline in credit quality, brought on by big changes in business conditions as well as issuers taking on too much financial risk. These issues were known as fallen angels.

Sometimes a company begins by issuing lower-grade high-yield bonds and does well, with their sales numbers going up. Eventually this company reaches a level at which they can issue higher-grade bonds. This means that in the short term, you can see high yields from their original low-grade bonds. It also means that they will call the bonds as soon as they are able to issue bonds at a lower yield.

If you see a company with great potential that has not yet hit its stride, perhaps you will want to take a shot at a high-yield bond from that company. If you are not that daring, you might opt for a high-yield bond mutual fund, which diversifies your investment so that you are not tossing all your eggs into one high-risk basket. In this manner, if one company defaults you are still invested in others in the fund, some of which may prosper.

Municipal Bonds

Munis, as they're called, are very popular for their tax-free advantages. States, cities, towns, municipalities, and government entities issue them to build schools, parks, and numerous other important aspects of our communities. In exchange for your willingness to lend money to help with such worthy ventures, you not only receive interest on your loan, but your bond is usually exempt from federal—and often state—taxes. That last part is what catches people's attention, since most other investments have Uncle Sam camped on your doorstep waiting to take a bite.

ALERT!

The yields on municipal bonds generally won't pay as much as those on their corporate counterparts. However, when you consider the yield after the taxes are paid from the corporate bond, the munis often don't look too bad, particularly in a state with high state taxes. You need to report tax-exempt interest on tax returns, but it is just for record-keeping purposes.

Not unlike corporate bonds, many municipal bonds are also rated, and those with the highest ratings rival only the government bonds in their degree of low risk. Companies such as Standard & Poor's (S&P), Moody's, and other investment services grade the bonds in the same way they grade corporate bonds. They use AAA (S&P) or Aaa (Moody's) as the top grade.

Usually you will look for bonds with a grade of at least BBB or Bbb. As with corporate bonds, the lower the grade the higher the risk. To ensure safety, you can get your investment secured, or in this case insured, so that you cannot lose your principal and interest due.

Municipal bonds cost $5,000 (or a multiple of $5,000). Yields vary, like other bonds, based on the interest rates. Actual prices for traded bonds will be listed in the financial pages. Prices will vary based on the size of the order of bonds traded and the market. Like other bonds, you can sell a muni on the secondary market and, depending on the current rate, receive a higher price than that at which you bought the bond. If you sell a municipal bond, however, and show a capital gain, the taxman will cometh.

If you are interested in munis, you should get to know the options available to you. Municipal bonds come in a few different types, including these:

- **Revenue bonds:** These are bonds usually issued to fund a specific project, generally for the public, such as a bridge, an airport, or a highway. The revenue collected from tolls, charges, or in some manner from the project will be used to pay interest to bond holders.
- **Moral obligation bonds:** This is essentially a revenue bond in which, if revenues fall short and despite a lack of legal obligation, the state wants to honor the moral pledge to uphold their own reputation—and because they want to issue bonds successfully in the future.
- **General obligation bonds:** If the issuer has the power to tax, they can back up the interest payments on the bond by taxation. Known as gos, these bonds are "voter approved," and the principal is backed by the full faith and credit of the issuer.
- **Taxable municipal bonds:** Why would anyone want a taxable muni if nontaxables exist? Simple: They have a higher yield more comparable to corporate bonds, generally without much risk. Such bonds can be issued to help fund an underfunded pension plan for a municipality or to help build a ballpark for the local baseball or football team.
- **Private activity bonds:** If a bond is used for both public and private activities, it is called a private activity bond.
- **Put bonds:** These bonds allow you to redeem the bond at par value on a specific date (or dates) prior to its stated maturity. Put bonds

typically come with lower-than-average yields in exchange for this flexibility, but they can make a good strategic purchase for active bond traders who expect a jump in interest rates. When rates rise sufficiently, they can cash in the put bonds (usually at par value) and reinvest in higher-yielding instruments.

- **Floating and variable-rate municipal bonds:** If it appears that the rate of interest will be on the rise, then these are good investments because they will—as the name implies—vary the interest rates accordingly. Naturally, there's a greater interest risk involved with such bonds.

If you want to find prices to buy municipal bonds that are being traded, you can usually find them in the financial section of a major paper or in a financial publication. Municipal brokers can then give you their own price quotes. The current market price will vary often, so if you want to buy (or sell), you need to stay on top of the current market price.

Mortgage-Backed Securities

A popular bond category since the 1980s, mortgage bonds can be a profitable, if somewhat complicated, investment option. Financial institutions can create a mortgage-backed security by selling part of their residential mortgage portfolios to investors. Investors basically buy a piece of a pool of mortgages. An investor in a mortgage-backed security sees profit from the cash flow generated from the pool of residential mortgages.

Of the several types of mortgage-related securities available today, one of the most common is the pass-through Ginnie Mae, issued by the Government National Mortgage Association (GNMA), an agency of the federal government. GNMA guarantees that investors will receive timely interest and principal payments. Investors receive potentially high interest payments, consisting of both principal and interest. The rate of principal repayment varies with current interest rates.

Zero Coupon Bonds

Zero coupon bonds can be issued by companies, government agencies, or municipalities. Known as zeros, these bonds do not pay interest periodically as most bonds do. Instead, they are purchased at a discount and pay you a higher rate (both interest and principal) when they reach maturity. In other words, it's like lending someone $100 and having them tell you that they'll give you an extra $50 on a specific date when they pay you back, though they will give you nothing in between.

ALERT!

Don't buy zeros (or zero coupon bonds) for liquidity in your portfolio. As for taxes, despite the fact that you are not seeing any interest payments, you need to report the amount increased each year as the bond grows.

The interest rate is locked in when you buy the zero coupon bond at a discount rate. For example, if you wanted to buy a five-year $10,000 zero in a municipal bond, it might cost you $7,500, and in five years you would get the full $10,000. The longer the bond has until it reaches maturity, the deeper the discount will be. Zeros are the best example of what compound interest is all about. For example, a twenty-year zero coupon bond with a face value of $20,000 could be purchased at a discount, for around $7,000. Since the bond is not paying out annual or semiannual dividends, the interest continues to compound, and your initial investment will earn the other $13,000. The interest rate will determine how much you will need to pay to purchase such a bond, but the compounding is what makes the discount so deep.

Bond Mutual Funds

In the overall scheme of things, bond mutual funds are generally less risky than stock mutual funds, but they generally do not yield the same high rates of return as stock mutual funds. Like stock funds, bond funds buy bonds in bulk quantity. They are also categorized into different bond groupings, depending on the types of bonds they buy.

One of the nicest features about a bond fund is liquidity. When you purchase a single bond, your money is tied into the bond until maturity. You can sell the bond, but sometimes bonds can be more difficult to sell because they trade in the bond market. In a bond fund, buying and selling the bonds is the job of the fund manager, which takes many of the complications associated with understanding bonds away from you. Your concern becomes the overall success of the fund.

Bond fund managers, like equity fund managers, do the research and homework to stay abreast of the bond market. This is good because bonds aren't as "sexy" as stocks—the yields are lower and the investments are more conservative—and it's not always as easy to get all the latest information on the bond market.

For someone seeking income from a mutual fund, a bond fund, thanks to interest, can provide a monthly check. Such a dividend can be especially welcome to someone who is retiring, or simply as income support. It is comforting to get a steady income when the stock or bond market is down. If you are not looking for a dividend check, the money can be reinvested into the fund. Since a bond fund is buying as many as hundreds of bonds with all different dates of maturity, there is always a bond paying a dividend and very often one coming due and being reinvested. Like stock funds, the diversification is something you could not accomplish on your own without a great deal of money and a lot of research. On top of that, you would pay more to buy each individual bond, whereas in a fund you are saving money and only paying any applicable operating and load fees.

A key fact to remember, though, is that your principal is *not* secured in a bond fund. In holding bond funds instead of bonds, you're investing in a mutual fund. Should the fund price drop (and it can), you could lose some of your initial investment. With corporate bonds, unless the company goes bankrupt, your capital will be preserved; with a U.S. government bond, you will always see your capital retained. With bond funds, though, it's the price of the fund that dictates the worth of your investment rather the underlying bond holdings. The value of the bonds in the portfolio will fluctuate until they reach maturity, based inversely on the interest rate. This means bonds in the fund may be sold at less than their value. However, the numbers of winners have beaten losers by a healthy amount in recent years. Again, be reminded that bond funds typically do not see returns that are as high as stock funds. As of December 31, 2004, the top short-term bond funds posted three-year returns of about 4 percent; in contrast, low volatility stock funds had three-year returns ranging up to 18 percent.

While looking through bond funds, you will notice the three primary types of bonds represented: municipal, government, and corporate. International bond funds also exist. As is the case with stock funds, there are different levels of risk associated with different types of bond funds. Inversely, the greater the risk (when dealing with junk bonds, for example) the greater the potential returns, and vice versa. When dealing with low-risk government bond funds, the rate of return is relatively low.

Municipal Bond Funds

These are bond funds that invest in either intermediate or long-term municipal bonds. Such money is often allocated to worthwhile projects, such as building new roads, repairing older ones, upgrading sewer systems, or other projects that both produce revenue and add to the community. An incentive of such munis, as they're often called, is that they generally offer you income that is not taxed. The tax-free bond funds, while paying lower yields, are often paying as much or more than many taxable bond funds because you are not paying those ugly federal—and, in many cases, state—taxes. Municipal bond funds can be national, investing in municipalities nationwide; statewide, investing in specific state municipalities; or local, investing in local municipalities. If you are in a state with high taxes, you may find these funds to be appealing because you avoid such taxes. Crossing state lines, however, may require you to pay taxes. In other words, you may be taxed in your home state if you buy a municipal bond from another state.

U.S. Government Bond Funds

You want low risk? Invest in the government. Despite high deficits and being owed money by countries that are no longer on the globe, the U.S. government has never defaulted, and there is no risk in the securities in a government bond fund. These funds hold treasury securities, bonds, and notes, as opposed to savings bonds. There is some volatility because the fund managers do trade on the market, but for the most part this is a very safe route, and many people will use a government bond fund to balance out other funds they hold. Since there are not as many choices in regard to government bonds, and since the risks are significantly lower, many investors do not bother looking for such a fund. Instead, they simply purchase their own government investment vehicles from the government directly, since it is so easy to do.

Corporate Bond Funds

The majority of the holdings in this type of fund are, as the name implies, in corporations. Like the equity funds, there are a variety of types of corporate funds, and they differ depending on the corporations from which they are purchasing bonds and the length of the holdings. Bond funds that buy high-grade (or highly rated) bonds from major corporations are safer on the fundamental risk scale than other corporate bond funds. They also tend to produce slightly better returns than government bond funds.

Long-term investment-grade funds have produced 8.24-percent returns over the past three years and returns of 8.68 percent over the past three years. These returns are similar to the stock funds holding blue-chippers and other stocks of long-established companies. However, some of these funds cheat a little, albeit legally, through their ability to own a small percentage of lower-grade bonds to balance out their portfolio and—if they pick the right ones—enhance the numbers slightly. As is the case with most funds, there is some flexibility beyond the category in which the fund falls.

Beware of bond funds that buy from corporations issuing bonds that are below investment grade. These junk bonds produce a high-yield fund that can be more volatile than many equity funds. The risk of the company backing this bond is higher and, therefore, the yield is also higher to compensate. In short, junk bond funds mirror junk bonds (which are high-risk bonds), only that you have more of them.

Choosing Bond Funds That Work for You

Just as you would consider the track record of a mutual fund before choosing to buy into it, you need to examine a bond fund's history before making your investment decision. In addition to learning the fund's track record, you need to ask some key questions when it comes to picking bond funds:

- Is the fund picking bonds with long or short maturities?
- What quality bonds is it selecting?
- Are you in the market for taxable or nontaxable bonds?
- Who is doing the picking?
- What do interest rates look like today?
- How will the current interest rate environment impact your investment?

Bonds with longer maturities and bonds of a lower grade, or lesser quality, are more risky, which taps into your risk/tolerance equation. Risk tolerance is always a key factor in your investment selection process. Although bonds are generally perceived as a less risky alternative to equity investments, there are risks in the bond market and in bond funds. Since bond funds do not hold onto most of their bonds until maturity, longer-term bonds will have more time to fluctuate and therefore be more risky. If the bond were held until its final maturity, these changing rates would not matter.

The taxable/nontaxable question reflects primarily on municipal bonds. Why in the world would anyone want a taxable bond if they could own one and pay no taxes? Well, a 12-percent yield on a junkier bond, after taxes, still earns you more than a 5-percent yield on a tax-free bond. Also, if you are buying the bond fund in a tax-free vehicle, such as your IRA, why purchase a tax-free fund? You are already not paying taxes on your IRA investment, so it's a useless advantage. Depending on your current investment strategy and the amount of time you have remaining until retirement, consider holding taxable bonds (to preserve principal) or a bond fund (to balance out an equity-laden portfolio) in your tax-free retirement vehicle.

As for management, you must once again evaluate how the fund is run. Bond funds generally have fewer operating costs than equity funds. However, they generally have fewer high payoffs.

FACT

Many people select bond funds to round out an equity fund portfolio, with perhaps two stock funds and two bond funds, or one balanced fund and one bond fund. Often the inclusion of a bond fund is meant as a conservative safeguard in the portfolio.

Just like the equity fund player, however, someone who is primarily investing in bond funds may allocate a certain amount to the safer funds while putting the rest toward the lower-grade or riskier funds. The higher-yield funds do have their share of successes, and with the right fund manager, they, like a good equity fund, can be profitable. Unlike owning one junk bond, a high-yield fund will consist of a carefully balanced portfolio. If one or two of the issuers actually default, you will still be fine due to the great deal of diversification in that area.

Like all other areas of investing, bond funds offer higher rewards for higher risk. While there are many funds to choose from, it's also to your advantage to understand more about bonds in general.

Chapter 13

Creating Your Own Mutual Fund

Recently, the mutual fund industry has been subjected to heavy scrutiny. Investors have turned away from this investment method, which they once considered safe, as they've become increasingly more knowledgeable about how the market works. To gain greater control over the money you're investing while keeping all the benefits of investing in a mutual fund, consider building your own mutual fund. This may sound daunting. Still, if you're actively interested in investing, you probably already have the skills and the right attitude to build a mutual fund of your own.

Mutual Funds in the Past

Make no mistake. Mutual funds have been a real boon to investors ever since they were introduced some fifty years ago. Individual investors loved the concept of pooling their money with like-minded individuals while receiving the same management services as wealthier clientele. During the sustained stock market bull runs of the 1980s and 1990s, many Americans used mutual funds to work toward their financial goals, earning double-digit annual gains in stock mutual funds.

QUESTION?

How do you build your own mutual fund?
You simply take a number of stocks you like, bundle them together, and manage them with the help of a financial advisor. In Wall Street vernacular, this basket is called a personal portfolio.

But under the radar, a different picture began to emerge. In the early 2000s, a recession-wracked economy pulled investment returns down, and mutual fund performance began to suffer. The double-digit returns of the 1980s and 1990s drifted away. Instead of enjoying returns, fund investors found themselves suffering losses—as high as 20 and even 30 percent annually in 2000 and 2001.

What didn't change were the mutual fund fees and tax implications that are part and parcel with mutual funds. Fund fees, which can run as high as 3 percent of an investor's total assets, continued to roll in. For the first time in years, fund investors began to notice how fund companies took their fees in good times and in bad.

As if this wasn't enough rain on their parade, investors received yet another nasty bear market shock: taxes. In good times, taxes hadn't been a big issue for fund managers. The money kept pouring in, so capital gains taxes were easy to pay off and keep out of the eyes of investors. After all, who notices a few tax payments when your mutual fund is earning 25 percent a year? But when those same funds began losing money, taxes became a liability, and some investors grew more anxious about mutual funds. With money tight, investors weren't chomping at the bit to pay taxes on mutual funds that weren't pulling in any profit.

This was especially so for investors who purchased their fund shares later in the year, in November or December, for example. Even if they had only owned their mutual fund shares for a month or two, SEC statutes made these investors just as liable for a fund's tax bill as a shareholder who had owned fund shares since January of the same calendar year. Imagine paying a full year's worth of taxes on a mutual fund that lost money—even though you had only owned the fund for a few weeks. That's exactly what happened to many fund investors during the bear market of the early 2000s.

Personal Portfolio Pluses

Anxious to take more control over their investments, investors had many reasons to turn to personal portfolios: to regain control over their investments, to cut high fund fees, and to reduce tax liabilities. If they could earn some decent returns in the bargain by managing their own portfolios, so much the better.

Mutual funds are big business. According to the Investment Company Institute, mutual fund assets reached $8.125 trillion in February 2005. Investment-wise, mutual funds account for 22 percent of all U.S. retirement fund assets.

Let's face it: We live in a do-it-yourself culture these days. With the ascent of the Internet, you can now easily make your own travel reservations, shop for mortgages online, and even buy your own cars and houses over the Internet. Using the World Wide Web to create your own mutual fund is the next logical step in the investing world. So why not make your own personal portfolio? Here are a few of things you can do with a personal portfolio:

- **Purchase ready-made funds.** Anxious about choosing the right thirty stocks for your fund? Relax—use a personal portfolio service that enables you to buy ready-made baskets of funds. If, for example, you are interested in the biotech sector, portfolio service providers have ready-to-go portfolios geared toward the biotech industry.

- **Save on financial management fees.** Personal portfolios cost about $30 a month. This makes them cheaper than most mutual funds, whose costs can often run as high as 2 or 3 percent of your total fund assets.

- **Help you manage your portfolio online.** Forrester Research conducted a study indicating that stock market assets managed online amounted to more than $1.5 trillion by the end of 2003. Forrester Research also estimates that there are 20 million financial services accounts managed online. This tells you that Americans want to use Internet technology to help manage their own money, as it makes things easier than ever.

- **Help save on taxes.** With personal portfolios you don't have to sell a stock for tax purposes, as does a manager of a traditional mutual fund. Why? Mutual funds are treated differently by the government than self-styled funds. As a result, it's easier to hold onto the stocks in your personal portfolio than a mutual fund.

From a tax point of view, it is easier and more beneficial to hold on to stocks in your personal portfolio. You can very easily rid yourself of stocks that might cause you a tax liability with personal portfolios without fear of Uncle Sam looking over your shoulder. Another tax benefit is that with traditional mutual funds, you have to pay taxes on your share of any capital gains and dividend income distributions. Not so with self-styled funds. There, you incur no capital gains taxes unless you elect to sell some of the stocks within your basket.

Hidden Benefits

You've already seen how personal portfolios offer lower management fees, have better tax structures, and allow you greater flexibility in managing your own mutual fund. But there are also other benefits you might not notice as easily.

For example, there are no minimum investment requirements or expense ratio fees with personal portfolios. So if you only have a few hundred dollars to invest, no problem—you can build your own mutual fund anyway. There is also less risk associated with personal portfolios. With upwards of fifty stocks in a given personal portfolio, as opposed to a mere thirty or so in your average mutual fund, the risk factor is lowered. That decreases the chances that something might go wrong and that one or two poor-performing stocks might drag the rest of your portfolio down with them.

Simplicity is another big benefit. There are no complicated formulas for managing your own personal portfolio, especially if you work with a credentialed personal portfolio provider. Your account is available online, where at the click of a few keystrokes you can check your balance, see how your stocks are performing, or buy and sell a stock instantly. In most cases you can purchase such a self-management service for under $30 a month.

Finally, as the master of your own mutual fund domain, you can invest in whatever companies you like. From a socially responsible point of view, that's a powerful lure. If you disapprove of alcohol or tobacco stocks, you don't have to have them in your portfolio. Try doing that with a traditional mutual fund.

Steps for Building Your Own Mutual Fund

The first step in creating your own mutual fund is deciding whether you have the time and discipline to craft and manage your own mutual fund. It's a big decision because you're going to need a lot of both. If you build your own mutual fund, expect to spend about ten hours a week or so in overseeing your investments. You'll be picking stocks, evaluating companies, tracking stock performance, and deciding whether you want to sell some stocks and replace them with others. However, you can likely cut that time if you decide to work with a personal portfolio specialist like FOLIOfn. This company offers about thirty baskets of stocks you can choose from, in categories like large-cap growth, international, or industry-specific funds like health care or manufacturing.

Every stock basket you buy for your personal portfolio can hold up to 50 different stocks, whether you start with the pre-selected variety or build your own from scratch. Even if you do get help from an online service in picking such stocks, it's highly advisable to perform due diligence and check on the value of each stock in the portfolio. One place to start is Hoovers Online (✍*www.hoovers.com*). At this business information site, you can find thumbnail sketches of companies you want to invest in, including bios and contact information for company executives; recent financial performance, company and industry news; and recent stock performance, among other features.

FACT

FOLIOfn charges about $300 annually for the option of choosing from its personal portfolios. They'll also help you organize and manage your portfolio for no extra fee. Companies like this one will charge you extra if you buy and sell stocks frequently, or if you want more active financial advisory help as part of your package.

Whether you create your own portfolio or select one already made from a personal portfolio provider, you then have the ability to trade in and out of your portfolio as much as you like. Be careful, though. Stock trade execution prices can add up. Sure, $10 a trade may look like a good deal at first glance. But if you buy and sell all day, you can amass hundreds of dollars in fund trading fees. That can wipe out any gains you might make in your portfolio.

It's better to team up with a personal portfolio provider that offers you free, limited trading capabilities. FOLIOfn, for example, allows you to trade in and out of your own portfolio twice a day (during their trading windows, at times they select). If you trade more than that you'll be charged. But if you've learned anything from this book, it should be that you ought not to jump in and out of your investment portfolio every day, anyway. The best portfolios are built from good, solid stocks that have been researched thoroughly and that serve a direct purpose in your portfolio. It's the old buy-and-hold mentality at work. Find good stocks and keep them.

However, there are occasions when a more active strategy can be more beneficial, such as during market declines. Yes, the buy-and-hold strategy seems like simplicity itself (presuming you've chosen the right stocks), but there are certainly times when active trading can boost your overall returns—and sometimes even create them where the holding strategy falls flat.

The High End of the Market:
Separate Accounts

A separate account is a professionally managed portfolio of individual securities. The difference between these and personal portfolios is the decision-maker at the helm: With a separate account, you hand your money over to a manager, and he or she makes all investment decisions based on your unique financial needs; by contrast, with a personal portfolio, you call all the shots, even if you have someone advising you on which shots to take. Just a few years ago, separate accounts were the privilege of the ultra-wealthy. But technology, reduced operating costs, and fierce competition has reduced the price of admission—greatly expanding the potential market. Account minimums commonly at $1 million just a few years ago, have fallen to $100,000 and lower.

ALERT!

Growth rates for separate accounts are outstripping mutual funds, with more of the same forecast. Assets in separate accounts—totaling about $415 billion in 2001—have more than doubled over the past five years. Financial Research Corp. projects separate account assets to more than double again over the next four years—approaching $1 trillion by 2005—and totaling nearly $3 trillion by 2011.

Often compared with mutual funds, separate (or managed) account programs offer customized portfolio management for an asset-based fee. Often compared with mutual funds, separate (or managed) account programs offer customized portfolio management for an asset-based fee. The advantages to having separate accounts instead of mutual funds include these:

- **Customization:** Clients can design a portfolio to contain stocks and bonds to suit their personal, economic, or ethical needs.
- **Tax efficiency:** Money managers can time a client's trades for optimal tax treatment based on the client's specific needs.
- **Stability:** Separate accounts aren't affected by other investors' cash flows, as in a mutual fund, that can sometimes force managers to

take steps that impede the fund's return.

- **"All-in" cost:** Most separate-account sponsors charge a simple fee based on assets under management, rather than discrete fees for each service (such as advice and trading commissions). In addition, the fee tends to decline as assets under management increase.

Separate accounts are popular, which goes along with the increase in fee-based investment advice. While mutual-fund assets currently dwarf total separate-account assets, sophisticated investors are increasingly searching for a more personalized alternative. Many formerly self-directed investors, bewildered by today's turbulent financial markets, want the assistance of an investment professional and are willing to pay for it.

Tread Carefully

As mentioned earlier, you should only consider building your own personal portfolio if you have a good understanding of how the financial market operates. You must have the time and discipline to craft a portfolio plan. Beyond that, you must stick to it like a barnacle to the hull of a boat and see your long-term financial plan through to the end.

Where can you find a company to help you with your personal portfolio? Start with FOLIOfn (☞*www.foliofn.com*), E*TRADE (☞*www.etrade. com*), or Charles Schwab (☞*www.schwab.com*). Each has programs that tout direct stock ownership, and each is relatively affordable. In addition, all have good online portfolio management packages.

If you feel skittish about taking the responsibility of managing your own money, you can always consider hiring a financial advisor to help you along the way. You'll read much more about financial advisors in Chapter 18, but for now you should know that a good financial advisor can help take some of the pressure off and help you steer a course toward financial freedom using your own self-styled portfolio. After all, that's what it's about.

Chapter 14

Socially Responsible Investing

Perhaps you consider yourself a purist. Do you lecture your friends about how important it is to recycle? Do you take home the empty soda can from your lunch to put in your curbside bin? Have you launched your own one-person campaign against child labor in sweatshops by only buying American-made products? You might even refuse to read magazines that contain cigarette endorsements because you're opposed to how glamorously they portray smoking to impressionable young readers. If so, you might also be interested in making a difference through your investment decisions.

Doing Well by Doing Good

Socially responsible investing (commonly referred to as SRI) began during the 1960s, when many people were involved in political and social causes such as protesting the Vietnam War, demanding environmental preservation, fighting for nuclear disarmament, and working toward equality for women and racial minorities. As more and more people grew to care about social responsibility, they began to impact the investment world. For example, when American investors took their money away from companies involved in South Africa during the time of apartheid, companies with holdings there (like Coca-Cola and Firestone) were compelled to sell them off.

The past two decades have brought further environmental, human rights, and unjust labor condition concerns that to social investors are just as important as bottom-line returns. If a company provides good returns for investors but unsafe working conditions for its overseas laborers, socially responsible investors are likely to take their money elsewhere.

If a company makes conscious efforts to improve the ways it performs, both environmentally and socially, rather than simply limiting negative practices in these areas, social investors take notice and move their money to these companies. Mainstream investors want to do good in the world and for their portfolios, and corporate leaders are learning how to coordinate socially responsible practices with long-term profits. More and more, corporations that pair social and environmental responsibility with good stock value are attracting more long-term investors. Indexes and actively managed mutual funds track these kinds of stocks.

FACT

Some of America's most popular mutual funds follow a policy not to invest in tobacco, gambling, or alcohol—without sacrificing double-digit returns. Check out these funds, each of which earned at least 10-percent returns for the year ended December 31, 2004: Aquinas Value Fund, Ariel Fund, Flex-funds Total Return Utilities, New Alternatives Fund, and Pax World Growth.

When you choose to invest socially, your assets won't necessarily grow more slowly—they may even grow faster. SRIs often outdo the rest of the market, at times growing at significantly higher rates than all other professionally managed assets in America. In fact, according to the Social Investment Forum's *2003 Report on Socially Responsible Investing Trends in the United States,* for the period from 1995 to 2003, the total assets dedicated to socially responsible investing grew 40-percent faster—posting a whopping 240-percent growth rate—than the total professionally managed investment universe, which showed 174-percent growth.

Growth isn't the only way SRI has trumped mainstream investing. Since its inception in May 1990, the Domini 400 Social Index has shown cumulative returns of 458.33 percent, compared to the 389.75 percent returns of the S&P 500 over the same time period (according to KLD Research and Analytics).

The Domini 400 Social Index is the result of the efforts of Amy Domini, an author and a money manager for private clients of a Boston firm. Reviewing the investments of her own church in the 1970s, she found the church was investing in companies that made weapons and realized that they, like most of us, did not know all the branches, divisions, and practices of major companies. She set out to enhance public awareness of the practices and policies of large corporations.

In 1990, Amy Domini created the Domini 400 as a way of screening 400 stocks with socially redeeming features. Companies in her listing must have a clean record when it comes to the environment. They must also provide fair treatment to women and minorities and not be involved with alcohol, tobacco, gambling, or the manufacture of weapons.

While this is a very broad description of "socially acceptable," the Domini 400 has performed slightly better than the S&P 500 over three- and five-year periods. The Domini Social Equity Fund, which uses the Domini 400 as a guide, has returned more than 17 percent in recent years. Nonetheless, Domini gets both praise and tough criticism for her efforts. For everyone who believes that she's taking a step in the right direction, making an effort toward enlightening the public as to which companies are practicing what vices (so to speak), there are others who find either fault with some of her criteria or find additional criteria to eliminate companies on her index. There will always be a level of debate.

All in all, social awareness is an important issue, and the Domini Index is making a case for it. Perhaps it will spill over into other areas. Perhaps consumers will simply stop supporting companies that have questionable track records in their hiring policies or in their manufacture of certain products. Just as there has been an anti-fur movement, people could stop buying products such as sneakers from companies with overseas child laborers or stop using a leading Internet provider that allows teenagers to discuss sex in chat rooms and on which pornography is rampant. Social responsibility runs deep if you allow it to. Where one draws the line is a personal decision.

The socially responsible funds have met a growing public demand for companies to get their acts together. The trend toward this type of investing is expected to grow in the future with the baby boomers as well as later generations looking at more than just the bottom line of financial figures and investing with their minds and their consciences.

What Is Socially Responsible Investing?

SRI earns you money and supports your social values. When you're a socially responsible investor, you evaluate a company's values, policies, and products as well as its potential profits. Maybe you don't want to support tobacco companies and have been looking for a large-cap fund that doesn't hold the Altria Group (the new name for Philip Morris and holdings). Or perhaps you're interested in environmental protection or human rights, leading you to invest your hard-earned dollars in companies that excel in these areas.

ESSENTIAL

When you are socially responsible in your investing, you have a double bottom line. You want your money to support your morals and values at the same time it brings you financial profit. This additional bottom line is generally rooted in religious or moral beliefs or in personal principles that you apply to other areas of your life.

There are plenty of stock and mutual fund options to match people's vastly differing belief systems. Depending on the causes nearest and dearest to you, you can choose a company that protects the environment, that does not test products on animals, or that doesn't rely on alcohol or tobacco to reap profits. Some people invest based on their personal beliefs, and others seek out mutual funds tailored specifically for their religious beliefs. Some companies offer benefits to same-sex couples; people who support this issue can put their money, for example, in the Meyers Pride Value Fund, which only invests in companies that don't discriminate against people based on sexual orientation.

Even though the specific demographics of socially responsible investing are not known, many people practice it in some way. There are some populations more likely to invest this way. Many baby boomers, for instance, developed a taste for social awareness after living through the social and political upheavals of the 1960s and 1970s. Women might seek out companies that provide equal advancement and compensation opportunities regardless of gender, and minorities may want to invest in businesses catering to diverse ethnicities.

FACT

Interest in SRI continues to grow, and mutual fund companies are keeping up with the demand. In 2001, there were 181 funds in this category, according to the Social Investment Forum; in the last three years, that number has increased by more than 10 percent, giving the investor more than 200 funds to choose from.

While money is the bottom line in any investment, socially responsible investors emphasize the importance of supporting their personal values in the process. As you educate yourself about SRI, you'll find plenty of options you can choose from that will support your values as well as put money in your pocket, from mutual funds to individual companies to community projects. This will also help you make decisions as a consumer as well as an investor.

Investing Versus Socially Responsible Investing

When you consider how to pair your financial goals with your social objectives, keep in mind that socially responsible investing doesn't differ much from regular investing. All it requires is more research, letting you select companies for your portfolio that match your values. Getting started is relatively easy. Make sure you are clear, and be direct with your money manager about your social concerns. This guidance will help your manager or advisor merge your ethics into your portfolio.

An article in the *Santa Fe New Mexican* from January 2004 concludes, "More than $1 out of every $9 under professional management in the United States is involved in socially responsible investing (SRI). More than 11 percent of all investment assets under professional management in the United States—$2.16 trillion out of $19.2 trillion—is in professionally managed portfolios utilizing one or more of the three socially responsible investment strategies that define socially responsible investing in the United States—screening, shareholder advocacy, and community investing."

Socially responsible investors tend to confront a common set of issues. Your loyalties may lie with companies with a clean environmental record, impeccable human rights practices, a history of supporting labor issues, or a firm policy against animal testing. When screening companies, the following issues commonly help guide investors interested in social responsibility:

- **Abortion:** Investors exclude companies with involvement in abortion tools and procedures.
- **Anti-family values:** Investors exclude companies that don't provide or promote "family friendly" policies for employees.

- **"Sin stocks":** Investors exclude companies that produce, sell, or promote alcohol, tobacco, or gambling.
- **Nuclear:** Investors exclude corporations involved in the sale or production of nuclear power, and/or the utilization of nuclear power in the fuel mix.
- **Military contracts:** Investors exclude those corporations involved in the production and/or supply of conventional or nuclear military products and parts.

Once you've determined what issues are critical to you, you (alone or with your advisor), pick companies that fulfill your financial needs as well as your social concerns. This process requires a good amount of research and learning, so you must be willing to put in some personal time to educate yourself.

ALERT!

Investing is an area in which you will benefit significantly by using your intelligence. Investors often cite a "gut feeling," and that feeling is usually based on something they *know* but either consciously or unconsciously don't want to divulge. Emotions alone should not guide your investments, but a message from your "gut" is always worth listening to.

But how do you find out if a company is tied to tobacco, covertly sells objectionable material, or is involved in business practices you consider unethical? Is it easy to find companies that support the causes you believe in? It's easy enough to get started. Try investigating the Web sites of the companies that interest you, or do a search for "socially responsible investing" on some investment sites. Look for press releases and other information that might hint at issues you want to research further. There are professional screeners who work for socially responsible mutual funds, and they ensure that companies remain corporately responsible. The stock listings on their Web sites should put you on the right track.

Components of a Socially Responsible Portfolio

The things that are important to you when it comes to investing your hard-earned money are probably different from what matters to your friends, your brother, or the guy in the next cubicle. It's important to remember that socially responsible investing is extremely subjective. Issues that matter to you may mean nothing to someone else. Don't base your decisions on other people—instead, make sure you base your investing actions on your personal value system.

Socially responsible investing traditionally has three basic components: screening, community investment, and shareholder activism. Knowing about these aspects will help you make the right decision for you.

Screening

Screening is simply the process of choosing whether to include a company in your portfolio, based on social or environmental criteria. It's most important to do this with mutual funds and venture capital funds. Screening is one of the most dynamic aspects of social investing; it's where you, as an individual investor, wield the most power. It's up to you to decide what goes into your portfolio.

There are two types of screening: avoidance and affirmative. Avoidance screening is the more common method; it would be used, for instance, by someone who hated smoking. Such an individual wouldn't want to invest any hard-earned money in a company that was tied to tobacco. Therefore, this person would screen to eliminate investment candidates in the tobacco industry.

Affirmative screening takes the opposite approach. Imagine this same investor has a young child at home and is looking for companies that promote products and services for youth. She'd probably be pleased to choose a company that produces organic foods for children.

Community Investment

Community investment supports sustainable development initiatives. These might include enterprises such as small local businesses in low-income neighborhoods, primarily inhabited by immigrants and minorities, or the little mom-and-pop operations often found in rural areas. By investing money in a community, socially responsible investors can feel confident that their dollars are going straight to those who need it: people who don't qualify for loans but who want to buy a home, start a business, or otherwise improve their neighborhood by creating jobs and facilities for children.

According to the Social Investment Forum, community investing is the fastest-growing area of social investing in the United States, with a growth rate between 2001 and 2003 of 84 percent. While these investments sometimes provide relatively low monetary returns (somewhere between 0 and 5 percent for direct investment vehicles like CDs), their social impact can be unparalleled. There are also several mutual fund families that devote a portion of particular fund holdings to community development but still provide strong returns for investors (like the Calvert Group, Aquinas Funds, or Domini Social Investments, to name a few).

FACT

Community investing is practiced in large part through four main types of institutions or vehicles: community banks, community credit unions, community loan funds, and microenterprise lenders.

It isn't always easy to learn about community investing, even if you want to invest locally. The best place to begin your search on any community investment topic is at the Web site *www.communityinvest.org*. You'll find plenty of resources and articles, as well as suggestions for bringing community investment to your own neighborhood. Other sources of Internet information include the Coalition of Community Development Financial Institutions (*www.cdfi.org*) and the National Community Capital Association, at *www.communitycapital.org*.

The Best Ways to Build a Socially Responsible Portfolio

Of the various ways to incorporate your personal values into your investment portfolio, most relate to how strict you are about a company's purity.

For example, the take-no-prisoners approach would dictate that you refuse to invest in any company that does not meet your standards, even in relatively minor issues.

There are plenty of resources available to help you build a socially conscious portfolio. For example, Responsible Wealth, a project of United for a Fair Economy, is a group of persons of wealth who are dedicated to social justice. Their Web site is *www.stw.org*. Other helpful sites include *www.goodmoney.com* and *www.socialfunds.com*. Check out Appendix C for more great investment Web sites.

You also need to consider how accountable you hold a company when it comes to the supply chain. Would you buy stock in a company that is supplied by an offending company? Or do you draw the line at companies that are actively committing offenses, as you define them? You might also take a more temperate approach and include companies under certain conditions; you'll consider a company that pollutes and that is actively addressing its waste issues, but not one that isn't taking any preventative measures. Your standards for choosing a company are as individualized as the issues that matter to you.

Quite a few mutual funds offer socially responsible investments, but this kind of investing is proving to be a big selling point for the personal portfolio industry. Why? Mutual funds don't offer their investors true freedom of choice. Instead, investors get a portfolio of companies approved by a fund manager. Personal portfolio investors can call their own shots and determine which stocks fit their specific needs, both financially and spiritually. Aligning one's investments with one's values is thus made significantly easier with personal portfolios—giving investors yet another reason to reconsider their mutual fund portfolios and take a harder look at building their own basket of investments.

Here's how your role works, as a socially responsible investor with a personal portfolio. Say you've opened a personal portfolio. Later you plan to fill it with stocks you've chosen yourself, but for now you have chosen one of the ready-made options. Skimming the list, you notice a big red flag. A strip-mining company that harvests precious minerals from hard-to-reach rural locations grabs your attention. As an ardent environmentalist, you are offended. You call your money management firm to voice your unhappiness, but you politely add that you are delighted with the rest of the portfolio. "No problem," a voice responds in a blink. "We'll take that stock out of your portfolio and replace it with another, along with a confirmation stating we've removed that stock from your holdings." You couldn't do this with a mutual fund, but it's no problem with a personal portfolio.

ALERT!

In the recent market downturn, socially screened mutual funds attracted and kept investor assets better than their unscreened counterparts. During the first nine months of 2001, the investment firm Lipper, Inc., reported a 94-percent drop in the dollars that investors put into all mutual funds, compared to only a 54-percent drop for socially screened funds.

Personal portfolios aside, an effective socially responsible investment strategy is certainly also possible using traditional mutual funds or other investment options. You will not have the flexibility to make decisions on individual stocks or bonds, but you can certainly decide to get out of a fund completely if it doesn't sit well with your value system.

Chapter 15
Retirement Planning

Think you're too young to start thinking about your retirement? Think again. People are living longer, which means you'll likely have quite a few golden years to enjoy. Get the most out of them by planning your future goals now. Numerous investment options will help you attain your goals. You can invest in employer-based plans, like a 401(k), or you can set up your own plan, like an IRA. Don't plan to rely on Social Security as your sole source of income for retirement. Instead, make sure you've got an investment plan to bolster what will likely be meager Social Security checks.

The Beauty of Tax-Deferred Investing

Taxable investments require that you pay taxes on annual interest or dividends and on any profit on investments you sell. For instance, if you have a savings account, you'll be taxed on the interest it earns. Tax-deferred investments, on the other hand, offer you a way to avoid paying current taxes on your current earnings, at least until you reach a certain age or meet other qualifications. This chapter discusses the different types of tax-deferred investments and how you can best take advantage of them.

Any investment that is not part of a special tax-deferred account is most likely taxable, and you'll be required to pay taxes on its earnings every year. Taxable investments can include stocks, bonds, mutual funds, and money market accounts. Even real estate rental properties, businesses you own a piece of, and collectibles; basically, any investment you make where you can enjoy the profits (or suffer the losses) immediately (and not have to wait until some time in the future) can impact your current taxes.

If you have a tax-deferred investment and don't withdraw any money from the account, you don't pay taxes on it. In many cases, contributions you make to tax-deferred accounts are partially, if not completely, tax deductible. Keep in mind that these accounts are meant to be used for large and specific financial goals, like education or retirement. If you withdraw money too soon from these accounts, or use the money for other purposes, you can expect to pay some stiff penalties.

FACT

A tax-free (or tax-exempt) investment is one in which income earned on the investment is not taxed—for instance, a municipal bond. Keep in mind that even tax-free investments aren't necessarily free and clear of taxes. Depending on the investment, you may be exempt only from certain taxes, like federal income tax or state and local taxes.

A big plus of tax-deferred investing is the ability to put pre-tax dollars into retirement accounts. For instance, with a 401(k) plan, your contribution to a tax-deferred retirement plan is deducted from your taxable income.

This lets you invest money for the future that you would have otherwise paid to Uncle Sam. Let's say your income puts you in the 27-percent marginal income tax bracket, and your annual contribution to your tax-deferred retirement plan is $1,000. Your federal income taxes will drop by $270, or 27 percent of your retirement contribution. Your marginal tax rate—the rate you pay on the highest dollar of earnings—determines your savings. To find your marginal tax rate, visit the IRS Web site at ✍*www.irs.gov.*

Advantages of Investing Early and Often

It's simple. The earlier you begin investing, the more money you'll have for retirement. That's because you're giving your money more time to grow. Consider the story of two twenty-five-year-olds, Madison and Cooper. Madison invests $2,000 annually over ten years, stashing the money away in her company's 401(k) plan. Then she stops at age thirty-five, never adding another penny into her plan. Madison can expect an average 10-percent annual growth rate on her investments. Because she started early and gave her money time to grow before taking it out at retirement, she can cash out at age sixty-five with $556,197.

Cooper, on the other hand, gets a late start, but works hard to make up for lost time. Starting at age thirty-four, he socks $2,000 away in his 401(k) plan every year for the next thirty years. Cooper ends up putting away three times as much money as Madison. But his retirement stash—which has earned the same rate of return over the years—is over $225,000 less than hers, at $328,988.

Both Madison and Cooper had the power of compound interest on their side. Madison harnessed it earlier and thus reaped higher gains. Here's the moral of the story: If you can afford to live without those tens or even hundreds of thousands of dollars in retirement, then by all means procrastinate. The easiest way to figure out the compounding effect on the money you're putting away is with an online retirement calculator (try the one at ✍*www. finance.cch.com*).

The 401(k) Plan

For nearly twenty years, one of the most significant retirement investing tools has been the 401(k) plan. The 401(k) is set up by your employer and is designed to help you save (and build) money for retirement. The money you contribute to your 401(k) is pooled and invested in stocks, bonds, mutual funds, or other types of investments. You choose the type of investment from your company's list of options. Usually your contribution is deducted from your paycheck before taxes and goes directly into your 401(k) account.

If such a plan is offered where you work, there is no reason not to jump at the opportunity. Putting the money in a plan earmarks it for your retirement, and you don't have to pay taxes on it as the money grows. In addition, employers generally make a matching contribution, which can be as much as 10, 25, or even 50 percent of the amount you contribute.

ESSENTIAL

A 401(k) plan can be set up by an employer in a number of different manners, with some going into effect immediately and others kicking in after you've worked in the company for a certain length of time. As of 2005, you can contribute up to $14,000 of your salary to your 401(k) plan in a given year.

There is a big difference between investing in a 401(k) and in a mutual fund that you can buy or sell at will, and that difference is the IRS. The IRS will not tax your 401(k) earnings as long as they remain invested in your 401(k). As soon as the money starts coming out, you'll start paying taxes on it. And if you withdraw money before a set date (usually fifty-nine-and-a-half years of age), you may have to pay a penalty (there are a few exceptions, as you'll learn below). With a current mutual fund investment, you'll pay taxes every year on the dividends and capital gains your fund earns, whether you take the money out or let it continue to work for you.

You have every reason to start a retirement plan through a 401(k). If your employer is making a matching contribution of, say, 10 percent of what you put in, you are already seeing a 10-percent growth on your investment, plus whatever gains the total investment accrues over time. It is a simple solution to retirement planning that you do not have to set up yourself. You do, however, need to keep tabs on where your 401(k) money is being invested (as described below). Too many people just make a choice and let it ride.

For people working in nonprofit organizations such as schools or hospitals, a 403(b) plan may be available, which works similarly to a 401(k). Such plans generally have fewer investment options, but they are also tax-deferred and similar in their makeup. Government workers may be offered a 457 plan, which is also similar in principle to a 401(k) or 403(b), with some additional restrictions.

Your 401(k) Investing Strategy

You can be more or less conservative about your 401(k), depending on what is going on in the market. Since you are in a retirement plan for the long haul, you need not worry too much about the days, weeks, or even months when the stock market is down. In fact, drops in the market can be in your favor as you continue to put money into the plan through payroll deductions. This concept, called dollar-cost averaging (described in Chapter 10), enables you to buy more shares of a stock or mutual fund when the rate is lower. In the long term, of course, the market will go up, and all those inexpensive shares will increase in value.

Since a 401(k) plan is a long-term retirement vehicle, it's important that you remember your long-term goals and stick to them. Don't be easily swayed by some hot stock or mutual fund. Focus on the long term and, as you approach retirement, maintain a solid assessment of how much money you will have when you retire and how much income will be coming in. Determine how much you will need, and remember that the 401(k) will most likely not be your only place to turn for retirement income. Besides Social Security benefits, you may have a pension plan, as well as other savings. Many retirees make sure they have other investments, such as stocks or bonds, to provide some income, while others find part-time jobs for income and to be busy—which is investing in yourself.

All in all, the 401(k) plan is an excellent opportunity to build for your retirement and do so at the level you feel most comfortable. As one financial analyst puts it, "No matter what I say or suggest, the bottom line is that the individual has to be able to sleep comfortably at night." It all goes back to risk/tolerance. First, be proactive and don't just forget about the money in your retirement plan; second, determine what level of risk is okay for your 401(k).

Keeping Your 401(k) Through Job Changes

Regardless of when, why, or how often you change jobs, your 401(k) investment can retain its tax-deferred status. If your new employer offers a 401(k), you can have your existing investment directly transferred, or rolled over, to a new account.

In a rollover, the money in your 401(k) is never in your possession, and you can thus avoid paying taxes on it (at least for the time being). It goes from your old employer to your new one; in industry lingo, from direct trustee to direct trustee.

By law, employers have to allow you to do a rollover. If you take possession of the money yourself, the company will issue you a check for your investment less 20 percent, the amount they're required to withhold and send to the IRS (where they treat it like an estimated tax payment) in case you don't roll the money over into another 401(k). You have to roll the money over within sixty days or you'll be hit with taxes and penalties, and you have to deposit the full amount of your rollover—including replacing the 20 percent your company withheld to avoid having that amount considered an early (and taxable) distribution.

Play it safe and do a trustee-to-trustee transfer if at all possible, or you may end up paying a lot in taxes. Otherwise, the clock is ticking. (If you are not starting a new job or are joining a company that does not have a 401(k) plan, roll yours over into an IRA.)

Taking Money out of a 401(k)

When you retire, you'll need to figure out what you want to do with the cash in your 401(k). As soon as you hit age 59½, you're eligible to start taking money (called distributions) out of your 401(k), whether you're formally retired or not. Once you hit age 70½, you have to take money out, at least the minimum required distribution (more on that in a moment); oddly, you still have to take that money out, even if you're still working and contributing to a 401(k) plan.

How you get your money is also up to you: You can take your money out in one lump sum, or you can take the money out over time. If you go the lump-sum route, you'll have to pay a huge chunk of taxes all at once; if you spread the distributions out over time, you'll also be spreading tax payments out. What you decide to do will largely depend on your financial situation when you reach retirement age. If you have plenty of taxable investment accounts, and aren't in need of additional cash infusion, leave as much money in your 401(k) for as long as you can. And, of course, if you don't want to leave your cash sitting in your old company's plan, you can always roll it over into an IRA, though the basic distribution rules will still apply. Let's suppose you don't really need to take distributions, but now you've hit age 70½ and you must begin taking them or face pretty nasty tax consequences. And just what can happen tax-wise? You can get hit with a 50% tax penalty on the amount you were supposed to take out but didn't. To avoid this pitfall, make sure to take the minimum required distributions (MRD) by December 31 every year. To figure out your MRD, you basically divide your account balance (from December 31 of the previous year) by the life expectancy factor from the current IRS table (you can find this table at *www.irs.gov*). Even better, ask your accountant to figure it out for you, because there are some circumstances that can alter your MRD, or which of the IRS tables you'd have to use.

There are also some circumstances under which you may want or need to take the money out of your retirement plan long before you retire. For example, you may change jobs and want (or have) to take your 401(k) with you. In that case, a direct rollover into your new plan or an IRA is your best bet. Sometimes people need to tap into their retirement funds early due to financial hardship; here's what the IRS considers a hardship: buying a primary residence, preventing foreclosure on your home, paying college tuition due in the next 12 months, and paying unreimbursed medical expenses. These withdrawals will cost you, though—the full tax bill on the distribution plus a 10% penalty. You can escape the penalty, but not the taxes, under really extreme circumstances (for example, total disability, court orders to give the money to an ex-spouse, or medical expense debt greater than 7.5% of your income). A better choice when you really need the money? A loan from your plan; many 401(k) plans allow loans, and there are no taxes or penalties at stake. The only caveat: The loan has to be repaid in full before you stop working for that employer.

Individual Retirement Accounts (IRAs)

The most popular retirement plan of the last decade has certainly been the individual retirement account, or IRA. Now available in two varieties (traditional and Roth), IRAs offer you a safe, tax-favored way for your money to grow for your retirement years. And now they're even safer: The U.S. Supreme Court unanimously ruled (in April 2005) that IRAs are fully protected should you need to file for personal bankruptcy.

Traditional IRAs

You are allowed to contribute up to $4,000 per year to a traditional IRA (for 2005; that increases to $5,000 in 2008). If you are married, you and your spouse may each contribute up to $4,000 into your own separate IRA accounts. If you are receiving alimony, you also qualify to contribute to an IRA. All or a portion of your contributions may be tax-deductible, depending on your adjusted gross income and whether you participate in a qualified retirement plan (such as an employee-sponsored retirement plan, SEP IRA, or Keogh). You'll have to look over the tax tables closely to determine the tax advantages a traditional IRA will have for you. For an easy-to-use online IRA advantage calculator, check out this Web site: *www.finance. cch.com.* Go to the financial calculators section, and choose "retirement."

FACT

With a traditional IRA, your contributions are all tax-deductible and your earnings are tax-free. Thus your account will grow more rapidly than if taxes were deducted. If you have many years until retirement, it is worthwhile to watch your money grow without taxation.

Of course, like anything else, IRAs have their rules. A traditional IRA says once you put money in for retirement, it is there until you are 59½ years old. This essentially ensures that you are indeed putting the money away for retirement purposes (even if you keep on working past 59½). If you withdraw money prior to age 59½, you will be penalized unless you qualify for one of a few exceptions. These include first-time home-buying expenses, substantial medical costs, qualifying higher education expenses, or ongoing disabilities. All of these need to be validated.

Once you are past 59½ years of age, you can withdraw the money as you see fit until you are 70½, at which point the government starts putting minimums on how much you need to withdraw annually. When you do withdraw the money, you will pay income taxes on the investment earnings based on your tax bracket. The long period of tax-deferred income, however, still outweighs this taxation. Also, it is very often the case that the income level for someone in his sixties, and perhaps semiretired, is lower than it was in his forties, so he will fall into a lower tax bracket. Since the government changes the rules from time to time, and the methods of taxation in the United States are under a great deal of criticism, some experts feel that if you can defer tax payment now for another twenty years, why not do so. After all, tax laws could certainly change by the second decade of the twenty-first century.

As for actually starting your IRA, you can choose to start one through a bank, brokerage house, or mutual fund, depending on where you want your money to be invested. Traditionally, banks offer fewer options than brokerage houses for where your IRA investment can go, usually sticking with the safer options such as a CD. Brokerage houses offer a wider range of options should you choose to be more savvy with your IRA investment, or you can play it safe with a money market fund. Mutual funds are, by definition, supposed to be riskier than a CD or money market account. Essentially, you need to do some investing homework if you want to get the most out of the account. The long time frame of an IRA makes equities or equity funds more attractive for some investors. Like other investments you can move your investments around within the IRA and suit your level of comfort in regard to risk.

Too many people put money into an IRA and forget that they can still work with that investment. There is often a feeling that once the money is in an IRA, because you cannot take it out until age 59½, you also can't touch it. That is not the case. There's nothing wrong with being proactive with the money you are investing within the IRA. In fact, you should be.

Roth IRAs

The Roth IRA is named for legislation sponsored by U.S. Senator William Roth. With this relatively new IRA, you are still limited to the same $4,000 annual investment ceiling. Your contributions to a Roth IRA are not tax deductible; you pay taxes on every dollar that goes into one of these retirement accounts. When it comes time to take money out of this account, however, you will not be subject to any more taxes—ever!

In fact, there are very few regulations when it comes to withdrawing the money from a Roth IRA. The money must be in the plan until you are at least 59½. However, the money can be withdrawn after five years, penalty-free, if you are disabled, if you use the distribution to pay up to $10,000 of the qualifying first-time home-buying expense, or if the distribution is to another beneficiary following the death of the account owner.

You may choose to leave your money in a Roth IRA for as long as you'd like. Whereas the government eventually requires you to make minimum withdrawals from a traditional IRA (at age 70½), you can leave your money in a Roth IRA with no minimum distribution requirements. This can even allow for a large tax-free benefit to pass directly to your heirs, if you so choose.

Your income determines your eligibility to contribute to a Roth IRA. This income structuring began with the advent of the new Roth IRA in 1998 and is subject to change, so you must ask about your eligibility when you decide to investigate a Roth IRA. As of 2005, the Roth option is phased out as adjusted gross income hits between $95,000 and $110,000 on a single return and between $150,000 and $160,000 on a joint return.

It is possible to roll money over from a traditional to a Roth IRA. The determination of whether to invest in or roll over your money from a traditional IRA to a Roth is based on your own financial situation. For current contributions, if you can't deduct a traditional IRA but still want to put some money away, go for the Roth (if you're eligible). Also, if you think your retirement tax rate will be higher (rates could increase, you could have fewer itemized deductions), or that you may need some of the money before retirement, a Roth IRA could be a better choice. As for the future, many experts agree that taking the tax hit now, if you can afford it, is far better than taking it on the much larger sum later on. Right now, the tax hit is a known quantity: the amount of your rollover times your marginal tax rate. The future tax hit is a question mark, as both the tax rates and income are unknown factors; almost certainly, though, that future tax hit will be bigger.

If you choose to roll over an existing IRA, simply call the company that holds your account and tell them. They'll talk with you about your unique tax situation, and send you all the required paperwork to make the switch. Your accountant will be able to provide you with the most accurate tax information, including the possible need to adjust your withholding taxes or make some estimated tax payments.

Which Is Better?

Assuming you are eligible for both traditional and Roth IRAs, the biggest determining factor is whether it is to your benefit to take a deduction now and pay taxes later, on withdrawal, or to pay taxes on your contribution now and never worry about taxes again.

The two IRAs have given Web sites and financial magazines a whole new area on which to write volumes. The question is, "Which IRA Is Right for You?" Once again, there is no definitive answer without looking at your own personal financial situation. Nonetheless, Web sites have calculators and fancy ten-page sections devoted to figuring out the answer to this question. It shouldn't be all that complicated. And a good accountant should be able to help you figure it all out in less time than it takes to download and evaluate the methods of calculations.

The bottom line is that no matter how much you calculate, you cannot know for sure what the next thirty years have in store in terms of taxes, the rate of inflation, the cost of living, your own health, and the stability of your job. While it is to your advantage to put money away for your retirement years, the decision to choose the traditional or the Roth IRA is not as tough as it is made out to be. Either way, you will have saved money for your retirement years. If you qualify for both plans, the simple equation, as stated earlier, is whether it's to your benefit to take tax deductions now or whether you can afford not to and have benefits later on. Thus, figure out basic, approximate numbers with your accountant, consider other factors in your life, make an overall assessment of your future as you'd like it to be, and pick one. Since your future is not a certainty, go with your best assumption.

Health Savings Accounts (HSAs)

There's been a lot of buzz about a relatively new tax shelter created to cover out-of-pocket medical expenses. Many employers are now offering these plans as cost-saving measures for both the business and (theoretically) the employees. Health Savings Accounts (HSAs) work well for some people; for example, young professionals in their twenties and thirties can use these as a way to save up for future medical expenses. However, these accounts are not right for everyone.

HSAs became available in 2004. To open one of these IRA-like accounts, you must have a special form of qualified health coverage called a "high deductible health plan" (HDHP) and no other standard health insurance. An HDHP is basically emergency health insurance, and it comes with a very high deductible minimum: $1,000 for single coverage and $2,000 for families. Essentially, you pay for all of your medical expenses yourself until you hit that deductible—and that's where the HSA comes in.

Your HSA is really just what it sounds like: a savings account to be used for your health expenses. But unlike basic savings accounts, this one comes with a hefty tax break. The deposits you make are tax deductible (like IRA contributions), the earnings are tax-free, and all withdrawals for qualified medical expenses are tax-free, regardless of when you make them. That's a lot of tax benefit packed into a single account.

The amount you're allowed to save depends on how high the deductible of your HDHP is; the higher that is, the more you're allowed to save—up to a maximum of $2,650 for single people and $5,250 for families, as of 2005. And if you're afraid that you might lose your contributions if you don't use them by year end (like with old-style medical savings accounts), have no fear: The money you put into your HSA and all of the compounded earnings are yours until you die, then it goes straight to your beneficiaries.

Who may be better off forgoing these tax benefits for more traditional insurance plans? Families with young children, people with chronic illnesses, and others who use professional medical care regularly will probably fare best going the standard HMO or preferred provider route.

Stay Focused

There's no rule that says you can't invest in both a 401(k) plan and an IRA. The most important point is to take advantage of all the tax-deferred investment opportunities you can. Start as early as you can, and keep filling them up with money come rain or shine.

"Investment black holes" is a term that appeared in the investment market in the late 1980s to refer to the virtually complete disappearance of investment capital due to sudden heavy losses. Since then, the market has seen the rise and fall of a myriad of these market-shaking phenomena that rapidly cause enormous losses for investors. Included in this genre of market catastrophes are the so-called Asian Flu of 1998, the backlash against high-flying dot-coms, the default of Argentina, and the bankruptcy of Enron.

The future of Social Security looks uncertain at best—the decreasing number of younger workers means fewer workers are supporting each Social Security retiree. Compare the numbers: In 1950, sixteen workers were supporting each retiree, as opposed to three workers per retiree in 2000. The number continues to decrease. If you instead focus on tax-deferred investing, you'll be taking a crucial step toward building a safe, secure, and sustainable financial future.

Chapter 16

Ground Rules: Investing in Real Estate

Real estate generally holds steady against inflation and any lows the stock market might suffer, but it can lose value during deflationary periods or in areas that are afflicted with housing slumps. Because the market has such a particular focus, the average investor faces some hurdles. Not everyone will want to deal with all the rates real estate brings with it—interest rates, occupancy rates, vacancy rates, construction rates—but those who have a mind for it can find real estate investment a profitable experience.

The Basics

The details of real estate investment can easily be overwhelming. There's a whole new language to learn: closing costs, resale value, liquidity, and inspections. But if you're willing to overcome your apprehensions, you'll find that real estate can be a wise investment. If you are considering investing in real estate, it's important that you do your research so that your investment will turn into a profitable venture. It's harder to get out of real estate than a stock or bond purchase, so educate yourself and make sure you understand exactly what you're doing.

A real estate investment is tangible—you buy land or property or property that you can actually see. (You can also invest in a real estate investment trust (REIT), described on page 216.) Think about how stocks and bonds work. You invest your money in a company you do not physically own. By buying shares, you are in essence lending the company your money and hoping for a profit. With real estate, you own the "company," so you need to sell "shares" of it to see a profit—be it by selling the property, or renting it.

Inflation is another issue to take into account when investing in real estate. Believe it or not, a real estate investor can reap profits from inflation alone. Check out this example. An investor has $30,000 worth of equity in a $100,000 property. With a 3-percent inflationary increase in property values, his holdings are now worth $103,000—a $3,000 increase. That $3,000 increase on his $30,000 investment translates into a 10-percent return—due solely to inflation.

What to Look for in a New Property

Real estate is a risky business, and there are no guarantees on every piece of land or property. Be careful and educate yourself before dropping a big chunk of change on any property. First, you need to know the difference between speculators and investors.

Real estate speculators aren't the same as investors. Speculators buy and sell quickly in order to make a fast profit. An investor, on the other hand, looks for a long-term gain, and usually buys only what he or she can afford to keep for an indefinite period of time. You must consider your finances carefully to determine which option is right for you. If real estate investing is new to you, hold off on speculation until you're more familiar with the market. It is wise also to consult specialists before you act.

For the average investor today, there are essentially two viable real estate options: smaller rental properties, or a house that needs some TLC. Of all the forms of real estate investing, the single-family house may offer the most opportunities to novice investors simply because it is the easiest to acquire and the easiest to sell. You'll get your feet wet and find that you will get more for your money.

FACT

Time is money. If you take a day to paint instead of hiring a painter, do you really save that much? You save $30 an hour for an eight-hour day of painting—a total of $240. In essence, you're paying yourself $30 an hour to paint. But if you hire a painter, you can spend the day finding another bargain property—perhaps one with a $20,000 profit margin. If it takes you 100 hours to find and fix this property and then sell it, you have, in essence, paid yourself $200 an hour!

Large profits can be made by purchasing run-down homes and restoring them for eventual resale. This is how most investors approach real estate, and while it can bring in some nice profits for some, it's not for everyone. Here are some factors that you'll need to consider before making the decision to invest in a fixer-upper:

- **Knowledge:** You must know something about architecture and remodeling and get an idea of how much it will cost to get the house back into shape. Consider what you will be able to do yourself and what it will cost you if you have to have it done. You'll need to factor the costs for contractors, materials, and your own time into the purchase price for the property.
- **Patience:** How much patience do you have for the inevitable problems that will crop up as you gut and restore the property? Will you

be able to get a full night's sleep when you're trying to reassemble what's left of the building?

- **Inspection:** Make sure you get a thorough inspection of the property by a qualified inspector before finalizing the purchase of a fixer-upper. You'll need to be aware of all the potential problems you might encounter once you start trying to remodel. And keep in mind that no inspector will be able to spot all the problems. They can only document what they're able to see.

- **Location:** The location of the property is the most important factor to consider. Study the neighborhood, shopping, and transportation facilities, and consider how the property might be used in relation to its location. For example, land that borders a highway is extremely valuable for commercial purposes such as warehouses and gas stations.

With location being such a huge factor, you should look for land that's no more than thirty miles away from a city. If you are willing to leave cities, you'll easily find inexpensive land. If you discover a tract of land appealing to you but not listed for sale, you can find out who the owner is by contacting the county register or the county appraiser's office. Get in touch with the owner—he or she might be willing to sell.

ESSENTIAL

If you decide to rent your investment property, be prepared to get rental insurance and property insurance. Your homeowner's policy most likely won't cover renters, and you need protection against any damage by your tenants. You don't want to be caught unprepared for tenants like the one in Tennessee, who heard a call from a divine source to light a fire in the living room. This also covers you if tenants try to blame injuries on you.

Most real estate professionals will tell you to stay conventional in your real estate investment strategies and not to buy white elephants. Of course, you must look for hidden defects in the property before you buy. If you find any problems after the purchase, you'll need to make the property attractive before offering it for resale. Study local conditions, and be sure your planned purchase is practical. Will there be a demand for this kind of property in five or ten years? Always be on the lookout for things that make a sale easier, like a bargain property, or extraordinary features that make a property more appealing.

Opportunities in real estate exist during good times and bad, but you must make wise decisions and pick carefully to get the best deals. This can be a tricky proposition for any investor, especially when real estate values and demand are at their peak, or, alternately, when high interest rates and a tight money market make getting a loan seem harder than winning the lottery.

Location, Location, Location

This well-worn phrase has gotten to be a little bit of a joke among real estate professionals and people interested in buying and selling property. But it's a joke based in fact—the importance of the location of a property cannot be overstated. Location can absolutely make or break the value of a home, rental property, or commercial parcel.

Take this example. After watching their children grow up and go off to college, a couple decided they did not need such a big house any longer, so they bought a beautiful place in upstate New York. They made improvements and additions, and after eleven years the house had increased in its appraised value. However, the house next door was empty. The bank had foreclosed on it, and the structure sat empty and unkempt. Furthermore, an important local industry was laying off workers. To make a long story short, the couple saw that if they wanted to sell, they would have to drop their asking price. A house with an empty property next door, in an area that people were moving out of, was not desirable enough to sell for its appraised value. Any property is only worth what the buyer is willing to pay for it. In other words, demand is a powerful force in the real estate market, and much of demand is based on location.

One of the best things a potential real estate investor can do is look for an area that is marked for revitalization. A careful examination of the local political scene can help you determine an area's development future. See what significant changes are being made. A major theme park opening up might mean it's advantageous to buy the family restaurant down the road, or transform a property into such a place. Perhaps you find out that a major New York City–based company is buying property in Tenafly, New Jersey, for their corporate headquarters. Is there property for sale in that area? It might be valuable with the influx of 20,000 people every day. Places people are moving to or are coming to for some reason are where you want to look for commercial property. People bring money into an area.

Because it's close to everything New York City has to offer, a modest one-bedroom apartment in midtown Manhattan can sell for more than a nine-room house on a three-acre property just outside Kansas City. There's nothing wrong with the suburbs; it's simply that supply and demand dictate property value. The same holds true for rental property. There are numerous factors involved when it comes to real estate as an investment.

The same holds true to an extent with residential property. However, the needs are different. Families buying homes are concerned about things like shopping, good schools, transportation, and so on. It's important to see the property from the perspective of a potential resident. If you were going to be living at this address, would the area have what you need?

And make sure you do all your homework about a property's location even if you think it's a great deal. A house that seems like a steal today may not seem like such a great deal in a few months when a major highway construction project comes through its front lawn. Find out from the local municipality what building projects are slated nearby—particularly projects like schools, highways, shopping centers, and industrial or commercial centers. All of these things can impact traffic issues and property values. Sometimes a great property offered at a great price means that the seller knows something that you don't about an upcoming event that will impact the resale value of the property.

Buying and Selling Rental Properties

If you are considering making a real estate purchase for rental purposes, you will choose between either commercial or residential property. You need to assess your own financial situation first, as this is not the most liquid investment. It's important to determine how much money you will need up front, how much money you can borrow, and what the terms will be. Investment capital is the first item on your agenda. If you do not have it, you'll need to borrow it. For a new investor, borrowing for the purpose of buying real estate is not usually advised. Unlike stocks or bonds, you cannot start out with a $100 investment.

In addition to the money, there are other complex aspects of buying real estate for the purpose of renting or selling. It's important that you have good management skills and an eye for detail, as there are numerous details involved with any property. You need to be able to maintain the property, which means proper upkeep. You have to factor that into your costs. Unless you are very handy, you will need to know how and where to find the right electricians, plumbers, and contractors. Maintaining a property is a major responsibility; unlike stocks or bonds, you are responsible for keeping this investment in good condition.

ESSENTIAL

Real estate investing can come with a big tax benefit. Tax incentives for real estate investors can often make the difference in your tax rates. Deductions for rental property can often be used to offset wage income. Tax breaks can often enable investors to turn a loss into a profit. Talk to your tax advisor to learn how investing in real estate can affect your tax liability.

If you are purchasing a commercial or residential property with the idea of renting it out or selling it in the future, you need to consider the following:

- **Is this a prime location?** "Location, location, location" still means everything in real estate.

- **Has this property been rented successfully before?**
- **How old is the property?**
- **Has it been thoroughly inspected and given a clean bill of health?** You may need to arrange for this yourself, including electricity, plumbing, foundation, roofing, etc. Everything must comply with local safety ordinances.
- **How much renovation and work needs to be put into this property?** This will follow, in part, from the inspections. Changing the interior to fit your business needs or rental needs (such as if you are making a one-family house into a two-family rental) is an important cost factor.
- **What are the zoning laws in the area?** This is particularly important if you are opening a new type of business in a commercial property.
- **What is the crime rate?** How safe is the neighborhood?
- **What is the accessibility to and from the property (roads)?** You may find the perfect little hideaway for a summer rental, but a business property will need to be accessible.
- **How much will you need to spend to maintain the property?** Do you need gardeners? Will there need to be a janitor on the premises at all times? Upkeep is important when evaluating the potential resale, as well as rental value, of the property.
- **What is the economic state of the area?** Even a business with the best intentions cannot survive if everyone in the area is being down-sized and moving elsewhere.
- **What plans are being made for the future of the area?** Is a new highway coming through that would help your business by providing high visibility? Or is a new highway coming through that would ruin the rental value of your secluded, quiet villa?
- **How much insurance will you need?** What are the rates for that property in conjunction with the purposes of your investment? Running a day-care center, for instance, means high insurance rates as a safeguard for children who might injure themselves on the property. Various businesses have various needs. You also need to be insured if you are renting for residential purposes.
- **What property taxes are applicable?** What can be deducted?

If this list hasn't scared you off, you might be the ideal real estate investor. Not unlike investing in stocks, there is an issue of timing when it comes to investing in real estate—even more so. The stock market, over time, tends to end up ahead. Real estate should as well. However, the economic climate can change, so real estate like any other investment can be risky.

What to Expect from a New Landlord

If you decide to make the leap and purchase a rental property, you will be entering the world of the landlord. Those who have had direct or indirect experiences with landlords as tenants know that a good landlord can make life easy, while a bad landlord can make life miserable. How you act as a landlord will have a great impact on the well being of your investment.

Problems will arise in any rental situation, and the way you handle them is important to maintaining the property without having to pour a lot of money into it. It's far easier to make the effort to maintain a property when it's your own residence. However, you'll have to do as much work—if not more—to protect your investment. If the investment is taking up too much of your time, you are basically losing income. That's time you could be spending earning money somewhere else. If you are spending hours maintaining a property, you are cutting into your income-earning time and losing money in the process. One of the reasons people choose stocks, bonds, and mutual funds is that other than tracking them, you do not need to do too much work to maintain your investment.

ALERT!

Always check a renter's credit history, background, and references. If you don't screen your tenants and select them carefully, you could encounter numerous problems later—a tenant who pays the rent late or not at all, trashes your place or moves in undesirable friends, or worse.

Good communication with your tenants is crucial to your ability to be a good landlord and to protect your valuable investment. Tenants need to understand your expectations, as well as your rules and regulations, in advance of entering into an agreement to lease your property. Any changes in the rules need to be expressed and explained in writing with sufficient notice to tenants. Make sure all communications with tenants are done in writing and that you can prove the communication was delivered to the tenant.

No matter what shape it's in, you cannot expect to buy a rental property, immediately find tenants, and then just walk away and let the monthly rental checks roll in. The upkeep on a rental property is at least what you put into your home or place of business; it's usually more, especially if you invest in a multitenant property that sustains more wear and tear over time.

If you are not prepared to manage your rental property, or if you simply don't have the time, you should hire a professional property manager. Property managers take care of daily repair and upkeep issues, landscaping needs, tenant concerns and complaints, and collecting rent. Fees vary based on the level of work required and size of building involved. You can hire an individual to do this work or contract with a management company. If you think you're going to need a professional manager to handle your rental property, make sure you factor that cost into your decision to buy the property, as well as the rental costs that you pass on to your tenants.

Investing in Real Estate Investment Trusts (REITs)

If you're not quite ready to jump into a real estate investment as an owner or landlord, there is another option that allows you to benefit from the benefits of real estate returns without the drawbacks of ownership. A real estate investment trust (or REIT, pronounced "reet"), offers investors a way to invest in commercial real estate in much the same way they would invest in the stock market. In short, a REIT lets you invest in real estate without having to actually buy property or land. There are over 200 REITs to choose from, and shares of REITs are traded much like shares of stock. In fact, you can find REITs listed on the stock exchanges.

Less popular than stocks, funds, and even bonds, REITs are not new, having been established more than thirty years ago as a safe way to get into the real estate market. They are more liquid, and therefore more attractive, than direct investments in real estate; selling shares of a REIT is as easy as selling a mutual fund or stock. Since you don't actually own the real estate, you don't suffer the hassles that come with property ownership. On the other hand, a REIT gives you none of the rights that come with property ownership, either.

REITs share the characteristics of both stocks and mutual funds. A REIT is a publicly traded company, so owning shares is similar to owning shares of stocks. On the other hand, REITs were created to follow the paradigm of the investment companies, or mutual funds. Most small investors cannot invest directly in income-producing real estate, and a REIT allows them to pool their investment resources. A REIT is, therefore, like a mutual fund. This investment type is called a "pass through" security, passing through the income from the property to the shareholders. The income is not taxed at the corporate level, but at the investor level provided they pass their profits through.

Unlike mutual funds, which purchase stock in companies, REITs focus on all types of real estate investment. These investments usually take one of two forms. An equity REIT buys actual property (with the property's equity representing the investment). A mortgage REIT invests in mortgages that provide financing for the purchase of properties. In the latter, the income comes from the interest on those mortgages. Of course, like everything else, there's always one option that fits in the gray area in between. In this case that's known as a hybrid REIT, which does a little of each.

What does all this mean to you? It means that REITs can be attractive investments. As with any investment, you must do your homework. NAREIT, the National Association of Real Estate Investment Trusts, offers a great deal of information on REITs (on the Web at ✐*www.nareit.com*, or by phone at 1-800-3NAREIT). Many REITs have their own Web sites as well. Brokerage houses also have REIT information. Since REITs are not as common as corporate stocks and mutual funds, however, not all brokers have the expertise to provide you with good guidance. Be sure you choose a broker who is familiar with this type of investment.

When comparing REITs and deciding which is best for you, you need to consider several factors. Here are some important areas to look at when you start comparing different REITS:

- **Dividend yield:** Review how much the REIT offers when paying dividends and how that compares to the price of the stock. Dividend yield is the dividend paid per share divided by the price of the stock.

So if the price goes down, the dividend yield goes up. Dividends in 2004 averaged 4.7 percent for REITs—compared with 1.7 percent for S&P 500 companies (according to ✍*www.realestatejournal.com*, run by the *Wall Street Journal*).

- **Earnings growth:** With REITS, the magic earnings number is called funds from operations, or FFO. The FFO indicates the true performance of the REIT, which can't really be seen with the same kind of net income calculation used by standard corporations. Basically, a REIT's FFO equals its regular accounting net income excluding gains or losses from sales of property or debt restructuring, and adding back depreciation of real estate.

- **Types of investments held:** Identify what properties the REIT invests in. REITs can invest in office buildings, shopping malls, and retail locations; residential property, including apartment complexes, hotels, and resorts; health-care facilities; and various other forms of real estate.

- **Geographic locations:** Check out where the REIT invests. Some REITs invest on a national level, and others specialize in regions of the country. Although the economy of late has been strong, that does not mean that every area of the country is doing as well financially. Therefore, many investors like to find REITs that diversify geographically.

- **Diversification:** There's that word again. Whether you choose a REIT that diversifies across state borders or buy several REITs with the idea of investing in everything from small motels to massive office complexes, you should always favor diversification when investing, and that includes investing in REITs.

- **Management:** Much like buying shares in a mutual fund, you are purchasing an investment that is run by professional management and that buys investments in the real estate market. You should look at the background of the manager. In this case, you'll be looking for someone with a real estate background. REIT managers often have extensive experience that may have begun in a private company that later went public as the person continued on with the company.

Just as you investigate the company issuing shares of stock, you have to investigate the company behind your REIT. You must also look at the real estate market and the economic conditions in the area, or areas, where your REIT is doing business.

ALERT!

Over the thirty-year span ending December 31, 2003, the compound annual total return for equity REITs was 14.2 percent. The S&P 500 return during the same stretch of time was 12.2 percent; for the Dow Jones Industrial Average, the return was 8.7 percent (data from *www.nareit.com*).

REIT share prices are quoted on a daily basis. In this way, you follow your investment much as you would a stock or a mutual fund. Funds from operations, or FFO, is the best measure of REIT performance, and is often referred to simply as earnings (and sometimes appearing in newspaper listings under that heading). The FFO differs from corporate earnings mainly in the area of depreciation: Real estate typically maintains its value, even increases; for accounting purposes, all physical assets (except land) get depreciated, meaning they record a decline in value. That makes sense for corporations that have assets like computers and tractors, which really do lose value over time, but not for a company whose main holding is real estate. The calculation of FFO starts with the standard net income number, adds back depreciation on real estate (and some other non-cash items), and removes the effect of some capital transactions. This way, you can see a clearer picture of what kind of cash the REIT is really generating.

All in all, if you are a beginning investor who believes the time is right to invest in real estate, the best choice is a REIT. This form of investment provides a cost-effective way to invest in income-producing properties that you otherwise would not have the opportunity (or the capital) to become involved in. Regardless of how you get into real estate, whether through a REIT or as a property owner, it can be a lucrative and worthwhile investment strategy.

Chapter 17

Cashing In on Collectibles

Maybe you're one of the millions of Americans who tunes in each week to one of the hottest shows on television: *Antiques Roadshow*. The show travels to different cities all over America and broadcasts real people having their items appraised. You've probably wondered if any of the items in your home is secretly worth a fortune. If you've got a houseful of items your relatives nostalgically stashed, you could be in luck. The market for collectibles is growing by leaps and bounds. If you've got the good sense to preserve your old dolls, baseball cards, and other items, you could cash in big.

Household Treasures

The possibilities for collectible items are seemingly endless. Some items are more commonly collected, like figurines, stamps and coins, and baseball cards, but others are more specialized and rare. The current estimate is that 50 percent of the American population collects something—from books to furniture. There are more than 1,500 clubs devoted to various types of vintage collectible items.

Some people collect for fun, hoping that someday their items will have increased in value. These people usually started collecting items that interested them when they were young, and they continue to add to their collections when they find an item they like. More serious collectors maintain their trove as an active hobby, constantly seeking out new pieces and staying up to date with current values for items. Most collectors fall into one of those two categories.

Usually people collect because of personal history or childhood interests—a passion for sports, a period of history that piques their interest, a type of craft they enjoyed making themselves. Higher-level collectors look mostly for pieces that will increase in value—items that they can sell later when the market will yield a profit. They view collecting as an investment that will bring them a future profit.

Because collectibles have become so popular in recent years, they are now a multimillion-dollar industry. Collectors who want to make a profit must be cautious about what they purchase if they want their investment to appreciate over time.

The Vintage Collectibles Market

Vintage collectibles earn their value because they are no longer made or because the way they are made has changed with the times, like Civil War memorabilia or old sporting equipment. These old items are usually harder to come by, and since they become harder to find, their value will theoretically increase. However, the value only increases if there is a market of buyers looking for these particular items. Almost every type of collectible has a market, and chances are there's someone somewhere in the world who wants to buy your old items—be they old soup cans or antique toilet seats.

Collectibles as an investment have their own set of risks. There are no SEC guidelines monitoring this region of the financial world. Authenticity is therefore a prime concern, and finding a reputable, knowledgeable appraiser through a recommendation is important. A licensed appraiser isn't necessarily reputable or fair. Treat the value of your collectibles the same way you would a serious medical diagnosis, and get a second opinion—even a third and a fourth—from other dealers, clubs, and groups. Appraisers will give you the true value of an item, and dealers will tell you (based on supply and demand) what the going market value is from their perspective. The market value can change from dealer to dealer and depending on the items they work with.

ESSENTIAL

If you do get scammed when purchasing collectibles, notify local law enforcement officials in the seller's jurisdiction and also the auction site where you purchased the item. Other organizations you may want to contact are the National Fraud Information Center, the Federal Trade Commission, or the United States Postal Inspection Service, if you bought the items through the mail.

The Contemporary Collectibles Market

The modern-day collectible market is growing by leaps and bounds. In 2005 it is expected to be more than a $17-billion industry. The market includes cast art, animation art, and other types of collectibles made in association with current trends, films, sports heroes, and so on. These items are designed to be collected. Good investments? Not really. Great for hobbies and for enjoyment? Yes.

Contemporary collectibles, like their vintage counterparts, do not have a large value at the time of production. But like vintage collectibles, their value often increases over time. For instance, a Barbie doll from 1959 has become rare and grown in value over the years: valued at $5,500 in 1997, one of these dolls sold in May of 2004 for $9,500—not bad for a doll that originally cost around $8. After forty-five years, it is rare to find one in good condition (not damaged after years of play or torture at the hands of little brothers), and the value is therefore higher. Also, fewer of these dolls were produced in 1959, when they didn't have our current mass production capacity.

A 2005 special-edition Barbie may someday be valuable, but currently it won't be worth more than the price you paid for it. However, if you took this same doll to another country where Barbies are not popularly marketed or produced, collectors there would likely pay you more money for it. Again, value is a matter of supply and demand. In the case of this particular Barbie, there is no current demand in America because it's easy for anyone to buy the doll in the store.

ALERT!

Can you expect a better return on your collectibles investment than in the stock market? Kiplinger's made this calculation: "In 1929, a beautiful Chippendale highboy sold at auction for $44,000. If that same chest of drawers came on the market today, it would probably sell for well over $3 million. But think about this: even at such a fabulous price, the highboy would have earned just 7 percent a year, a return that was easily exceeded by the 10-percent average return on quality stocks over the last sixty years." Keep that in mind when you're buying and holding Beanie Babies as opposed to shares of Microsoft.

Ideally, you would want the 2005 Barbie to be manufactured in a limited edition. Those are key words when buying contemporary collectibles. Some limited editions even come with a letter or certificate telling you how many were issued and what number you have. If you keep your purchase on a display stand or in a safe place where its condition remains pristine, you might have a collectible in twenty-five years or so. Maybe Barbie will make a major comeback in the year 2025. Your doll could be a hot vintage collectible worth $5,000.

From a collectibles and investment standpoint, the idea is to buy something that may eventually become rare, with an increased value due to increased demand. Baseball card collectors seek out rookie cards of the players whose stocks they believe will go up, knowing that the player can have only one rookie year (and a ton of rookie cards, nowadays). Nonetheless, if in twenty years the player makes the Hall of Fame, the card will be worth something. Would that be a lot of money? Probably not, because there are so many cards available. Unlike vintage collectibles, which people tend to have only because no one bothered to throw them out, these items were bought with the intention of saving them as a collectible. In essence, the future value of contemporary collectibles is controlled by manufacturers, who determine how many of each item to produce.

You run into more problems when more than one company makes the same version of contemporary collectible items. The question then becomes a matter of determining which is the authentic item. Beyond the issue of copies or imitations, you must decide which brand is really more valuable. Are Donruss baseball cards more valuable than Topps?

All of this brings us back to the idea of collecting as a hobby. Yes, you can and may find a contemporary item that is truly limited in quantity, but for the most part contemporary collectibles are for fun. They give people a pleasurable hobby. There are thousands of clubs and organizations, as well as Web sites and publications that are devoted to collectibles. People who collect as a hobby stick to items that have a personal significance or that they enjoy.

Collecting Art

The right piece of art can be extremely valuable. However, these items are not easy to come by. Art appreciates over time and with the fame of the artist. It is not an area new investors generally delve into unless they become the heir to a masterpiece.

Most people buy art because they simply like a painting or sculpture. They may enjoy a particular style or appreciate the work of a specific artist. From an investing standpoint it's very difficult to know, without a background in art, which artist's work will greatly appreciate over the years.

Sometimes the best work by a lesser artist will command more attention than the lesser work of a great artist. You may also be able to buy such a work for less money, thus allowing a greater potential appreciation—unless you are talking about a lesser work by Picasso.

If you have a work of art that you believe is valuable, you should have it appraised twice. See if the appraisals match. Look it up in books. Do some research on the artist and, if possible, the artwork itself. Limited prints and lithographs can also be valuable, and they tend to be more affordable.

Setting Prices

Do your homework if you plan to sell collectibles. There is no "big board" listing the latest prices. There are, however, plenty of guidebooks and magazines featuring information and pricing for many types of collectibles. The pricing of vintage collectibles can be tricky. Items are judged by their scarcity or rarity, their condition, and their authenticity—and not always in that order.

Things get further complicated when you consider that values placed on an item (whether by an appraiser, book, or magazine) can be greatly swayed by two important factors: supply and demand, and sentimentality. The first item is the key. Mark McGwire's seventieth homerun ball garnered millions of dollars because it was one of a kind and in very high demand, which made its price rise to an extraordinary height.

Most often a collector is seeking out a potentially marketable item at an undervalued price. Shrewd investors look in areas of low demand for an item that in another area will be of great demand. For example, a gentleman purchased an antique set of golf clubs from a woman at a garage sale for $50. Then, at a golf memorabilia show, he sold the clubs for $400. How does this happen? At the garage sale, the clubs were not in demand. They were simply being sold, perhaps to clear a space in the garage. At the golf show, however, a knowledgeable group of golf collectors knew the value of the clubs, and several people wanted them. Thus there was a demand, and up went the price. Watching an auction lets you see for yourself how demand raises the price of an item. Does this mean that the woman at the garage sale was ripped off? No. It means that she profited on an item that was of no value to her. She did not have the wherewithal, the means, or perhaps the time to take the clubs to a golf show and deal with golf enthusiasts.

Sometimes people sell off collections at prices below their top market value because they need the money or simply do not want to be bothered storing the items. Value comes in many forms. The flip side is someone who turns down a handsome profit because the item is of great sentimental value and the owner cannot part with it.

Another good example of how people buy low and sell high in collectibles comes from a man in the Midwest who purchased an old Boston Red Sox jacket for $25 in a store selling old clothes. The store's owner knew the jacket was probably worth more, but in his part of the country, there were no higher bidders and no one beating down his door for it. The jacket had been part of a pile of old clothes he had bought for $8. Therefore, he was happy to make a profit. The purchaser, however, decided that the next time he made a business trip to Massachusetts, he'd stop by Boston. Visiting areas around Fenway Park, he easily found that there was a great deal more enthusiasm for the old Sox jacket, which he sold for $300. Sometimes making a profit is a matter of being in the right place.

From an investment standpoint, collectibles are risky and only as liquid as the market allows them to be. A baseball card collection is liquid if you go to a card show and sell it. The current value of the collection as you hold onto it is based on the market price set forth by the dealers and traders. Hobbyists enjoy looking through books to find the value of their collections. Often the values are guided by an organization or graded, such as coins or stamps.

You have to have the right attitude about collecting in order to be successful at it. Not every item you come across will make you rich. In fact, very few have that potential. As you begin collecting, follow some simple guidelines:

- **Get several appraisals.** Get a good idea from various sources of the value of the items you want to buy or sell.

- **Look for authenticity.** This can be difficult with autographs and less commonly marketed items.
- **Keep your collection in a safe place.** Unlike many investments that exist only as computer transactions, collectibles are tangibles that you can touch.
- **Be patient.** The longer you hold onto something, the more valuable it (usually) gets.
- **Look for propitious selling opportunities.** A ballplayer about to go into the Hall of Fame for his particular sport will see his stock rise, so to speak. Collectibles from the *Titanic,* although always valuable, went way up during the wave of excitement (pun intended) that followed the film. Noncollectors entered the bidding and drove the price of such items up.
- **Have fun.** There are plenty of other investment choices out there. This one can be highly inconsistent in your rate of return, so at least enjoy collecting.

Auction Portals: eBay and Others

If you want to find collectibles for purchase, or a place to sell one of your antiques, an Internet auction may be just the place for you. Since their inception in 1995, online auctions have exploded in popularity. They are like online flea markets, allowing people to buy and sell almost any kind of item imaginable from and to a worldwide community of collectors.

Online auctions can mean a risky business, as reported by the U.S. Federal Trade Commission (FTC). This federal agency prevents fraud, deception, and unfair practices in the marketplace. Online auction fraud usually tops the lists of thousands of consumer fraud complaints the FTC receives each year. People usually complain of late or missing shipments, items whose condition differs from that advertised, fraudulent online payment services, and fraudulent dealers who entice buyers with false offers. Often the complaints are about sellers, but some complaints are filed against buyers, too.

Whether you're a buyer or a seller, understanding how Internet auctions work can help you avoid these problems.

Auction Rules

Internet auctions are online bazaars. Some are the scenes of business-to-person activity, and a Web site operator controls the items and oversees the financial transactions. Most of these sites, however, run person-to-person activity, where individual sellers or small businesses auction their items directly to consumers. In these auctions, the seller—not the site—has the merchandise.

The person-to-person sites require sellers to register before they can place items for bid. Sellers agree to pay a fee when an item is sold.

Many sellers set a time limit on bidding and, in some cases, a reserve price—the lowest price they will accept for an item. When the bidding closes at the scheduled time, the highest bidder wins. If no one bids at or above the reserve price, the auction closes without a winner. At the end of a successful auction, the buyer and seller communicate by e-mail to arrange for payment and delivery.

Payment Options

Bidders can pay by any of a number of options: credit or debit card, money order, personal or cashier's check, or cash on delivery. Credit cards may offer buyers the best protection. With most, the buyer can get credit from the credit card company (also known as a "charge back") if the product isn't delivered or isn't what was ordered. Most online merchants and private sellers accept credit cards, either directly or though a service such as PayPal; those that don't require payment by cashier's check or money order before they send an item.

In many cases, an online payment service or an escrow service is used to facilitate payment.

Online Payment Services

Buyers and sellers both tend to favor online payment services. Buyers can use credit cards or electronic bank transfers to pay sellers who are otherwise unable to accept credit card or electronic bank transactions. This also offers the buyers some protection by preventing illegal use of their financial information. The online payment service holds the account information, not the seller. Many sellers prefer online payment services because payment services tend to provide more security than, say, personal checks.

FACT

The top six most popular categories on eBay, in order, are collectibles; clothing, shoes, and accessories; entertainment; sports; home; jewelry; and watches. Scan your home. Do you have any items that may have value? Get them appraised right away!

In online payment services, both the buyer and seller set up accounts that allow them to make or accept payments. Buyers provide payment information, such as bank account or credit card numbers, and sellers give information about where payments should be deposited. To complete a transaction, buyers authorize the online payment service to send the funds to the seller. Sellers can then access the funds, less any service fees.

Guidelines to eBay

Many people get excited about eBay and jump right into using it without learning the rules first. This can be a big mistake. You need to understand the eBay process, regulations and guidelines, and other details before starting.

One of the worst mistakes a collectibles investor can make is to start juggling too many commodities. In other words, if you invest in coins, cars, candleholders, and key chains, you might be spreading yourself thin. The best route is to choose your favorite hobby and invest in that. That way you'll be a more knowledgeable investor who'll know a good coin from a bad one, for example, before you buy.

As much as you know about your favorite hobbies, it may not be enough. If you're going to be investing in Barbie dolls, make sure you go to shows, subscribe to collectible magazines or newsletters (and there are plenty of them), and maybe even join a Barbie club. The Internet is also a treasure trove of information on collectibles and hobbies. In fact, eBay has a great educational page on hobbies and investing.

Indiscriminate collectible dealers are the first to go broke. Don't be afraid to pay a few bucks more for something in better condition. Bring a magnifying glass with you and check carefully for chips and scratches. Make sure that the manufacturer's name is on brand-name products like Barbie dolls or Beanie Babies. The collectibles industry is rife with con artists and unscrupulous predators who'll think nothing of selling you a cheap knockoff.

Luck is a big part of the mix, too. In 1996, the *Wall Street Journal* told of a cash-strapped Irish sheep farmer who discovered that the cigars he had been doling out from his cellar were the oldest and most expensive smokable cigars on the planet. Indeed, one investor reportedly offered $1 million for a box of 500—which the *Wall Street Journal* calculated to be $22 a puff.

E ALERT!

The phrase "Buyer beware" (which should be every eBay shopper's mantra) is especially pertinent in the collectibles market. Do your homework and identify dealers with dependable records, integrity, and good references. Internet trading sites like eBay try hard to provide clean transaction experiences, but there's no guarantee you won't be swindled or duped.

When you become a collectibles trader, you won't be the only one interested in how your investments pan out. Uncle Sam will be watching, too. If you turn a profit on that 1961 Mickey Mantle baseball card, it'll be taxed as capital gains. If you lose money, on the other hand, that's your tough luck. Under IRS rules, you can't deduct the loss. You can, however, deduct related expenses, such as insurance premiums and appraisals. Maintain records of your purchases, sales, and expenses so you can determine your tax bite and survive an audit.

Above all, know that collectibles investing is a far more emotional experience than you might have guessed. If you're passionate about your Elvis Presley commemorative plates, you may not want to sell them no matter how high the price. That's okay. In fact, it's part of the fun of collecting. The first rule of investing in collectibles is to purchase what pleases you. In that event, who cares about future returns?

Chapter 18

Teaming Up: Working with a Financial Advisor

You may wonder why an entire chapter of a book about self-directed investing would be dedicated to working with a financial advisor. The reason is straightforward. Before you've gained some solid knowledge and experience, you can benefit from the wisdom of someone who's been doing this for years. Think of your financial advisor as a mentor, someone to guide you through the rough spots as you begin investing. When it comes time to make your first purchase decisions, you'll be in the driver's seat—but it can be comforting to have a seasoned navigator sitting next to you.

Go It Alone or Get Help?

You may like to do things yourself, but is this a wise choice in the complex world of investing? Often it is, particularly after you've gained some experience managing your money and trading securities. If, for instance, you already know you want to allocate 50 percent of your assets to domestic-growth stocks, 30 percent to international stocks, and 20 percent to treasury bonds—and you're comfortable with your ability to make that determination—there may be little reason to pay someone to make those allocations for you. But if you're not yet comfortable making those decisions on your own, a financial advisor can come in handy.

Before you choose between teaming up with a financial advisor and going it alone, take some personal inventory. Emotions play a major role in any investment plan, and building your own financial security is no small job. Ask yourself if you have qualms about the financial market. Do you shrink at the thought of crunching numbers, or are you pumped up over diving head-long into stock analysis? Do you eagerly tear through the newspaper's business pages to see how certain companies are faring? Just how much time are you willing to put into investing? If the answer to any of these questions is negative, you may be better off ringing up some financial advisors.

ESSENTIAL

Your financial advisor assumes the role of a true consultant, assisting you in developing long-term investment plans and determining asset allocation strategies for your investment portfolio. Your advisor can also help you prepare a budget, plan for college education savings, and even help with taxes and estate-planning issues. If you decide to do without an advisor, the consultant's responsibilities all fall on your shoulders.

In the go-go information age, time is a big factor. Essentially what you're buying from a financial advisor—apart from his or her expertise—is time. In other words, your financial advisor has the time to scour the world for the best investment opportunities and the best fund managers, even to run different options through the computer to figure out the best choice. Maybe you don't have that kind of time. If not, it's a good idea to hire a financial advisor to take the time to help you make the right decisions for you and your family.

Let's assume that you want to work with a financial advisor. In order to appreciate the real value of this unique approach to investing, it is important to understand the role of your financial advisor, which can vary based on the type of advisor you choose and on your comfort level with personal financial decisions. Financial advisors run the gamut from simply helping you find potentially profitable investments to actually making all of your investment decisions. As you gain confidence and experience in the financial arena, you can modify the role of your advisor. But when you're just getting started, having an expert in your corner can not only help you make good choices, it can also keep you from making bad ones.

ALERT!

Unlike the impersonal relationship you have with your stock brokerage firm, discount trader, or mutual fund company, you should expect to develop a direct and lasting relationship with your financial advisor.

It is especially critical for a new investor to establish a good relationship with a financial advisor who has the expertise and experience needed to grow assets. The whole idea behind wealth creation in this, the information Age, is that individuals and smaller investors have the same opportunity as institutional investors. Job one for your financial advisor is to know the market better than you do, even if you are somewhat market savvy.

What Can You Expect from a Financial Advisor?

Taking an active role in your finances not only increases your chances of becoming wealthier, it also makes you a better investor. But that doesn't mean you have to go it alone. The best financial advisor for you is one who complements your existing knowledge and skills, and helps you gain insight and confidence in making financial decisions.

As you learned earlier, there are several types of financial advisors, and each type puts a slightly different spin on their roles. Basically, the type of advisor you choose will dictate the services you'll receive. The most encompassing is the money manager, who actually makes all decisions for you once you've agreed to a general style and purpose; with these professionals, you will have virtually no part in the day-to-day decision making process though you will be kept abreast of the activity in your portfolio. Financial planners help map out long-term strategies, and advise you on all aspects of your personal finances (from college planning to retirement funds to asset allocation to stock selection), but you make the final call about what actions are taken. Investment analysts and advisors focus primarily on trade recommendations, and don't really look at your overall financial picture; again, here you have the final say-so as to which trades are made.

When you work hand-in-hand with a financial professional, regardless of the type, you will receive frequent reports to keep you up to speed regarding both your personal financial status and current market activities. More frequent personal interaction with your advisor will help you build a better relationship with your money and, by extension, your financial life. Your participation level is up to you, but the more involved you get, the sooner you'll be able to captain your own financial ship.

Two key pieces of your decision are control and access—the advantages traditionally associated with institutional investors. When you invest in a no-load fund, for example, your access is basically limited to a toll-free telephone number and you have no control over the underlying investments. When you hire a financial advisor, though, you're engaging an investment consultant with whom you can interact, ask questions of, and learn from.

Your financial advisor should monitor your portfolio's performance, help you change your asset allocation strategies when appropriate, and alert you to major changes in the markets. Additionally, your advisor should help you stay focused on the long term. Many investors get emotionally involved with their money—which is certainly understandable, given the high stakes involved. But a good advisor will stop you from buying high and selling low, or making unsure, emotional decisions based on short-term results.

Shopping for a Financial Advisor

Once you've decided to use a financial advisor, and in what capacity, it's time to start looking for a good fit. Many investors make the mistake of choosing a financial advisor based on performance alone. Equally important, though, are the investment style, the organization the person works for, the levels of service provided, the fees, and the "click" factor (how comfortable you feel with the advisor, and whether his or her philosophies mesh with yours). You may need to do some investigating to make sure that the advisor and the company he or she works for are trustworthy, experienced, and solvent. Look for evidence of an efficiently run, profitable organization with an attention to client servicing. Look into how much insurance coverage the firm has for possible fraudulent acts of its employees. Ask about the investment successes, setbacks, and strategy changes that came about from market turnarounds. And check whether there have been any complaints filed with the SEC by going to their Web site at *www.sec.gov*.

Don't be afraid to ask for references. Any advisor worth hiring will be happy to provide references or testimonials from both clients (only with the client's permission, of course) and industry professionals (like insurance agents and accountants). If the advisor seems insulted, or refuses to provide references, go somewhere else.

When it comes to credentials, acronyms abound. It's important to understand the distinctions among the various designations and certifications—that knowledge will help narrow your search to the type of advisor who will work best in your situation. Read on for information on some of the most common advisor designations.

Certified Financial Planner (CFP)

An advisor with "CFP" tacked on to his or her name has proven competency in virtually every area of financial planning. The education required is extensive—over 100 crucial topics are included, from the ins and outs of stocks to estate planning. After completing their studies, those seeking the CFP designation have to pass a rigorous certification exam, then obtain qualifying work experience. The licensing agency (the Certified Financial Planner Board of Standards, Inc.) then monitors its licensees to make sure they adhere to strict ethical and professional standards. In addition, the CFP board posts information about their professionals, including any whose licenses have been revoked.

CFPs can make excellent financial planners. They can help you develop an overall financial strategy from the ground up, both long-term and short. Then they'll advise you on the best ways to achieve your financial goals.

Chartered Life Underwriter (CLU)

A chartered life underwriter starts out where the name implies—insurance. These professionals have undergone demanding study programs in the insurance field, and more. Licensed by the American College, prospective CLUs have to pass eight courses, meet minimum experience standards, and adhere to a strict code of ethics to get their licenses, as well as keep up with continuing education requirements once they are licensed.

While the main focus here is insurance, CLUs know about a lot more than just life policies. They're typically well versed in overall financial and estate planning, and often work heavily in retirement planning. When it comes to current investment selection, though, these people probably aren't your best choice. So, use a CLU if you have insurance planning questions, maybe even to help you formulate an overall comprehensive long-term financial plan. But as for stock picking (and the like), you may be flying solo.

Chartered Financial Consultant (ChFC)

Also certified by the American College, many chartered financial consultants are also CLUs—but with a lot of extras. The ChFC program covers virtually every area of financial planning from the client's perspective. Students are taught how to assemble a true picture of each client's financial know-how, position, and goals. The coursework goes on to make sure each candidate knows how to turn that basic information into a comprehensive plan, as well as how to set the plan in motion and keep it on track.

Once they've completed the program and passed the requisite exams, potential ChFCs must demonstrate evidence of three years industry experience before they can append the initials to their business cards. When they receive the designation, you can be sure they are well versed in everything from income taxes to stock analysis. What does that mean to you? You'll have the ear and advice of an expert who can take you from square one all the way to the finish line.

Personal Financial Specialist (PFS)

Personal financial specialists are certified public accountants (CPAs) with additional financial planning qualifications. On the plus side, they're starting out with an intimate knowledge of the tax code, and often may also have vast experience with tax planning; this can come in handy when you're looking for ways to add income without increasing your income tax bill. In order for a CPA to become a PFS as well, he or she must either complete additional education as demanded by the American Institute of Certified Public Accountants (AICPA) or already have a CFP or ChFC designation.

To maintain both the CPA and PFS designations, the professional must keep up with continuing education requirements and adhere to strict ethical guidelines. PFSs can be very helpful in determining your current net worth, your future needs for retirement, and appropriate investment strategies. Plus, you get the added benefit of expert tax planning to help minimize the current and future burden.

How Much Will You Pay?

The short answer is: that depends on the advisor you choose. Financial advisory services don't come cheap; but it's important to know ahead of time how much you'll be paying, and that you'll get what you pay for. There are many fee arrangements out there. You must discuss this issue with the advisors you're considering before you make your final choice. Remember: While you don't want to nickel and dime when you're paying for expert knowledge and advice, you also don't want to be taken to the cleaners. Any advisor who won't discuss fees with you before you sign, or won't show you a preprinted fee sheet, is not the right advisor for you.

There are basically three ways fees are determined: commissions, flat fees, and percent of assets (though this is mainly seen with money managers). In addition to base fees, there may also be other charges associated with your account, so make sure to ask about all related expenses. You don't want to pay for services you won't use and don't need. Keep in mind, though, you will be charged standard brokerage fees every time you make a trade using a broker, regardless of the way you're paying for advice.

Advisors who get paid commissions rather than flat fees earn more money with active accounts than passive (or buy-and-hold) ones. And although there are many scrupulously honest commission-paid financial advisors out there, you may also encounter some who place their own financial interests above yours (meaning that they'd make unnecessary, even harmful, trades in your account to bump up their commissions). Because their inexperience can keep them from differentiating between solid trades and frivolous ones, novice investors often feel more comfortable with fee-only advisors.

If you decide to go the money management route, you can expect to pay for the heightened level of service. In terms of price, the total cost for a money management service averages out to between 1 and 3 percent of assets managed on an annual basis with flat fee advisors. This fee often drops with the size of the account and through discounting. For example, if you have an initial investment of $25,000 you might pay a slightly higher rate than the person who's bringing $100,000 to the table. The discounts usually get bigger the more money you toss into the asset pot. Pricing schedules may include trading, money management, custody, and financial consultation.

The bottom line here: The more services you receive, the more you'll pay. If you go with a commissioned advisor (but not a money manager), insist on approving every trade before it's made—and actually take the time to understand the advice before acting on it. The most important thing to take away from this section: Get the fee structure in writing before you sign on.

Where to Find an Advisor

It's not too difficult to find the right financial advisor, but it may take some time. As in romance and matrimony, finding the right advisor for you can be a real trial-and-error process. If you can, get a referral from a trusted family member or friend with financial holdings similar to yours. Then you'll be starting out with somebody with a proven track record of performance productivity and a reputation for playing well with others.

If that doesn't pan out, try going directly to the organizations and associations that have access to good financial planners. You have several resources at your disposal, including the Financial Planning Association, the National Association of Personal Finance Advisors, the American Institute of Certified Public Accountants, the American Society of Financial Service Professionals, and the International Association of Registered Financial Consultants. Talk to as many professionals as you can until you find the right advisor for you.

Chapter 19

You, Your Portfolio, and Uncle Sam: Investing and Taxes

Naturally, you can't expect to get high returns from your investments scot-free. Uncle Sam expects a little compensation too. But as much as you may grumble about paying taxes on your investments, it makes sense. The government is allowing you the opportunity to invest and assure your future financial security and success. You could double your investment in just a few years if you pick the right stocks and funds. While taxes can be a burden, and the system could use some reform, they're just part of a larger and more effective system.

Why Do Taxes Exist?

Oliver Wendell Holmes, a former U.S. Supreme Court justice, called taxes the price Americans pay to ensure a civilized society. Maybe you think people are civilized enough without taxes, but Holmes had the right idea.

QUESTION?

How many people work for the Internal Revenue Service (IRS)?
For the 2002 fiscal year, the IRS had approximately 100,000 employees (full-time equivalent) and a budget of $9.4 billion. Are these numbers similar to what you guessed?

It would be very hard for society to function without taxes. How would citizens fulfill all the promises in the Constitution—a common defense, providing for the general welfare, a perfect union overall—if there wasn't a built-in budget for all this? The country couldn't do it if Americans refused to gather together every April, armed with pay stubs and receipts, and troop en masse to their accountants' offices.

Perhaps you're still not convinced that taxes serve a valuable purpose. Consider this: You can't live in the United States unless you pay taxes. It's kind of like an extension of your rent. You need a place to live and call home, and taxes are one of the things that allow you to do this.

How Taxes Impact Your Portfolio

Wall Street and the U.S. Congress have always been engaged in a tug of war, battling over the amount of money investors make and how much of that money should be taxed and given to Uncle Sam.

Naturally, Wall Street takes a minimalist approach to taxes—the less taken out of investor earnings, the better. Uncle Sam sees things differently, and expects investors to dig deep and fork up a chunk of their profits. This is the way it's been for decades, and it doesn't show signs of changing any time soon.

As an investor, you might disagree vehemently with Uncle Sam, but there's no way around it—you'll have to pay taxes. This being the case, what's the best way for you to hang on to as much of your hard-earned investment as you can? You can actually do a lot to help yourself here.

To keep your cash in your wallet, keep efficient tax records. These can equal big savings for you. For example, keep track of your tax credits and allowable deductions in order to use them, and you'll find that more of your money stays yours.

First, get a sense of the terrain—learn the types and workings of investment taxes, like capital gains and retirement plan taxes. Once you're a tax expert, you'll be ready to work with your accountant to prepare a tax strategy that keeps your wallet full.

You can owe taxes on a number of investments. Primarily, though, most tax-related events apply to American stocks, bonds, mutual funds, and other investments that you've bought and sold, as well as tax-deferred retirement plans like IRAs and 401(k)s. And don't forget your house—possibly your biggest investment of all.

Types of Investment Taxes

There are generally three ways in which investment income can be taxed: through dividends, capital gains, and investment interest. When a company profits, it distributes dividends to its shareholders. You can choose to receive the dividends as a check or have them invested directly in a dividend reinvestment plan, or DRIP. When you sell an investment security like bonds, stocks, or mutual funds at a profit, you generate a capital gain. When the opposite happens and you sell at a loss, it's called a capital loss.

With a capital gain, the holding period for the investment security will determine the tax rate. For holding periods of more than twelve months, rates are 10 percent for people in the 15-percent bracket and 20 percent for people in other brackets. If an asset is held for under twelve months, the capital gain is the same as ordinary income. With a capital loss, long-term and short-term losses can be written off dollar-for-dollar against any capital gain.

As you learned in Chapter 3, interest earned from your investments, mostly fixed-income investments, are considered taxable at your marginal tax rate. Even though many people believe that mortgage interest only is deductible, the law still allows investors to deduct interest on loans used to make investments. You can deduct this interest to the extent of your investment income. When totaling up your investment income for purposes of this limit, you generally aren't able to include capital gains that are treated specially under the law. Uncle Sam won't let you subtract investment interest if you are in a higher bracket and have gains that are being taxed only 10 or 12 percent. You might opt to add your capital gains to your investment income, but this prevents you from getting lower capital gains rates. Contact your tax professional for help in determining which option is best for you.

Creating an Investment Tax Strategy

When it comes to any type of tax planning, the basic premise is this: Keep your taxes to the bare minimum and more money in your pocket. To make that goal a reality takes some planning on your part, perhaps in conjunction with your accountant or financial advisor.

FACT

Though it may seem like there's a tax for everything, some things in life are actually tax-free! For example, some investment-related income, such as life insurance proceeds paid upon the policyholder's death and interest on municipal bonds, is not taxable by the IRS.

The first step is to know where you stand on the gain/loss scale. If your investment losses exceed your gains, you can take small comfort in the fact that you've trimmed your tax bill. If you've scored a lot of gains throughout the year, though, you could get hit with a whopping tax bill—and that's where the main planning strategy comes in.

December is the time to look at your holdings with an eye toward your tax bill. If you've been holding on to some losers, hoping they might turn around, December is the time to sell them and at least reap a tax advantage.

Every loss you incur helps offset the gains you've earned, and lower gains means a lower tax bill.

Something to Save You Big Bucks

If you sell capital assets (such as stocks, mutual fund shares, real estate, and bonds) during the year, you'll have a gain or loss on each transaction. Near the end of the year, say in October or November, review all your sales of capital assets and see if you have a net loss or gain from all your transactions.

If you have a large net loss, consider cashing in some investments that are currently showing large paper gains. The reason? Your current losses offset your gains, which allows you to realize capital gains while avoiding the tax you would otherwise pay.

If you have a large net gain, consider the opposite tactic—sell some assets currently showing a large paper loss. The result is the same. Your losses will offset your gains and reduce your tax bill.

E ALERT!

Is a foreign tax credit on your docket? You may deserve it, for example, if your mutual fund invests in foreign securities. You can treat foreign taxes paid on your behalf as an itemized deduction or claim a credit. This credit will most likely be worth more than an itemized deduction, which merely reduces how much income you're expected to pay taxes on. In comparison, the credit offsets your tax liability dollar for dollar.

That's great tax advice, but don't rush in impulsively. Keep in mind that tax consequences are like a side salad compared to the investments that comprise the meat and potatoes of your lifelong investment portfolio.

Know Your Holding Period

Your capital gains tax rate varies based on how long you've had the investment; that time period is officially known as your holding period. This rule is fairly straightforward. If you've held the investment for more than one year before selling, you've got a long-term capital gain (and, therefore, a lower tax rate). Investments held for one year or less are considered short term. So if you bought Stock XYZ on January 5, 2004, and sold it on January 5, 2005, you've got a short-term capital gain. But if you wait the extra day and sell on January 6, 2005, you've lowered the tax bill by transforming the trade into a long-term capital gains transaction.

How to Benefit from Deductions

Are investment-related expenses tax deductible? You bet. From phone calls to your broker to dividend redistribution plan charges, you can deduct in quite a few areas. In fact, many costs associated with helping you with your investments that produce taxable income (for example, expenses related to tax-free municipal bonds can't be deducted) are tax deductible. Here are some expenses you may not have realized are deductible:

- Trading account maintenance fees.
- Books, magazines, newsletters—basically anything you read to gain financial knowledge and apply to your trading.
- Travel expenses when you meet with your financial advisor.
- Any fees you pay to maintain your investments, like for professional recordkeeping, IRA account setup, and custodial fees.

Tips for Reducing Your Investment Tax Liability

Face it—no matter how much you'd like to try, you won't be able to get around paying taxes on your successful investments. If you're smart with your investing strategies, you can significantly minimize the taxes you'll have to pay, however. It's important as a savvy investor that you be aware of the upsides and downsides of your investment plans as they relate to potential tax liability. The following sections provide some tips for how to go about investing wisely while keeping an eye on your taxes.

Stocks

When it comes to stocks and taxes, it's all about recordkeeping. You must keep purchase documents for every security you buy, especially if you've bought shares in the same company at different times. This information is crucial when you sell the securities—and it gives you some additional control when it comes to tax planning. At sale time, you'll subtract the cost basis of your stock from your sale proceeds to determine the gain or loss. Your cost basis equals the amount you paid for the stock, plus commissions. A higher basis means lower gains, and that means a lower tax bill. Another key factor is the holding period, or length of time you owned the stock. That determines your tax rate, and the long-term holding rate is lower than the short-term tax bite. A longer holding period also means a lower tax bill. But you have to have the paperwork to prove it all.

Let's take a look at some numbers. Let's say you picked up 100 shares of XYZ, Inc., in January 2002 for $1,000 including commissions. Your basis in that stock is $10 per share. Now let's suppose XYZ was doing so well that you bought another 100 shares in January 2003, this time for $2,000 including commissions; for those shares, the basis comes to $20 each. Finally, in January 2004 you added another 100 shares to your holdings, this time for a total (including commissions) of $3,000, for a per-share basis of $30.

Now it's October 2004, and the stock has hit $50 per share, so you decide to sell off some of your holdings and take a profit. If you simply tell your broker to sell 100 shares, he'll follow the IRS guideline called first-in, first-out (or FIFO). That means he sells the shares you bought in 2002. However, you can specifically tell him to sell particular shares, when that will be more advantageous to you in terms of taxes. (You can give the same instruction to an online trading firm.) Regardless of which shares you sell, your proceeds will be $5,000 (for easy math, let's pretend the commission is zero). But your total gains, and the tax rate on them, depends on which stocks you've sold. With the 2002 shares, you'll have a $4,000 long-term gain; the 2003 shares bring a $3,000 long-term gain; and the 2004 shares net you a $2,000 short-term gain.

Which shares you choose to sell will depend on your overall tax picture at the time. If you have short-term losses to offset, you may want to shed the most recently purchased shares. If you have no other capital transactions, you may choose the 2003 shares for the smallest addition to your tax bill.

In any case, the bottom line is that as long as you have your records, the impact on your taxes is up to you.

Mutual Funds

Mutual funds are treated a bit differently than stocks in that they are taxed in three ways: sale of shares, capital-gains distributions, and dividend distributions. Just like a stock transaction, you must pay capital gains taxes on any profit that you make when you sell shares of a mutual fund. Also like a stock, you can declare a loss on the investment if the shares decreased in value. The amount of gain or loss is determined by the difference between the sale price and the basis of the fund shares.

If you invest in any mutual funds (except municipal bonds), you'll pay taxes on dividends and capital gains. Dividend distributions are primarily from the interest and dividends earned from the investments that comprise the fund portfolio. These must be reported as income on your federal tax form 1040. Capital-gains distributions represent any gains from the sale of shares held more than a year that the fund itself made during the year, and are taxed, usually at rates lower than marginal tax rates, as capital gains.

Municipal Bonds

Just as U.S. government securities don't owe state and local income taxes, interest on IOUs issued by states and municipalities escape the grasp of federal revenuers. These are referred to as municipal bonds. They are tax-exempt and have lower interest rates than fully taxable bonds. Investors make up the difference—and sometimes more—via tax savings.

It would be nice if municipal bond investing were as easy as that—but it's not. Although interest from municipal bonds is exempt from the federal income tax, the IRS doesn't ignore the gain or loss that results when you sell the bonds. If you sell a bond for more than your basis, the profit is a capital gain; if you sell it for less, it's a deductible capital loss.

Life Insurance

Once a virtual afterthought at the Wall Street party during the late 1990s, life insurance is in big demand these days, thanks to recent changes by

Congress that merge some elements of stocks and bonds into life insurance options and boost its appeal. If you choose a policy that pairs your investments with some type of life insurance policy (for instance, whole life, universal life, or single-premium life), it will gain you tax-favored status.

Part, and sometimes a very substantial part, of the premiums go not to pay for insurance but into investments that build cash value. These earnings are protected from the IRS.

You don't have to die to get these privileges, either. You are allowed to borrow against your policy's cash value. They are very special loans because you don't have to pay them back, ever. Any outstanding loan at the time of death is simply deducted from the proceeds paid to beneficiaries. Although borrowers have to pay interest on the loan, in the sweetest deals the cash value in the policy earns just as much as the interest charged.

Annuities

A stronger investment-insurance hybrid, annuities also sport big tax advantages. With annuities, you are guaranteed that your heirs will receive at least as much as you have invested in the annuity, even if your investments have lost money. But that's just window dressing. The real attraction of an annuity is that earnings accumulate tax-free until you begin to withdraw the funds.

An annuity contract prevents the taxman from taking your earnings, which differs from bank CDs and mutual funds. No tax is due until you pull funds out of the contract, presumably in retirement, either in a lump sum or by annuitizing the contract and having the company make payments to you for life. Funds in an annuity have the same tax-deferred growth advantage as the money invested in an individual retirement account. But you aren't able to deduct amounts that are in an annuity, unlike an IRA.

ALERT!

If you cash in the annuity before retirement, watch out. For starters, most contracts impose surrender charges during the first several years. Any earnings pulled out of the annuity are taxable, and if you're under age 59½, you'll be hit with a 10-percent penalty tax.

Even aside from potential tax penalties, annuities don't come cheap. There are myriad fees associated with these instruments: surrender charges (usually very high fees—think 8 or 9 percent—for taking your money out before your contract allows); mortality and expense fees (charged based on customer risk characteristics); and administrative and management fees. Other than the surrender charges that an action by you will instigate, the rest are annual fees—and they typically run 0.50 to 0.75 percent higher than similar mutual fund fees.

Keep More of Your Own Money

It seems like Uncle Sam wants to take more of your money away each year. As the government grows larger all the time, its funding falls more heavily on American taxpayers. The best way to keep more of your money is to gain a better understanding of the tax code and how it works. If you can get a grip on that, you're way ahead of the game.

FACT

While trading fees and commissions paid are not directly tax deductible, they can be subtracted from the amount you got when you sold your securities, reducing the capital gain (or increasing the loss).

As discussed in Chapter 18, a financial advisor can help guide you through all the rough spots of being an individual investor. These professionals have a good handle on tax law, as well as investing procedures. Do as much research and get as much guidance as you can before diving into anything. You'll be glad you did when you're not losing sleep over a shaky investment plan and unclear goals.

Chapter 20

Online Investing: Resources, Road Maps, and Red Flags

Believe it or not, Wall Street's fastest form of broker-to-investor communication in the eighteenth century was through carrier pigeons. Things have come a long way since then. It's amazing to think that just twenty years ago, no one imagined how integral the Internet and computers would become to almost every aspect of life, including investing. Think of the speed and ease of modern-day online investing. In about five minutes, you can log on to your online account at noon and put in a limit order for a certain stock you've got your eye on.

Your Portfolio and the Internet

You may be wondering why investors love the Internet. There are quite a few benefits, including lower service and transaction fees. There was a huge migration of investors to the online brokerage firms, where they found they could trade their stocks and mutual funds free of transaction fees. This can slash an investor's trading costs by 50 percent—definitely a change from the old-fashioned brokerage.

Be forewarned. You can get addicted to online investing. People who trade stocks online use the Internet for an average of 11.6 hours each week, as opposed to the rest of the population, which spends 8.34 hours a week online.

The Internet has revolutionized investing. Superior services are now available to more customers than ever before. Any Americans can now access financial planning tools that previously weren't accessible to any investors but the very rich. Even Americans with a net worth of $1 million—a population that continues to increase—can access services at a level that used to be reserved for those with $100 million or more.

Consumers are able to access more services than ever before, and the most important of these is the wealth of educational information. Investors are now able to learn about stocks, bonds, and mutual funds and how to properly incorporate them into an investment portfolio, all on their own. Almost all investment Web sites offer investment tutorials or other research resources to educate investors on everything they ever wanted to know about investing—but didn't know they were supposed to ask.

These Web sites also do a great job promoting basic investment guidelines, like the importance of investing regularly, investing for the long term, and creating investment goals. Thanks to the Internet, investors know more about things like mutual funds—something investors just twenty years ago basically ignored. Self-empowerment and the evolution of technology and the Internet mean that investors are more highly educated than ever and are subsequently playing a greater role in their long-term financial choices.

Advantages of Investing Online

There are many advantages to investing online, and the more you invest online, the more Internet investor resources you'll find. Here are just a few of the benefits of managing your fund portfolio through an online broker:

- **Control:** You don't have to rely on your broker's schedule anymore. If you're confident in your decision-making process, control over your portfolio should be an advantage. It's your portfolio, and you should ultimately be responsible for making it grow. You do the research and initiate trades. And with online services, you won't have to call your broker, wait for a call back, or deal with your broker droning on about the mutual fund his company is pushing.

- **Access to information:** The Internet provides you with previously unavailable information on financial products and services. Investors interested in trading online can receive breaking industry news, analyst's reports, and real-time stock quotes and account updates, all from one Web site. You can take stock of your investments, check up on your trading activity, and even make a trade twenty-four hours a day.

- **Convenience:** The Internet gives you the ability to access your financial information from anywhere at any time. By employing the Internet, consumers are no longer restricted to making financial transactions at a physical location or during a firm's hours. And if you travel frequently, the Internet is the most convenient and reliable way to stay up to date.

- **Efficiency:** The Web gives you a platform for managing all of your finances. With a click of a mouse, consumers have access to past account statements and transaction histories without stockpiling paper. And the Internet now gives consumers the ability to review information from multiple financial providers on one site.

- **Low cost:** Because of heated competition among online brokers, you'll enjoy commission rates that have gone through the floor.

Purchasing fifty shares of stock from a traditional broker may cost you $80. You could do it online for $10 to $15. By taking the online route, you could buy another three shares. And those savings can really add up.

What to Look for in an Investment Web Site

To really reap the benefits that online investing provides, be sure to look for sites that have the tools you need to successfully manage your investments. Specific features to look for include these:

- An accessible Web site with easy navigation
- A well-organized trading screen with built-in safety guards to prevent data entry errors
- Access to real time quotes—current stock prices displayed on the screen
- A quick confirmation system
- Current portfolio updates and account balances
- Easy access to customer service, preferably twenty-four hours a day, seven days a week
- A low minimum dollar amount to open an account
- The ability to conduct buy or sell stops, which instructs the system to buy or sell a specific security automatically when it hits a predetermined price
- A full range of investment vehicles including stocks, bonds, and mutual funds
- Automatic sweep of uninvested cash into a money market fund

Best Practices of Internet Investing

Even though the Internet has made the practice of investing your money faster, more convenient, and less costly, you still need to take the time to learn some of the best ways to maneuver through the Web and make your investment decisions.

FACT

Estimates show that more than 80 percent of all online investors lose money at the outset. While we know that a great number of online investors have realized great profit and achieved financial success, in order to be a winner you need to demonstrate prudent judgment to join that 20 percent who really are successful.

To make your online investment experience more efficient, easy, and profitable, keep a few things in mind. Firstly, research is the key to trading success. Never invest in anything without doing plenty of research first. Most online brokerages offer research and financial news in addition to stock and mutual fund quotes. Beware of any information gleaned from the many active investment message boards. These boards are full of unfounded and often ill-conceived rumors. Don't count on any hot tips you find on message boards, as you can't verify the authenticity of any of the postings.

ALERT!

Be careful when you're making orders online. It can only benefit you to double-check your orders. Is that the right ticker symbol? Do you have the right number of shares? If you're rushed or distracted, you could make a serious mistake.

Know the details of market and limit orders. The prices of market orders depend on the time of day the order is placed. If the stock price is volatile that day, you might pay more than you planned to. With limit orders, you set the buy or sell price, but your order might not happen as a result. Familiarize yourself with your broker's trading guide before getting started to be sure you pick the order type that's right for you.

Finally, trade wisely. There are times when the buy-and-hold strategy works well, and times when you may need to trade a little more actively to grow and protect your nest egg. Keep abreast of general market conditions, especially those directly affecting your holdings, and revisit your strategy accordingly. No matter how carefully you choose a stock, when it drops below your stop point (typically 10 percent), it's time to sell.

Is There a Downside?

Does all this Internet stuff sound too good to be true? You're probably feeling like there's more to this story than we're letting on. Well, you're right. Online investing has gained a lot of acceptance among individual investors, with its instantaneous trading and low fees. The Internet offers investors a new kind of freedom and personal empowerment, but Internet investing also carries risks.

FACT

The average income of an online investor in the United States is $78,300. The number of U.S. online brokerage accounts is 13 million. And the percentage of Americans trading online is 5 percent.

Network Crashes

Who hasn't experienced the horror of having their computer die in the middle of a workday? Computers are not infallible, and neither are the networks that drive them. One of the primary causes of network breakdown is an overload of traffic, and online investing is a fast-growing activity. On busy market days, online brokerages can find it a struggle to keep up with demand, and occasionally they find that they can't meet the needs of the many investors trying to access their sites.

Online brokers took a heavy beating in the press on October 27, 1997, when a one-day crash led to trading halts on the New York Stock Exchange and brought many brokerages to a screeching halt. Too many devastated investors clamored to access their accounts at one time, and brokerage sites were overwhelmed by the demand. In recent years, major Internet brokers have worked hard to increase their network capacity. They are now strong enough to cope with emergency market conditions, but the bottom line is that online brokerages may not be available when you need them the most.

Online chat rooms offer investors communities that discuss just about every investment opportunity around the globe. At every hour of every day of the week, some new investment is being primed and pumped in an Internet chat room. The SEC, however, wants Web site owners to know that it will hold them liable for what they say when they engage in online bull sessions.

You're Flying Solo

If you commit to online investing, you will no longer be the wingman to your broker. You are in command of the flight, without the comfort of a broker advising you every step of the way. Internet brokers are do-it-yourself operations, for the most part. In many cases you have access to a live broker when you need one, but that's no substitute for an ongoing relationship with a professional who knows your personal history, resources, and goals. Even if you do make your trades online, a financial advisor can still help you make good investment choices, and help you make sure that your choices are in line with your big-picture goals.

Even if people would rather let a professional make their investment decisions, the Internet can still be a great tool for them. It offers information and resources that will increase their knowledge of the investment world as well as allowing them to evaluate the professionals handling their money.

A Word to the Wise on Internet Scams

Care to go trolling on the Internet for some great stock tips? Fine by me. Just beware that the online analyst who says he's found the next eBay may be a paid tout for the very stock he's promoting. Paid touts thrive in the murky underworld of stock-tip Web sites, where you don't have the opportunity to make eye contact and take the measure of a person.

It's tempting—seemingly objective analysis from a reputed source that asks nothing in return for the great tip he's providing you. All you have to do is plunk down some money for the stock, sit back, and wait for the big payoff. By the time you've figured out that you've been duped, you need a microscope to locate what's left of your investment. Plus, the "analyst" is long gone, paid off handsomely by the same company executives who took your money and got out early.

Did You Hear the One About . . . ?

Take the example of Roland R. Baughmann. Fraud detectors at the SEC (SEC) knew him as "The Phantom." Web investors knew him as "Roland," a jovial self-anointed stock expert who regularly hung out on stock message boards. Back in 1996, he provided stock tips on Prodigy's Money Talk Bulletin Board. The SEC suspected Baughmann and his cronies of artificially pumping up the stock of a company called Interactive Multimedia Publishers (IMP).

From February 7 to March 1, 1996, shares of IMP shot through the roof, leaping 1,322 percent from 56 cents to $8 per share. After that (and after Baughmann and co. sold their shares) the bottom fell out, leaving the stock virtually worthless within a matter of months. After Prodigy members complained, the SEC put together a paper trail that ultimately landed Baughmann in front of a U.S. District Court judge in February 1999. Regardless of consequences for Baughmann, authorities say, there's little or no chance of duped investors seeing any of their money again. Says Duncan King, deputy director of public affairs for the SEC, "For every tout we get, there's hundreds more still operating out there in cyberspace."

What You Can Do

King adds that investors can take some valuable steps in helping the SEC track down and nab securities scam artists. Keep the following in mind, in case this happens to you:

- Call your state securities regulator, or check the SEC's EDGAR database (follow the links from *www.sec.gov*) to see whether an investment is legally registered.
- Ask your state securities regulator whether the person or firm selling the investment is licensed to do business in your state and whether they have a record of complaints or fraud.

- Assume investments offered through the Internet are scams until you've done your homework and proven otherwise.

Also, to report suspicious Internet activities pertaining to securities fraud, the SEC encourages you to contact its Enforcement Complaint Center through its Web site (*www.sec.gov*) or to e-mail them at *enforcement@sec.gov*. For more about avoiding fraud online, visit the Investor Information section of the SEC's Web site. So get cracking. As King says, "It could be you next."

The Ten Best Investment Web Sites

There are lots of investment-related sites out there in the ether. If you search around, you'll find plenty to choose from, although the level of quality can vary dramatically from site to site. Be careful whose advice you take, and make sure you know where their information comes from.

Internet message boards can be interesting places to interact with other investors and get various points of view. You should use extreme caution, however, in evaluating message board information. You don't know the sources, and much information exchanged on message boards is bogus.

To get you started, here is a list of the top ten investment sites, in no particular order:

1. **E*TRADE** (*www.etrade.com*). This site offers a great trading experience with lots of extra features. Easy to use and navigate too.
2. **Netstock** (*www.netstock.com*). A great place to bypass the old-fashioned broker, this site provides an extensive list of online DRIP and DSP resources.
3. **Schwab** (*www.schwab.com*). This is the largest online brokerage in the world, with online answers to your investment questions.
4. **Waterhouse** (*www.waterhouse.com*). This site offers great human customer service without the high fees.

5. **DLJ Direct** (✍*www.dljdirect.com*). If you want to research your investments before you buy, this is the site to do it.

6. **MSN Investor** (✍*www.investor.com*). In five minutes, you can download the free portfolio software and get extensive portfolio import capabilities and wizards to track your investments.

7. **Morningstar** (✍*www.morningstar.com*). Morningstar provides excellent analysis and portfolio management tools to research your investments.

8. **Reuters Moneynet** (✍*www.moneynet.com*). This fast, easy-to-use site lets you see how your investments are faring anytime during the day.

9. **Interactive Investor** (✍*www.zdii.com*). This cutting-edge site provides IPO information, tech market date, the magazine *Red Herring*, and much more for the investor who wants to play a little edgy.

10. **Hoover's Online** (✍*www.hoovers.com*). A site designed to provide information to help guide the investor through the marketplace, Hoover's uses twenty-two financial criteria and includes in-house research, and news and analysis from other sources.

The Big Picture

Hopefully, you're not too overwhelmed as you conclude this book. Investing is a wide world of intricacies, but it's absolutely conquerable. People do it every day—you just have to keep the basics in mind. Throughout the entire book you've repeatedly read about risk tolerance and the fact that people must do what is best for meeting their own goals and needs. You also know now that it's important not to think of investing as gambling or a means to quick cash. It's simply a way of planning for your future as you wander down the uncertain paths of life.

It's also worth remembering that although this entire book is focused on investing to make more, there is a lot more to life than earning money. After all, and it has been said many times before, "You can't take it with you." Thus, if you are wealthy and miserable, you need to change your perspective. Many people have a few investments, are comfortable financially, and are enjoying life. With just a little time and effort, this could be you. If you have your sights held a little higher, that's great. Just remember that maintaining balance will help you arrive at your goals feeling calm and satisfied.

Appendix A
Discount Brokers

This listing includes some of the numerous discount brokers available. Many offer you the opportunity to trade online, while most have toll-free numbers for easy phone trading. Some online brokers are very popular with those who believe technology rules supreme (a growing segment of the population).

The following list contains just some of the many popular, easily accessible discount brokers throughout the United States. This list includes brokers with toll-free numbers, and most offer online trading.

Accutrade
✍ *www.accutrade.com*
✆ (800) 228-3011

American Express Financial Direct
✍ *www.americanexpress.com*
✆ (800) 658-4677

Ameritrade
✍ *www.ameritrade.com*
✆ (800) 669-3900

Bull and Bear Securities
✆ (800) 262-5800
No online trading thus far.

Ceres Securities
✍ *www.ceres.com*
✆ (800) 669-3900
No-frills trading.

Charles Schwab and Co.
✍ *www.eschwab.com*
✆ (800) 435-4500
High volume and low prices from one of the biggest of the brokerage houses.

E*TRADE
✍ *www.etrade.com*
✆ (800) 786-2575
High volume, very popular site with low prices.

Fleet Brokerage
☏(800) 766-3000
No online trading thus far.

Freedom Investments
✉ *www.tradeflash.com*
☏(800) 381-1481

Ichan and Company
☏(800) 634-8518
No online trading thus far.

Marquette De Bary Company
✉ *www.debary.com*
☏(800) 221-3305

Max Ule
✉ *www.maxule.com*
☏(800) 223-6642

National Discount Brokers
✉ *www.ndb.com*
☏(800) 888-3999
Major discount brokerage house with research information available.

Quick and Reilly
✉ *www.quick-reilly.com*
☏(800) 926-0600
Offering two online services for trading.

Regal Discount Securities
✉ *www.regaldiscount.com*
☏(800) 786-9000

Savoy Discount Brokerage
✍ *www.savoystocks.com*
📞(800) 961-1500

Tradex Brokerage Service
📞(800) 522-3000
No online trading thus far.

USAA Brokerage Services
📞(800) 531-8343
No online trading thus far.

Vanguard Discount Brokerage
✍ *www.vanguard.com*
📞(800) 992-8372

Wall Street Access
✍ *www.wsaccess.com*
📞(800) 487-2339

The Wall Street Discount Corporation
✍ *www.wsdc.com*
📞(800) 221-7870

Waterhouse Securities
✍ *www.waterhouse.com*
📞(800) 934-4410

Your Discount Broker
📞(800) 800-3215
No online trading thus far.

Ziegler Thrift Trading
✍ *www.ziegler-thrift.com*
📞(800) 328-4854

Appendix B

E Investment Publications

There are myriad publications that can be of assistance to investors. These financially oriented newspapers and magazines offer valuable insights about the stock market, including stock tips and articles with a more psychological slant. Publications are a good place to get ideas about investments, but you still need to do your own investigations. You also need to consider whether or not a given stock that you read about in a magazine fits in with your strategy and your overall approach to investing. Many publications make stock recommendations and show you how the stocks have fared after a year. To look at a copy before buying a subscription you can check your local library. Among other resources, you can gain valuable insight about investing from the following:

The *Wall Street Journal*

✆ (800) 568-7625

Published by Dow Jones and Company, the *Wall Street Journal* is a leading global newspaper with a focus on business. Founded in 1889, the newspaper has grown to a daily circulation of about 1.8 million readers. In 1994, Dow Jones introduced the *Wall Street Journal Special Editions,* special sections written in local languages that are featured in about thirty-three leading national newspapers worldwide. The *Wall Street Journal Americas,* published in Spanish and Portuguese, is included in approximately twenty leading Latin American newspapers. The *Wall Street Journal* offers thirteen-week subscriptions for $49, six-month subscriptions for $89, one-year subscriptions for $175, and two-year subscriptions for $299. Eligible students and professors can save nearly half the price on their subscriptions. Online access to the *Wall Street Journal, Barron's,* and *Smart Money* is available for $29 per year for print subscribers and $59 for nonsubscribers.

Barron's

✆ (800) 568-7625

Barron's is also known as the *Dow Jones Business and Financial Weekly.* With its first edition published in 1921, *Barron's* offers its readers news reports and analyses on financial markets worldwide. Investors will also find a wealth of tips regarding investment techniques. The weekly publication can be had for a thirteen-week subscription rate of $39. Six-month subscriptions are $74; one-year subscriptions are $145; and a two-year subscription is $245. Eligible students and professors can receive nearly half off on their subscriptions.

Investor's Business Daily

✆ (800) 831-2525

Founded in 1984, *Investor's Business Daily* is a newspaper focusing on business, financial, economic, and national news. The publication places a strong

emphasis on offering its readers timely information on stock market and stock market–related issues. The front page of each issue provides a brief overview of the most important business news of the day. It's published five days a week, Tuesdays through Saturdays, and you can have a six-month subscription for $109. For one year it's $197; a two-year subscription will run you $327; and a three-year subscription is $439.

Forbes

✆ (800) 888-9896

Forbes magazine is a biweekly business magazine for "those who run business today—or aspire to." Each issue has more than fifty stories on companies, management strategies, global trends, technology, taxes, law, capital markets, and investments. A one-year subscription, or twenty-six issues, is $59.95, a two-year subscription is $99.95, three years is $139.95, and a seventeen-issue student rate is $19.99.

Worth

✆ (800) 777-1851

Worth is a monthly personal finance magazine for individuals who "insist on being in control and refuse to put their finances on auto-pilot." The monthly magazine features such columnists as Peter Lynch and political economist Walter Russell Mead. Coverage ranges from the current state of the markets (domestically and abroad) to specific portfolio strategies for investing in equities, bonds, and mutual funds. A one-year subscription costs $18 (ten issues).

Equity

✆ (800) 777-1851

Equity, published by the same company as *Worth* magazine, is geared to high-income women. Women and their relationship with money is the overall theme of the publication, which was introduced in December 1998. Among other topics, feature articles revolve around investing money, spending money, and making money. As of this printing, *Equity* is free with a subscription to *Worth*.

Money

✆ (800) 633-9970

Money is a monthly personal finance magazine from Time-Warner publications, covering such topics as family finances, investment careers, taxes, and insurance. Each issue includes tips, advice, and strategies for smart investing. The magazine also features other related matters like finding cheap flights, buying a home, and preparing for tax season. They also offer a substantive annual mutual fund guide. A one-year subscription, or thirteen issues, is $39.89; a half-year subscription, or seven issues, is $21.47.

Fortune

✆ (800) 621-8000

Every month, *Fortune* magazine, a Time-Warner publication, offers analysis of the business marketplace. The publication's annual ranking of the top 500 American companies is one of its most widely read features. *Fortune* has been covering business and business-related topics since its origins in 1930. A one-year subscription, or twenty-six issues, is $59.95, and for students a one-year subscription is $29.98.

Smart Money

✆ (800) 444-4204

Smart Money, a monthly personal finance magazine, offers readers ideas for investing, spending, and saving. The publication also covers automotive, technology, and lifestyle subjects, including upscale travel, footwear, fine wine, and music. One-year subscriptions are $24, with discounts to *Wall Street Journal* subscribers.

Kiplinger's Personal Finance

✆ (800) 544-0155

One of the most respected names in financial publications, *Kiplinger's* offers investing ideas, updates on companies, insider interviews with top financial experts and fund managers, and very detailed listings of the best-performing mutual funds in a wide range of categories. One-year subscriptions are $23.95, two-year subscriptions are $39.95, and three-year subscriptions are $54.95. A discount rate for a one-year subscription of $14.97 is available to students and eligible teachers.

ValueLine Investment Survey

✆ (800) 634-3583

A weekly publication available at most libraries and through subscription, it offers ratings, reports, opinions, and analysis on about 130 stocks in seven or eight industries on a weekly basis. Approximately 1,700 stocks in about ninety-four industries are covered every thirteen weeks. CD-ROM subscribers can also purchase an expanded version containing reviews of 5,000 stocks.

Standard & Poor's Equity Investor Services

Standard & Poor's
25 Broadway, New York, NY 10004-1010
✆ (212) 208-8786

The services include numerous products, such as the Compustat database, which provides information on nearly nine thousand active U.S. companies—including over twenty years of market data and a lot more. Other S&P Equity Service products include ComStock, Stock Guide, corporate records, stock reports, and directories of the S&P 500, the S&P Mid-Cap 400, the S&P Small-Cap Index, securities dealers, pension funds, and just about any other type of investment opportunity. A catalog will provide you with a listing of their software and books.

Investment Web Sites

The Internet has made an unparalleled impact on the state of investing. It has significantly affected the manner in which business is conducted worldwide. It has taken the information once found buried in the business sections of newspapers and made it easily accessible to investors at all levels. In short, the proliferation of home computers coupled with the Internet have brought investing to the masses. Add to that a vast array of software, as well as investment Web sites designed for the investment professional, and you have a whole new world of investing, literally at your fingertips.

A majority of the major financial institutions and nearly all of the major brokerage houses offer their own Web sites. The most comprehensive of the many Web sites offered by major investment firms are the following:

- *www.aimfunds.com*
- *www.americancentury.com*
- *www.fidelity.com*
- *www.Franklin-Templeton.com*
- *www.prudential.com*
- *www.strong.com*

Historical information, fund holdings, performance updates, fund profiles, information on fund managers, libraries of articles and general information, and even glossaries and investor tips can be found on various Web sites. Needless to say, the investor tips and how-to information can lean in favor of the funds offered by a fund family. You usually won't find the virtues of REITs or advantages of muni bond funds discussed by a fund family that doesn't handle them. Nonetheless, you will get a lot of overall information at the Web sites of financial institutions.

While Web surfing, it's to your advantage to hone in on the specific areas that you are looking for, such as tax-free investments, socially responsible investing (try *www. coopamerica.org*), or information on particular funds. This will narrow down your search and reduce your time spent online, since some Web sites (in all areas) are loaded with promotional material and hype or are simply confusing with numerous bells and whistles.

There are numerous investing Web sites. Some will give you an overall picture of investing as a whole, and others will focus on a particular area. The following list includes a few of the many investment-related Web sites:

Armchair Millionaire
www.armchairmillionaire.com
Offers a wealth of information for personal investors.

Bloomberg
www.bloomberg.com
Bloomberg's online financial news and information site.

The Bond Market Association Sites
www.psa.com or *www.investinginbonds.com*
Legislative and statistical information, research, prices, and more.

Bondtrac Financial Information
www.bondtrac.com
If you're looking for bond information and the latest in bond offerings, this site should be of help.

Brill.com
www.brill.com
This Mutual Fund Interactive site is a Mecca for mutual fund information.

BusinessWeek
www.personalwealth.com
Here you can get words of wisdom from Wall Street experts, S&P stock information, and more.

CBS Market Track
www.cbsmarketwatch.com
This CBS financial site has information on stocks, bonds, mutual funds, and more, plus charts and commentary.

CNN Financial News
www.cnnfn.com
The CNN Financial News Network offers a site with an extensive amount of information about U.S. and global markets.

Coopamerica
www.coopamerica.org
Describes how to make a financial plan and how to integrate social investing.

Cyber Invest
✍ *www.cyberinvest.com*
Links and information and the latest news on stocks, bonds, banking, global investing, education, etc.

Dailystock.com
✍ *www.dailystock.com*
Quotes, news, and a wealth of financial information are available, with links to numerous other sites.

Dogs of the Dow
✍ *www.dogsofthedow.com*
Gives you the lowdown on the stocks in the Dow Jones, from historical information to the latest quotes, plus news and updates.

Dow Jones Business Directory
✍ *www.dowjones.com*
Offers you a comprehensive listing of all sorts of financial sites on the Web, even reviewing many of them.

The Global Investor Directory
✍ *www.global-investor.com*
As the name indicates, this site provides access to a plethora of international investing information, including performance information on worldwide markets.

Greenpages.org
✍ *www.greenpages.org*
Helps you look up financial planners and portfolio managers to aid you in socially responsible investing.

Guide to the Web Sites of Time, Inc.
✍ *www.pathfinder.com*
Time Warner's huge site for a number of other information sources, including *Fortune* and *Money* magazines.

Hoovers Online
✍ *www.hoovers.com*
Gives you the scoop on more than 10,000 companies, from IPOs to industry profiles.

INVESTools
✍ *www.investools.com*
Links personal investors with the latest from financial news services and with research information sites such as Standard & Poor's, among others.

Invest-o-rama
✍ *www.investorama.com*
A major directory to personal finance and investing sites, with more than 4,000 links.

Investor Guide
✍ *www.investorguide.com*
Offers a long list of subjects, with plenty of information and tons of links.

Links and Tips for Investing
✍ *www.moneypages.com*
Links to stocks, bonds, and mutual funds, plus investment tips for the individual investor.

Morningstar
✍ *www.morningstar.net*
One of several sites from Morningstar, an institution in the financial community.

The Motley Fool
✍ *www.fool.com*
Provides a wide variety of information, including a lot of investing basics.

Mutual Fund Channel
✍ *www.mutualfundchannel.com*
Helps you keep tabs on the mutual funds in your portfolio (with some possible downloading necessary).

The Mutual Fund Investment Center
✍ *www.mfea.com*
Helps you get all the information you need to select the right mutual funds.

Quote.com
www.quote.com
Up-to-the-minute quotes from numerous markets, along with analyses and commentary.

Reuters
www.reuters.com
Offers all the latest financial news you need.

U.S. Government Investment and Tax Information
www.irs.ustres.gov
The government's Web site for government investments and tax information.

U.S. Securities and Exchange Commission
www.sec.gov
Information on companies, brokerage houses, SEC policies, and news.

Smart Money
www.smartmoney.com
From *Smart Money*, this is a comprehensive site for all levels of investors.

Socialinvest
www.socialinvest.org
Shows a chart of community investing options and lists mutual funds; updated monthly.

Standard and Poor
www.stockinfo.standardpoors.com
Extensive site with across-the-board information about companies, sectors, funds, and so on.

Stocksite.com
www.stocksite.com
Stock picks, quotes, charts, split information, and research all available.

Stockmaster.com
www.stockmaster.com
The latest stock quotes plus news and historical information about the companies behind them.

Thomas Investors Network
www.thomsoninvest.net
Offers real-time quotes, stock tips, research, charts, a fund center, and more.

U.S. Treasury Department
www.ustres.gov
Plenty of information on what the government has to offer in the way of investment vehicles.

Easysaver.gov
www.easysaver.gov
The U.S. Treasury Department's new plan for direct deposits from your savings or checking account.

Winning Investing
www.winninginvesting.com
This site comes from *Winning Investing*, a comprehensive newsletter geared at the individual investor.

Workfamily
www.workfamily.com
Compiles a list of model companies with good family-friendly policies.

WSRN.com
www.wsrn.com
A major umbrella site with investment information and links to numerous other sites.

Zack's Investment Research
www.zacks.com
A research site with market commentary and information.

Appendix D

Glossary of Terms

Investing has a language all its own, but it doesn't have to be intimidating. The average investor only needs to know the basics, so if you have an understanding of the terms in this glossary, you're off to a good start.

annuity:
A contract or agreement between you and the issuing company. You give the issuing company a certain amount of money, and in turn it promises to invest your money and repay you according to the option or payment method that you choose.

arbitrage:
The act of taking advantage of the difference in price of the same security traded on two different markets. For instance, if Nortel Networks were trading at $100 (U.S.) on the Toronto exchange and $99 on the NYSE, an arbitrageur would buy shares on the NYSE and sell them on the Toronto exchange.

asset:
Anything you own that is of monetary value, including cash, stocks, bonds, mutual funds, cars, real estate, and other items.

asset allocation:
Asset allocation refers to the specific distribution of funds among a number of different asset classes within an investment portfolio: It is diversification put into practice. Funds may be distributed among a number of different asset classes, such as stocks, bonds, and cash funds, each of which has unique types of expected risk and return. Within each asset class are several variations of the asset, meaning that there are levels of risk within each asset class. Asset allocation involves determining what percentage of funds will be invested in each asset. Determining how to allocate funds depends on the individual investor.

average daily volume:
The average number of shares traded per day over a specified period.

bankruptcy:
A court process in which you acknowledge that you are unable to pay your debts and you allow your assets to be sold to repay creditors to the extent possible (liquidation bankruptcy), or you work with the court to set up a plan to pay all or some of your debt over a period of several years (reorganization bankruptcy).

bear:
Someone who believes or speculates that a particular security, or the securities in a market, will decline in value is referred to as a bear.

bear market:
A market in which a group of securities falls in price or loses value over a period of time. A prolonged bear market may result in a decrease of 20 percent or more in market prices. A bear market in stocks may be due to investors' expectations of economic trends; in bonds, a bear market results from rising interest rates. Investors are "bearish" when they view stocks as being in sustained decline.

beneficiary:
The person for whose benefit a trust is created. There is often more than one beneficiary.

beta:
Compares a mutual fund or stock's volatility to a benchmark (usually the S&P 500 Index). A beta greater than 1 is more volatile than the index. For instance, a beta of 1.5 means the fund or stock is historically 50 percent more volatile than the index.

bid price:
The price a prospective buyer is ready to pay. This term is used by traders who maintain firm bid and offer prices in a given security by standing ready to buy or sell security units at publicly quoted prices.

blue chip:
Blue chip refers to companies that have become well established and reliable over time, and have demonstrated sound management and quality products and services. Such companies have shown an ability to function in both good and bad economic times and have usually paid dividends to investors even during lean years. Most blue chips are large cap, *Fortune* 500-type stocks like IBM or General Electric.

bonds:

Loans from investors to corporations and governments given in exchange for interest payments and timely repayment of the debt. Interest rates are usually fixed.

bottom-up analysis:

The search for outstanding performance of individual stocks before considering the impact of economic trends. Such companies may be identified from research reports, stock screens, or personal knowledge of the products and services.

budget:

A forecast of income and expenses by category. Actual expenses and income are compared to the forecast and a plan is developed to reduce or control expenses to provide for savings to meet financial goals.

bull:

Someone who believes that a particular security, or the securities in a market, will increase in value is known as a bull. Investors are "bullish" when they view stocks as being on the upswing.

bull market:

A bull market is a long period of rising prices of securities, usually by 20 percent or more. Bull markets generally involve heavy trading and are marked by a general upward trend in the market, independent of daily fluctuations. For example, from 1982 to 2000, American investors enjoyed two lengthy bull markets: one lasting from 1982 through 1990 and the other from 1992 through 2000.

capital gain:

A capital gain is appreciation in the value of an asset—that is, when the selling price is greater than the original price at which the security was bought. The tax rate on capital gain depends on how long the security was held. Studies show that personal portfolios are much easier, tax-wise, when it comes to declaring capital gains, than are mutual funds.

capital gain distributions:

Payments to a mutual fund's shareholders of profits earned from selling securities in a fund's portfolio. Capital gain distributions are usually paid once a year.

CD:

Certificate of Deposit; money lent to banks for a set period of time, usually between one month and five years, in exchange for compound interest, usually at a fixed rate. At the end of this term, on the maturity date, the principal may either be repaid to the individual or rolled over into another CD. The bank pays interest to the individual, and interest rates between banks are competitive. Monies deposited into a CD are insured by the bank; thus, they are a low-risk investment and a good way of maintaining a principal. Maturities may be as short as a few weeks or as long as several years. Most banks set heavy penalties for premature withdrawal of monies from a CD.

closed-end fund:

Investors buy shares from other shareholders and sell shares to other investors. Share price is determined by supply and demand for fund shares (as opposed to net asset value for open-end funds).

commission:

Commission is a fee charged by a stockbroker or, in some cases, the financial advisor may be working with an investor on a personal portfolio, who makes transactions of buying or selling securities for another individual. This fee is generally a percentage based on either the number of stocks bought or sold or the value of the stocks bought or sold.

compound interest:

If interest earned on an investment is calculated only on the original amount invested, it's known as simple interest. If interest earned is calculated on the original amount plus any previously earned interest, it's known as compound interest, which makes the investment grow more quickly.

cost basis:
The amount you subtract from the sale price of a property to compute your gain or loss when you sell a piece of property.

creditor:
Any person (or entity) to whom you owe money.

credit risk:
Credit risk refers primarily to the risk involved with debt investments, such as bonds. Credit risk is essentially the risk that the principal will not be repaid by the issuer. If the issuer fails to repay the principal, the issuer is said to default.

default:
To default is to fail to repay the principal or make timely payments on a bond or other debt investment security issued. Also, a default is a breach of or a failure to fulfill the terms of a note or contract.

defined-contribution retirement plan:
A retirement plan offered by employers that allows employees to contribute to the plan but does not guarantee a predetermined benefit at retirement. 401(k), 403(b), 457, and profit-sharing plans are examples.

discount broker:
Brokerage firms that offer cut-rate fees for buying stocks, usually online over the Internet (although discount brokers also offer phone and fax trade order options). Some of the most prominent include Charles Schwab, Quick & Reilly, and Ameritrade.

diversification:
Diversification is the process of optimizing an investment portfolio by allocating funds to a number of different assets. Diversification minimizes risks while maximizing returns by spreading out risk across a number of investments. Different types of assets, such as stocks, bonds, and cash funds, carry different types of risk. For an optimal portfolio, it is important to diversify among assets with dissimilar risk levels. Investing in a number of assets allows for unexpected negative performances to balance out with or be superseded by positive performances.

dividend:
A dividend is a payment, made by a company to its shareholders, that is a portion of the profits of the company. The amount to be paid is determined by the board of directors, and dividends may be paid even during a time when the company is not performing profitably. Mutual funds also pay dividends. These monies are paid from the income earned on the investments of the mutual fund. Dividends are paid on a schedule, such as quarterly, semiannually, or annually. Dividends may be paid directly to the investor or reinvested into more shares of the company's stock. Even if dividends are reinvested, the individual is responsible for paying taxes on the dividends. Unfortunately, dividends are not guaranteed and may vary each time they are paid.

dividend yield:
The current or estimated annual dividend divided by the market price per share of a security.

Dow Jones Industrial Average:
The Dow Jones Industrial Average is an index to which the performance of individual stocks can be compared; it is a means of measuring the change in stock prices. This index is a composite of 30 blue-chip companies ranging from AT&T and Hewlett Packard to Kodak and Johnson & Johnson. These 30 companies represent not just the United States; rather, they are involved with commerce on a global scale. The DJIA is computed by adding the prices of these 30 stocks and dividing by an adjusted number that takes into account stock splits and other divisions that would interfere with the average. Stocks represented on the Dow Jones Industrial Average make up between 15 percent and 20 percent of the market.

DRIP:
Dividend reinvestment plans allow investors to automatically reinvest their dividends in the company's stock rather than receive them in cash. Many

companies waive the sales charges for stock purchased under the DRIP.

due diligence:
The process whereby an in-depth examination of a company's business prospects is conducted.

earnings growth:
A pattern of increasing rate of growth in earnings per share from one period to another, which usually causes a stock's price to rise.

equity:
Equity is the total ownership or partial ownership an individual possesses minus any debts that are owed. Equity is the amount of interest shareholders hold in a company as a part of their rights of partial ownership. Equity is considered synonymous with ownership, a share of ownership, or the rights of ownership.

escrow:
Money or other assets held by an agent until the terms of a contract or agreement are fulfilled. Many mortgage companies require borrowers to pay prorated property taxes monthly with their mortgage payment. These funds are held in an escrow account until payment is due to the local government.

financial advisor:
A fully accredited financial planning professional who helps people manage their money, prepare for retirement, manage their taxes, and prepare an estate planning strategy (among other financial services). Financial advisors are a good idea for do-it-yourself investors who want a good sounding board as they build their own mutual funds.

fiscal year:
Any 12-month period designated by a corporation as their accounting year. Once set up, a corporation's fiscal year does not change.

folio:
Popularized by companies like Foliofn and E*Trade, folios are an ideal mechanism for building your own mutual fund. Essentially, folios are "baskets" of stocks that do-it-yourself investors pick on their own. Some folio companies also provide "ready to go" folios of selected stocks. Folio programs can cost as little as $29.95 per month to use.

foreclosure:
A legal process that terminates an owner's right to a property, usually because the borrower defaults on payments. Home foreclosures usually result in a forced sale of the property to pay off the mortgage.

forex:
Foreign currency exchange markets.

fundamental analysis:
An analysis of a company's balance sheet and income statements used to forecast its future stock price movements. Fundamental analysts consider past records of assets, earnings, sales, products, management, and markets in predicting future trends in these indicators of a company's success or failure. By appraising a company's prospects, these analysts assess whether a particular stock or group of stocks is undervalued or overvalued at its current market price.

going public:
A company that has previously been privately owned is said to be "going public" the first time the company's stock is offered for public sale.

good for the day:
Buy or sell limit order that will expire at close of trading if not executed.

good until cancelled:
Buy or sell limit order that remains active until you cancel it.

growth investing:
An investment style that emphasizes companies with strong earnings growth. Growth investing is generally considered more aggressive than "value" investing.

hedge:

Hedging is a strategy of reducing risk by offsetting investments with investments of opposite risks. Risks must be negatively correlated in order to hedge each other—for example, an investment with high inflation risk and low immediate returns with investments with low inflation risk and high immediate returns. Long hedges protect against a short-term position, and short hedges protect against a long-term position. Hedging is not the same as diversification; it aims to protect against risk by counterbalancing a specific area of risk.

inflation:

A general increase in prices coinciding with a fall in the real value of money, as measured by the Consumer Price Index.

inflation risk:

Inflation risk is the risk that rising prices of goods and services over time—or the general cost of living—will decrease the value of the return on investments. Inflation risk is also known as purchasing-power risk because it refers to increased prices of goods and services and a decreased value of cash.

intrinsic value:

A term favored by value-oriented fundamental analysts to express the actual value of a corporation, as opposed to the current value based on the stock price. It is usually calculated by adding the current value of estimated future earnings to the book value.

IRA:

Individual retirement account; a retirement account that anyone who has earned income can contribute to. Amounts contributed to traditional IRAs are usually tax-deferred. Amounts contributed to Roth IRAs are not deductible but taxes are never due on the earnings.

junk bond:

A bond that is considered high yield but also has a high credit risk. Junk bonds are generally low-rated bonds and are usually bought on speculation. Investors hope for the yield rather than the default. An investor with high risk tolerance may choose to invest in junk bonds.

liability:

An amount owed to creditors or others. Common liabilities include mortgage, car payments, student loans, and credit card debt.

liquidity:

Liquidity refers to the ease with which investments can be converted to cash at their present market value. Additionally, liquidity is a condition of an investment that shows how greatly the investment price is affected by trading. An investment that is highly liquid is composed of enough units (such as shares) that many transactions can take place without greatly affecting the market price. High liquidity is associated with a high number of buyers and sellers trading investments at a high volume.

load:

A sales charge or commission paid to a broker or other third-party when mutual funds are bought or sold. Front-end loads are sometimes incurred when an investor purchases the shares and back-end loads are sometimes incurred when investors sell the shares.

market capitalization:

The market price of company's shares multiplied by the number of shares outstanding. Large capitalization companies generally have over $5 billion in market capitalization, mid-cap companies between $1.5 billion and $5 billion, and small cap companies less than $1.5 billion. These capitalization figures may vary depending upon the index being used and/or the guidelines used by the portfolio manager.

market risk:

Market risk is the risk that investments will lose money based on the daily fluctuations of the market. Bond market risk results from fluctuations in interest. Stock prices, on the other hand, are influenced by factors ranging from company performance to economic factors to political news and events of national importance. Time is a stabilizing element in the stock market, as returns tend to outweigh risks over long periods of time. Market risk cannot be systematically diversified away.

market value:
Market value is the value of an investment if it were to be resold, or the current price of a security being sold on the market.

mutual fund:
An investment that allows thousands of investors to pool their money to purchase stocks, bonds, or other types of investments, depending on the objectives of the fund. Because mutual funds are divided into shares and can be bought much like stocks, they have high liquidity. Mutual funds are convenient, particularly for small investors, because they diversify an individual's monies among a number of investments. Investors share in the profits of a mutual fund, and mutual fund shares can be sold back to the company on any business day at the net asset value price. Mutual funds may or may not have a load, or fee; however, funds with a load will provide advice from a specialist, which may help the investor in choosing a mutual fund.

NASD:
National Association of Securities Dealers; An organization of broker/dealers who trade over-the-counter securities. The largest self-regulated securities organization, this organization operates and regulates both the NASDAQ and over-the-counter markets, ensuring that securities are traded fairly and ethically.

NASDAQ:
National Association of Securities Dealers Automated Quotation; A global automated computer system that provides up-to-the-minute information on approximately 5,500 over-the-counter stocks. Whereas on the New York Stock Exchange (NYSE) securities are bought and sold on the trading floor, securities on the NASDAQ are traded via computer.

net worth:
The value of all of a person's assets (anything owned that has a monetary value) minus all of the person's liabilities (amounts owed to others).

NYSE:
New York Stock Exchange; Established in 1792, the NYSE is the largest securities exchange in the United States. Securities are traded by brokers and dealers for customers on the trading floor at 11 Wall Street in New York City. The exchange is headed by a board of directors, which includes a chairman and 20 representatives who represent both the public and the members of the exchange. This board approves applicants as new NYSE dealers, sets policies for the exchange, oversees the exchange, regulates members' activities, and lists securities.

P/E ratio:
Price–earnings ratio; A measure of how much buyers are willing to pay for shares in a company, based on that company's earnings. The price–earnings ratio is calculated by dividing the current price of a share in a company by the most recent year's earnings per share of the company. This ratio is a useful way of comparing the value of stocks and helps to indicate expectations for the company's growth in earnings. It is important, however, to compare the P/E ratios of companies in similar industries. The price–earnings ratio is sometimes also called the "multiple."

price-to-book ratio:
Current market price of a stock divided by its book value, or net asset value.

quotation:
A quotation, or quote, refers to the current price of a security, be it either the highest bid price for that security or the lowest ask price.

Real Rate of Return:
The Real Rate of Return refers to the annual return on an investment after being adjusted for inflation and taxes.

reinvestment:
Reinvestment is the use of capital gains, including interest, dividends, or profit, to buy more of the same investment. For example, the dividends received from stock holdings may be reinvested by buying more shares of the same stock.

return on equity:
The amount, expressed as a percentage, earned on a company's common stock investment for a given period. It is calculated by dividing net income for the period after preferred stock dividends but before common stock dividends by the common stock equity (net worth) average for the accounting period. This tells common shareholders how effectively their money is being employed.

risk tolerance:
An investor's ability to tolerate fluctuations in the value of an investment in the expectation of receiving a higher return.

rollover:
Reinvestment of a distribution from a qualified retirement plan into an IRA or another qualified plan in order to retain its tax-deferred status and avoid taxes and penalties for early withdrawal.

S&P 500 Index:
The Standard & Poor's 500 Index is a market index of 500 of the top-performing U.S. corporations. This index, a broader measure of the domestic market than the Dow Jones Industrial Average, indicates broad market changes. The S&P 500 Index includes 400 industrial firms, 20 transportation firms, 40 utilities, and 40 financial firms.

SEC:
Securities and Exchange Commission; A federal government agency comprised of five commissioners appointed by the president and approved by the Senate. The SEC was established to protect individual investors from fraud and malpractice in the marketplace. The commission oversees and regulates the activities of registered investment advisors, stock and bond markets, broker/dealers, and mutual funds.

security:
A security is any investment purchased with the expectation of making a profit. Securities include total or partial ownership of an asset, rights to ownership of an asset, and certificates of debt from an institution. Examples of securities include stocks, bonds, certificates of deposit, and options.

socially responsible investing:
Investing in companies that meet an individual's ethical standards. Personal portfolios are good ways to invest in socially responsible companies because they give investors a way to pick and choose the companies that comprise their portfolios. With mutual funds, money manages do all the stock picking and investors have no say in the matter.

split:
A split occurs when a company's board of directors and shareholders agree to increase the number of shares outstanding. The shareholders' equity does not change; instead, the number of shares increases while the value of each share decreases proportionally. For example, in a 2-for-1 split, a shareholder with 100 shares prior to the split would now own 200 shares. The price of the shares, however, would be cut in half; shares that cost $40 before the split would be worth $20 after the split.

stock:
An ownership share in a corporation, entitling the investor to a pro rata share of the corporation's earnings and assets.

technical analysis:
The research into the demand and supply for securities, options, mutual funds, and commodities based on trading volume and price studies. Technical analysis uses charts or computer programs to identify and project price trends in a market, security, mutual fund, or futures contract.

ticker:
The ticker displays information on a movable tape or, in modern times, as a scrolling electronic display on a screen. The symbols and numbers shown on the ticker indicate the security being traded, the latest sale price of the security, and the volume of the most recent transaction.

top-down approach:
The method in which an investor first looks at trends in the general economy, selects attractive industries and then companies that should benefit from those trends.

total return:
The change in value of an investment in a fund over a specific time period expressed as a percentage. Total returns assume all earnings are reinvested in additional shares of a fund.

underwriter:
An underwriter is an individual who distributes securities as an intermediary between the issuer and the buyer of the securities. For example, an underwriter may be the agent selling insurance policies or the person distributing shares of a mutual fund to broker/dealers or investors. Generally, the underwriter agrees to purchase the remaining units of the security, such as remaining shares of stocks or bonds, from the issuer if the public does not buy all specified units. An underwriter may also be a company that backs the issue of a contract by agreeing to accept responsibility for fulfilling the contract in return for a premium.

value investing:
A relatively conservative investment approach that focuses on companies that may be temporarily out of favor or whose earnings or assets are not fully reflected in their stock prices. Value stocks will tend to have a lower price-to-earnings ratio than growth stocks.

volatility:
Volatility is an indicator of expected risk. It demonstrates the degree to which the market price of an asset, rate, or index fluctuates from the average. Volatility is calculated by finding the standard deviation from the mean, or average, return.

yield:
Yield is the return, or profit, on an investment. Yield refers to the interest gained on a bond or the rate of return on an investment, such as dividends paid on a mutual fund. Yield does not include capital gains.

401(k):
A defined-contribution retirement plan that allows participants to contribute pretax dollars to various investments.

E

Index

Determination, 34–36
Discipline
    and exchange points,
        141–42
    goal of, 56, 123–24
    and guidance, 131–34
    handling, 123–42
    noninflammatory discipline,
        130–31
    and structure, 137–41
    and supervision, 134–37
Distract-and-return strategy,
    14–15
Distractions, 89–91, 184–86
Drug addiction, 291–92
Drug use, 167, 279–95

E

Earning systems, 65, 127–28
Education considerations,
    193–208
Electronic brain training,
    186–87
Emotional extortion, 39,
    153–54, 255–56
Emotional loading, 67–68,
    164
Emotional overreactions, 78,
    177–80
Emotional responsibility,
    167–69
Emotional sobriety, 163–80
Emotions, and expectations,
    59, 174–77

Emotions, and thought
    processes, 164–69
Employment benefits, 243
Exceptional treatment,
    45–48
Exchange points, 141–42
Exchange systems, 65
Expectations
    academic expectations,
        194–98
    and emotions, 59, 174–77
    of only children, 274–75
Experimentation, 247–49,
    287–88
Extortion, 39, 153–54,
    255–56

F

Family dynamics, 265–67
Fear-prone parents, 82–83
Flexibility, 52–54
Freedom, 221–31

G

Guidance, 131–34

H

Healthy family, 117
Helplessness, 3
Homeschooling, 203–5

I

Imitation, 74–75
Impatience, 18–20
Independence
    and adolescence, 212,
        261–63
    and determination, 35
    and late adolescence, 277
    problems with, 43–45
    propositions for, 13–14
Influences, 59
Initiative, taking, 93–94, 112
Interactions, 75–76, 166–67,
    253
Intolerance, 52–54, 77, 272–73
Intractable child, 111–16
Isometric encounters, 80–81

M

Medications, 191–92, 287
Money management, 19–20,
    190, 224–27
Mutuality, 50–52

N

Name-calling, 33
Negative attitudes
    about rules, 114
    and ADHD, 182
    of adolescence, 240–42
    results of, 23–24, 87–89,
        107–8

THE EVERYTHING SERIES!

BUSINESS & PERSONAL FINANCE

Everything® Budgeting Book
Everything® Business Planning Book
Everything® Coaching and Mentoring Book
Everything® Fundraising Book
Everything® Get Out of Debt Book
Everything® Grant Writing Book
Everything® Homebuying Book, 2nd Ed.
Everything® Homeselling Book
Everything® Home-Based Business Book
Everything® Investing Book
Everything® Landlording Book
Everything® Leadership Book
Everything® Managing People Book
Everything® Negotiating Book
Everything® Online Business Book
Everything® Personal Finance Book
Everything® Personal Finance in Your 20s
    and 30s Book
Everything® Project Management Book
Everything® Real Estate Investing Book
Everything® Robert's Rules Book, $7.95
Everything® Selling Book
Everything® Start Your Own Business Book
Everything® Wills & Estate Planning Book

COOKING

Everything® Barbecue Cookbook
Everything® Bartender's Book, $9.95
Everything® Chinese Cookbook
Everything® College Cookbook
Everything® Cookbook
Everything® Diabetes Cookbook
Everything® Easy Gourmet Cookbook
Everything® Fondue Cookbook
Everything® Grilling Cookbook
Everything® Healthy Meals in Minutes
    Cookbook
Everything® Holiday Cookbook

Everything® Indian Cookbook
Everything® Low-Carb Cookbook
Everything® Low-Fat High-Flavor Cookbook
Everything® Low-Salt Cookbook
Everything® Meals for a Month Cookbook
Everything® Mediterranean Cookbook
Everything® Mexican Cookbook
Everything® One-Pot Cookbook
Everything® Pasta Cookbook
Everything® Quick Meals Cookbook
Everything® Slow Cooker Cookbook
Everything® Soup Cookbook
Everything® Thai Cookbook
Everything® Vegetarian Cookbook
Everything® Wine Book

HEALTH

Everything® Alzheimer's Book
Everything® Diabetes Book
Everything® Hypnosis Book
Everything® Low Cholesterol Book
Everything® Massage Book
Everything® Menopause Book
Everything® Nutrition Book
Everything® Reflexology Book
Everything® Stress Management Book

HISTORY

Everything® American Government Book
Everything® American History Book
Everything® Civil War Book
Everything® Irish History & Heritage Book
Everything® Middle East Book

HOBBIES & GAMES

Everything® Blackjack Strategy Book
Everything® Brain Strain Book, $9.95
Everything® Bridge Book
Everything® Candlemaking Book

Everything® Card Games Book
Everything® Cartooning Book
Everything® Casino Gambling Book, 2nd Ed.
Everything® Chess Basics Book
Everything® Crossword and Puzzle Book
Everything® Crossword Challenge Book
Everything® Cryptograms Book, $9.95
Everything® Digital Photography Book
Everything® Drawing Book
Everything® Easy Crosswords Book
Everything® Family Tree Book
Everything® Games Book, 2nd Ed.
Everything® Knitting Book
Everything® Knots Book
Everything® Motorcycle Book
Everything® Online Genealogy Book
Everything® Photography Book
Everything® Poker Strategy Book
Everything® Pool & Billiards Book
Everything® Quilting Book
Everything® Scrapbooking Book
Everything® Sewing Book
Everything® Woodworking Book
Everything® Word Games Challenge Book

HOME IMPROVEMENT

Everything® Feng Shui Book
Everything® Feng Shui Decluttering Book,
    $9.95
Everything® Fix-It Book
Everything® Homebuilding Book
Everything® Lawn Care Book
Everything® Organize Your Home Book

EVERYTHING® KIDS' BOOKS

All titles are $6.95

Everything® Kids' Animal Puzzle & Activity
    Book
Everything® Kids' Baseball Book, 3rd Ed.

All Everything® books are priced at $12.95 or $14.95, unless otherwise stated. Prices subject to change without notice.

Everything® Kids' Bible Trivia Book
Everything® Kids' Bugs Book
Everything® Kids' Christmas Puzzle
    & Activity Book
Everything® Kids' Cookbook
Everything® Kids' Halloween Puzzle
    & Activity Book
Everything® Kids' Hidden Pictures Book
Everything® Kids' Joke Book
Everything® Kids' Knock Knock Book
Everything® Kids' Math Puzzles Book
Everything® Kids' Mazes Book
Everything® Kids' Money Book
Everything® Kids' Monsters Book
Everything® Kids' Nature Book
Everything® Kids' Puzzle Book
Everything® Kids' Riddles & Brain Teasers Book
Everything® Kids' Science Experiments Book
Everything® Kids' Sharks Book
Everything® Kids' Soccer Book
Everything® Kids' Travel Activity Book

KIDS' STORY BOOKS

Everything® Bedtime Story Book
Everything® Fairy Tales Book

LANGUAGE

Everything® Conversational Japanese Book
    (with CD), $19.95
Everything® French Phrase Book, $9.95
Everything® French Verb Book, $9.95
Everything® Inglés Book
Everything® Learning French Book
Everything® Learning German Book
Everything® Learning Italian Book
Everything® Learning Latin Book
Everything® Learning Spanish Book
Everything® Sign Language Book
Everything® Spanish Grammar Book
Everything® Spanish Phrase Book, $9.95
Everything® Spanish Verb Book, $9.95

MUSIC

Everything® Drums Book (with CD), $19.95
Everything® Guitar Book
Everything® Home Recording Book
Everything® Playing Piano and Keyboards
    Book

Everything® Reading Music Book (with CD),
    $19.95
Everything® Rock & Blues Guitar Book
    (with CD), $19.95
Everything® Songwriting Book

NEW AGE

Everything® Astrology Book
Everything® Dreams Book, 2nd Ed.
Everything® Ghost Book
Everything® Love Signs Book, $9.95
Everything® Numerology Book
Everything® Paganism Book
Everything® Palmistry Book
Everything® Psychic Book
Everything® Reiki Book
Everything® Spells & Charms Book
Everything® Tarot Book
Everything® Wicca and Witchcraft Book

PARENTING

Everything® Baby Names Book
Everything® Baby Shower Book
Everything® Baby's First Food Book
Everything® Baby's First Year Book
Everything® Birthing Book
Everything® Breastfeeding Book
Everything® Father-to-Be Book
Everything® Father's First Year Book
Everything® Get Ready for Baby Book
Everything® Getting Pregnant Book
Everything® Homeschooling Book
Everything® Parent's Guide to Children
    with ADD/ADHD
Everything® Parent's Guide to Children
    with Asperger's Syndrome
Everything® Parent's Guide to Children
    with Autism
Everything® Parent's Guide to Children
    with Dyslexia
Everything® Parent's Guide to Positive
    Discipline
Everything® Parent's Guide to Raising a
    Successful Child
Everything® Parent's Guide to Tantrums
Everything® Parent's Guide to the Overweight
    Child
Everything® Parenting a Teenager Book
Everything® Potty Training Book, $9.95

Everything® Pregnancy Book, 2nd Ed.
Everything® Pregnancy Fitness Book
Everything® Pregnancy Nutrition Book
Everything® Pregnancy Organizer, $15.00
Everything® Toddler Book
Everything® Tween Book
Everything® Twins, Triplets, and More Book

PETS

Everything® Cat Book
Everything® Dachshund Book, $12.95
Everything® Dog Book
Everything® Dog Health Book
Everything® Dog Training and Tricks Book
Everything® Golden Retriever Book, $12.95
Everything® Horse Book
Everything® Labrador Retriever Book, $12.95
Everything® Poodle Book, $12.95
Everything® Pug Book, $12.95
Everything® Puppy Book
Everything® Rottweiler Book, $12.95
Everything® Tropical Fish Book

REFERENCE

Everything® Car Care Book
Everything® Classical Mythology Book
Everything® Computer Book
Everything® Divorce Book
Everything® Einstein Book
Everything® Etiquette Book
Everything® Mafia Book
Everything® Philosophy Book
Everything® Psychology Book
Everything® Shakespeare Book

RELIGION

Everything® Angels Book
Everything® Bible Book
Everything® Buddhism Book
Everything® Catholicism Book
Everything® Christianity Book
Everything® Jewish History & Heritage Book
Everything® Judaism Book
Everything® Koran Book
Everything® Prayer Book
Everything® Saints Book
Everything® Torah Book
Everything® Understanding Islam Book

All Everything® books are priced at $12.95 or $14.95, unless otherwise stated. Prices subject to change without notice.

Everything® World's Religions Book
Everything® Zen Book

SCHOOL & CAREERS

Everything® Alternative Careers Book
Everything® College Survival Book, 2nd Ed.
Everything® Cover Letter Book, 2nd Ed.
Everything® Get-a-Job Book
Everything® Job Interview Book
Everything® New Teacher Book
Everything® Online Job Search Book
Everything® Paying for College Book
Everything® Practice Interview Book
Everything® Resume Book, 2nd Ed.
Everything® Study Book

SELF-HELP

Everything® Great Sex Book
Everything® Kama Sutra Book
Everything® Self-Esteem Book

SPORTS & FITNESS

Everything® Fishing Book
Everything® Fly-Fishing Book
Everything® Golf Instruction Book

Everything® Pilates Book
Everything® Running Book
Everything® Total Fitness Book
Everything® Weight Training Book
Everything® Yoga Book

TRAVEL

Everything® Family Guide to Hawaii
Everything® Family Guide to New York City, 2nd Ed.
Everything® Family Guide to RV Travel & Campgrounds
Everything® Family Guide to the Walt Disney World Resort®, Universal Studios®, and Greater Orlando, 4th Ed.
Everything® Family Guide to Washington D.C., 2nd Ed.
Everything® Guide to Las Vegas
Everything® Guide to New England
Everything® Travel Guide to the Disneyland Resort®, California Adventure®, Universal Studios®, and the Anaheim Area

WEDDINGS

Everything® Bachelorette Party Book, $9.95
Everything® Bridesmaid Book, $9.95

Everything® Elopement Book, $9.95
Everything® Father of the Bride Book, $9.95
Everything® Groom Book, $9.95
Everything® Mother of the Bride Book, $9.95
Everything® Wedding Book, 3rd Ed.
Everything® Wedding Checklist, $9.95
Everything® Wedding Etiquette Book, $7.95
Everything® Wedding Organizer, $15.00
Everything® Wedding Shower Book, $7.95
Everything® Wedding Vows Book, $7.95
Everything® Weddings on a Budget Book, $9.95

WRITING

Everything® Creative Writing Book
Everything® Get Published Book
Everything® Grammar and Style Book
Everything® Guide to Writing a Book Proposal
Everything® Guide to Writing a Novel
Everything® Guide to Writing Children's Books
Everything® Screenwriting Book
Everything® Writing Poetry Book
Everything® Writing Well Book

We have Everything® for the beginner crafter!
All titles are $14.95

Everything® Crafts—Baby Scrapbooking
1-59337-225-6

Everything® Crafts—Bead Your Own Jewelry
1-59337-142-X

Everything® Crafts—Create Your Own Greeting Cards
1-59337-226-4

Everything® Crafts—Easy Projects
1-59337-298-1

Everything® Crafts—Polymer Clay for Beginners
1-59337-230-2

Everything® Crafts—Rubber Stamping Made Easy
1-59337-229-9

Everything® Crafts—Wedding Decorations and Keepsakes
1-59337-227-2

Available wherever books are sold!
To order, call 800-872-5627, or visit us at *www.everything.com*
Everything® and everything.com® are registered trademarks of F+W Publications, Inc.